Prais
by Mary She

"If you have a baby who is more sensitive, alert, and intense, *Raising Your Spirited Baby* has the answers you need. Mary Sheedy Kurcinka, Ed.D., brings her expertise in raising spirited children to help you understand and soothe your spirited baby. Her research-based, parent-tested strategies will help your baby sleep better and develop a calmer, more resilient brain and nervous system. I'll be recommending this for all new parents."

—Dr. Laura Markham, founder of AhaParenting.com
and author of *Peaceful Parent, Happy Kids*

"Dr. Mary explains that it is how you respond to your young baby that will shape their future behavior. In this book she leads parents through a step-by-step approach to see, hear, understand, and enjoy every moment with their baby, because how you interact, respond, and parent your infant can make all the difference in their future temperament, relationships, behavior, and success."

—Dr. Tanya Altmann, author of *Baby and Toddler Basics* and *What to Feed Your Baby*

"*Raising Your Spirited Baby* is a gentle, encouraging guide to communicating and supporting babies who need a little more help in developing sleep patterns that work for them and the family. For parents stressed out and feeling guilty about their little one's inability to sleep soundly through the night, Mary Sheedy Kurcinka offers practical support that will make everyone "sleep easier," confident that baby's good sleep habits are developing as a result of working with this invaluable resource.

—Nancy Peske, coauthor of *Raising a Sensory Smart Child*

"*Raising Your Spirited Baby* offers insight and relief into the often very fraught first months of parenting an infant. Over the years, I've come to know and care for many babies with this spirited 'wiring'—and now, Dr. Mary's latest research and strategies will allow me to provide clear, useful guidance."

—Marjorie Hogan, M.D., professor of
pediatrics, University of Minnesota

"As a pediatrician, and mother of spirited twins, I have seen first-hand how Mary's wise words prove invaluable even years after your spirited infant has outgrown his bassinet and pacifier. Understanding that a spirited child is wired differently is key to helping him achieve regulation throughout the day and the calm needed for sleep. With Mary's gentle guidance, the things that right now seem out of control, unpredictable, and exhausting will become the very things you cherish about your extraordinary child. Respecting that spirit will set your child up for a lifetime of healthy habits and success."

—Jill Funk Simons, M.D., F.A.A.D.

"A well-written, comprehensive, and, above all, loving and positive approach to understanding that oh-so-challenging child."

—Evonne Weinhaus and Karen Friedman, coauthors of *Stop Struggling with Your Child* and *Stop Struggling with Your Teen*

Raising Your
Spirited Baby

Also by Mary Sheedy Kurcinka, Ed.D.

Raising Your Spirited Child

Raising Your Spirited Child Workbook

Kids, Parents, and Power Struggles

*Sleepless in America: Is Your Child
Misbehaving or . . . Missing Sleep?*

Raising Your Spirited Baby

A BREAKTHROUGH GUIDE TO THRIVING WHEN YOUR BABY IS *MORE* ... ALERT AND INTENSE AND STRUGGLES TO SLEEP

Mary Sheedy Kurcinka, Ed.D.

WILLIAM MORROW
An Imprint of HarperCollins*Publishers*

FIRST EDITION

Designed by Diahann Sturge

Library of Congress Cataloging-in-Publication Data

Names: Kurcinka, Mary Sheedy, 1953–, author.
Title: Raising your spirited baby: a breakthrough guide to thriving when your baby is more . . . alert and intense and struggles to sleep / Mary Sheedy Kurcinka, Ed.D.
Description: First edition. | New York, NY: William Morrow, [2020] | Includes index.
Identifiers: LCCN 2020002204 (print) | LCCN 2020002205 (ebook) | ISBN 9780062961525 (trade paperback) | ISBN 9780062961556 (ebook)
Subjects: LCSH: Infants. | Child rearing. | Parent and infant. | Infants—Development. | Infant psychology. Infant sleep. Temperament. Crying.
Classification: LCC HQ774 .K87 2020 (print) | LCC HQ774 (ebook) | DDC 306.874—dc23
LC record available at https://lccn.loc.gov/2020002204
LC ebook record available at https://lccn.loc.gov/2020002205

ISBN 978-0-06-296152-5

20 21 22 23 24   LSC   10 9 8 7 6 5 4 3 2 1

To you—
and all the parents of infants seeking information,
effective strategies, comfort, and a vision filled with hope
for a joyful life with your spirited little one who is "more."

Contents

PART TWO: THE SPIRITED WAY IN PRACTICE

Acknowledgments

This book has been years in the making. It would not have been completed without the support, encouragement, guidance, shared wisdom, and stories of many contributors. I am deeply grateful and must say thank you to:

All the parents, child-care providers, teachers, and babies who have shared their stories, asked their questions, participated in my research studies, and allowed me to peek into their homes and classrooms. A special thank-you to Caroline, Betsy, Victoria, Lindsey, Kelly, Kyla, Grant, Ashlie, Abby, Brooklyn, Becca, Matt, Courtney, Kim, Rob, Megan, Shea, Jennifer, Jenny, Christina, Rachel, Teri, Lydia, Patti, Wendy, and Elky.

Janet Goldstein, consulting editor, who helped me sort, organize, brainstorm, and prioritize an overabundance of information gathered over the years. Your insights, guidance, and support have been priceless.

Liz Stein, in-house editor and wise new mom, who believed in the merit of this project. This book would not be a reality without your guiding hand, wisdom, and sharp eye for detail.

Heide Lange, my agent, the visionary dealmaker who patiently waited for me to finally say, "The baby book is ready to be born."

Joe Kurcinka, my husband and best friend, who pulled me back on my feet when I floundered, and offered encouragement, perspective, humor, and understanding when I desperately needed it.

Lynn Jessen, lifelong friend, colleague, and one of the most effective, wise, and caring parent and child educators I have ever encountered. I have learned so much from you!

My daughter, Kristina; son, Joshua; daughter-in-law, Betsy; and grandchildren, Grace and Owen. You have made my life with spirit rich and deeply rewarding.

Jill Funk Simons, M.D., F.A.A.P., Laurel Wills, M.D., and Sara Bennett Pearce, CNM, IBCLC. I am deeply indebted to you for sharing your knowledge, support, and especially your willingness to be readers. Your detailed notes, questions, and insights have significantly enhanced the advice in this book.

Janet Crow, M.D., clinical professor, Department of Pediatrics, University of California, San Diego, for your assistance in refining the temperament and parent stress tools.

Researchers and practitioners Sara Harkness, Ph.D., Sarah Watamura, Ph.D., Bill Carey, M.D., Sean McDevitt, Ph.D., Katja Rowell, M.D., Christina Spaeth-Herrer, OTR/L, and many other brilliant individuals, for taking the time to talk with me and share your research.

Vivian Johnson, Ph.D., Monica Potter, Ed.D., and Laurel Wills, M.D., for serving on my dissertation committee.

Nicole Hall, administrative assistant extraordinaire, for transcribing interviews, summarizing research articles, organizing appointments and engagements, and more!

Kim Cardwell, Marietta Rice, Jenna Ruble, fellow parent educators and friends, for insisting on excellence and hanging in there with me for over fifteen years.

Vicki Cronin, friend, colleague, fellow parent of spirited children, infant specialist, and parent educator, for sharing your cross-cultural stories and tremendous empathy for parents.

Charrisse Jennings, child-care director and parent, for demonstrating how spirited infants can thrive in child care.

Cindy Christian, children's librarian and friend, for inviting me to teach at our community library.

Nancy Tanner, for teaching me so much about the arousal system and the importance of patience.

Eric Funk, for sharing his creative genius.

My sisters, Barbara, Kathy, Helen, and Suzanne, whose daily emails start my day in the office with warm greetings and news of family.

Kelsey Sathers, Brook Merrow, Patricia Agnew, and Margaret Dowling, my Montana writing group. Your in-depth questions and creative inspiration made writing fun and less lonely.

Rossi, my favorite doodle, who let me know when it was time to stop to take a walk!

Introduction

Greetings and welcome to *Raising Your Spirited Baby*. I'm so glad you have opened this book. I envision it as a gift for you—a guidebook for the first eighteen months of life with the little human sparkler who has come into your home. The one who is bright, delightful, but a bit challenging when not handled carefully. Whether your baby is an off-the-charts, all-the-time *spirited baby* (which you'll read about in the coming chapters) or a less intense version, I'm here to give you a new approach to life with your baby.

By the way, I'm Dr. Mary, a licensed parent and early childhood educator, researcher, bestselling author of the classic book *Raising Your Spirited Child*, collector of stories, and parent of one spunky and one spirited infant—both now grown-up, and prospering.

The idea of writing a spirited-baby book came to me years ago, after surviving my own spirited infant's first eighteen months, but I failed to write it. First, because I was too blown away to accomplish such a task. Second, I was not certain if it truly was more challenging to raise an infant who is what I call *normal but more*. Perhaps the issue was me and my own lack of skills. Despite my holding graduate degrees in child development and parent education and actively teaching classes for parents, my son's lack of sleep and frequent bouts of shrieking left me bewildered and exhausted—for months on end. I questioned myself when strategies that seemed to have worked for everyone else failed in my house. This was *not* how it was supposed to be. The experience was so humbling I even considered quitting my job as a parent educator.

Fortunately, I continued teaching, with a focus on parents and educators of infants, toddlers, preschoolers, and school-age children. When my classes on *spirited children* touched a nerve and word spread, I added *author* to my résumé, writing *Raising Your Spirited Child*, and later *Raising Your Spirited Child Workbook; Kids, Parents, and Power Struggles;* and *Sleepless in America.* Still I did not go back to the baby book. I conducted workshops and keynoted conferences nationally and internationally. I created a private consultation business providing guidance for families across the world, yet the idea for the spirited-baby book sat frozen in the back of my mind.

Over the years, though, I kept hearing from families who struggled in these early months. No matter what their circumstances, they were exhausted by endless nights of sleep deprivation, frustrated that recommended strategies were not working, and demoralized by the sense that they were doing something wrong. I finally accepted that my experience had not been unique. These babies truly were *more* intense, confusing, yet amazing little ones, and they did require greater skill from their parents. Yet accepted parenting practices simply did not address their needs. It was time to find a better way.

I began a fervent quest to understand several underlying questions: What made these babies spirited? Did the same factors that influenced older children's behavior also apply to infants? What was life like for their parents? And most important, what did both the babies and the parents need to thrive?

In my quest for knowledge, I returned to graduate school to complete a doctorate in education. In the process I reviewed the latest research on temperament, parent-infant interaction, neuroscience, self-regulation, attachment, child development, and sleep. I identified parents of spirited babies at pediatric clinics by asking them to complete a temperament survey describing the characteristics of their babies. I then interviewed parents of the spirited babies, asking them to describe their thoughts and feelings when their baby cried or did not sleep; how their baby was similar to or different from others they knew; and how life with their baby had affected their adult relationships. Eager to share their stories, they described feelings of shock at how challenging it was to be the parent of this baby, intertwined with a sense of awe for the powerful spirit that lay within their child. The parents' tales of successes and joys mixed with those of confusion, doubts, and disappointments. I listened for common themes as well as the gems of insights not previously mentioned in the research.

Following the interviews, each parent kept a journal for one week recording their baby's sleep, wake, and crying behaviors and their own emotions and thoughts in response to those behaviors. The parents' written insights both reinforced the themes I had identified and presented new concepts I had previously missed. My goal was to dig deep into their feelings, beliefs, thoughts, and actions to understand their experience, how they made sense of life with a spirited baby, and the meaning they attributed to it.

My data was extensive, but my sample small, so I did not stop there. I expanded my research and knowledge from multiple angles over the years by conducting hundreds of additional interviews with parents. Then I turned to other leading professionals in the field to learn from them. I took the information and the effective strategies that I had gathered and tested them in my classes for parents of spirited infants and in private consultations. Together we hashed over the information, applied it in real home settings, tossed what was not helpful, and collected the strategies that truly worked for spirited infants, parents, and caregivers.

Fifteen years in the making, the result of these efforts is the Spirited Baby Method and this book. To flourish, spirited babies *need* the Spirited Baby Method, which addresses their inborn temperament and highly sensitive arousal systems. It presents an attentive, responsive approach to parenting that is attuned to each baby's unique needs as well as the needs of the whole family. But another exciting discovery is that the effectiveness of this methodology is not limited to spirited babies. Every parent of an infant experiences *spirited-baby moments.* Any parent can benefit from this book, which helps them not only understand and care for their baby but also care for themselves, including their relationships, which are profoundly changed by life with a baby.

As you read *Raising Your Spirited Baby,* you'll realize how having effective strategies in hand can calm you and energize you, allowing you to see, hear, and understand your baby's needs. You'll gain a newfound appreciation for your baby's intensity, tenacity, and perceptiveness, and for the gifts they can be.

The stories included are amalgamations of tales shared and honest emotions expressed. Details have been slightly altered to protect the privacy of the families. Yet each story holds its own truth.

Through these stories you will find I am honest about the difficulty of the journey with a spirited baby. But you will also see I bring you hope—a vision of how rewarding and life-changing this experience can be once the challenging behaviors and mystifying responses of these loud, bright, passionate babies are understood.

I will be the first to admit, the Spirited Baby Method is not a magical quick fix. (That does not exist—I looked for it.) It is a process that requires time, practice, and gentle nudges. But it does work—it does lay out a pathway to less stress and more ease and joy for everyone.

I encourage you to keep this book on your bedside table, reading it first for the overarching insights and principles that will reassure you from the start, and then as an easy-to-turn-to guide in the middle of the night when nothing you are doing seems to be working. It is designed to offer you concrete steps when it feels like you are stumbling and a hand to hold when needed.

Be assured, my own experience makes me a fierce warrior protecting and advocating for spirited infants and their parents—no parent shaming or blaming lies within this book cover! Nor any crushing pressure to force these babies to fit standard practices. These babies are different, they are challenging, and, with the responsive care they require, they fully become the loving, rewarding, creative little ones we cherish. I have seen it. I have lived it. Come along, we'll walk forward together.

Raising Your
Spirited Baby

Chapter 1

Welcome to More . . . Spirit, Crying, Fussing, Giggling, Guilt, and Struggles to Sleep

The Joys and Challenges of Raising a Highly Alert, Intense, Spirited Baby

"My daughter entered life like a warm and gentle shower.
My son began his life like a raging thunderstorm."
—John, father of two

If at your childbirth class reunion you found yourself holding your baby in the back of the room, dipping into deep knee bends in the hope of preventing him from becoming a roaring lion while every other baby laid oh-so-placidly on the floor, you are likely the parent of a spirited baby. Spirited infants are the outliers—the exceptions to the rules, the extraordinary ones. As we will see, spirited infants are normal but somehow . . . more.

When you hear other parents extol how easily their babies sleep and feed, you cannot help thinking they are lying. Getting your baby to sleep is a wrestling match, requiring forty-five minutes of bouncing, singing, shushing, and swaying, only to have your bundle of joy wake minutes later. You want to scream, "This is NOT the baby I expected."

Yet there is something about this child that delights you, draws you to her, and wraps around your heart. You sense her intensity—a spirit so palpable that the delivery room nurses commented about it and wished you luck. The power of her gaze is irresistible. Even strangers remark about how alert she is. You love her so much but . . .

You are probably exhausted, likely to have gone longer without sleep than a Navy SEAL in training! You are certainly weary of hearing success stories that seem so foreign to you and unattainable. Do babies really just fall asleep anywhere? Do they really take to new foods, people, and places with ease? Do they really remain calm while riding in their car seat or while tucked into a stroller in the middle of a busy restaurant or store?

If you have another child, a non-spirited one, you know the answer to these questions is a resounding yes. But now, since your spirited one has arrived, you may have lost your confidence. You may find yourself questioning your abilities as a parent and possibly crying every day. If this is your first child, you may wonder why it feels like you are failing when you are trying so hard.

I am here to tell you: *You're not failing at anything!* Your actions do not make your baby spirited. You are not doing something wrong. You are not lacking some magical touch that other parents seem to have.

- -

I am here to tell you: *You're not failing at anything!* Your actions do not make your baby spirited. You are not doing something wrong.

- -

Nor are you alone. Worldwide it is estimated that spirited in-fants make up 20 to 25 percent of all full-term babies. That is one million babies born every year in the United States alone. You are not the only one with a baby who sends your partner to the couch, leaving you alone to cry. You are not the only one whose dream baby was dropped off at your best friend's house and instead you were given this special little one—a purely delightful package, but oh so exhausting. You are not the only one to find yourself pant-ing, and at times gasping, to catch your breath.

Spirited infants arrive in this world genetically wired to be highly alert and intense. It is not your imagination that your baby's shrieks are more piercing or that you are working harder. Raising a spirited baby does take more time, skill, and perseverance—and, I would say, more knowledge—*and yet almost no one talks about it.*

Every year 20 to 25 percent of all babies born are spirited. . . . Spirited infants arrive in this world genetically wired to be highly alert and intense.

YOUR BABY'S INNATE AROUSAL SYSTEM

It is easy to think the problem is you. But it's not. It's all about biology. Spirited infants who can rocket from quiet and calm to red-faced and screaming in seconds are genetically wired with a more reactive arousal system.

The arousal system is the body's built-in wiring that regulates our fight, flight, or freeze response, energy levels, sleep cycles, diges-tion, heart rate, breathing, and attention. Like a command center, it lies within our brains, scanning our environment and absorbing everything that is going on around us. When our arousal system perceives anything new or different—any change, any surprise—it sends a signal to the body's biological systems: *Pay attention! Be on alert for potential danger.*

When a possible threat is detected, the control center calls for a burst of energy, speed, and strength, telling us, *Gear up! Be ready to fight, flee, or freeze!* It then accelerates the heart, pulse, and breathing rates, increases blood flow to our muscles, and shifts our focus to the threat at hand. If the information is unimportant and can be ignored, our biological systems are directed to idle in a balanced, quiet state. This ability to accelerate or slow our biological reactions according to the needs of the situation is called *self-regulation.*

Your baby's spirited arousal system is apparent when:

- ☐ Your baby bursts into tears while another baby in the same situation sleeps soundly.
- ☐ The strategies your friends swear by do *not* work with your baby.
- ☐ It is nearly impossible to lay your baby down because the moment you lean forward, she startles herself awake.
- ☐ At ten months old your baby is "emptying" the dishwasher, finding his own snack in the pantry, and already refusing to take no for an answer.
- ☐ The upsets and shrieking come out of seemingly nowhere and take forever to subside.

The arousal system of these babies is set to trigger faster and calm more slowly. At any given moment, a spirited baby, compared to an "easy" baby, is in a state of heightened awareness and reactivity.

While everyone has an arousal system—babies, children, and adults alike—there are stark individual differences in how our systems are calibrated. We vary widely in the amount of information it takes to trip our control center's threat response and how swiftly our biological systems jump into action. Think solid Subaru versus high-strung Lamborghini. (Both are great cars, just different.)

To see these differences in action, meet Hannah and Jordan.

TJ and Meg were dining at a restaurant with their three-month-old twins. Hannah and Jordan lay contentedly in their infant seats until a waiter accidently dropped a tray, sending glasses and dishes crashing to the floor. Hannah gazed toward the noise, casually searching for the source. Jordan erupted in a fire-engine wail. His body flailed, nearly flipping him out of his carrier. TJ immediately picked Jordan up to calm him, but he continued to shriek, forcing TJ to abandon his food and dart for the door to help Jordan settle down. Despite the ruckus, Hannah fell asleep.

Same place, same parents, same ages, so why such different responses? At three months of age, Hannah and Jordan's polarized reactions are not learned, but reflect the differences in their genetic wiring. Hannah, who merely gazed about the room after the dishes crashed, was born with a *low-key* arousal system. It requires a formidable amount of stimulation to activate her system. When a source of stimulation does become overwhelming, she is able to withdraw her attention and switch to sleep. Jordan, on the other hand, arrived with a highly reactive, *spirited* arousal system. A mere click of the car seat buckle can trigger a response, much less the explosive sounds of breaking glass. Once upset, Jordan remains upset longer as well.

If we had a monitor to measure their responses, we would see that Jordan's heart and pulse rates were racing in comparison to Hannah's slow, steady beats. His pupils would be dilated wider, his vocal cords tighter, and his stress hormone levels elevated higher. On any given day Hannah's arousal system may not even become physiologically elevated by stimulation that overwhelms Jordan. Jordan experiences every sensation to a degree that is bigger, louder, higher, faster, hotter, and more penetrating. His keen attentiveness is an asset that can lead him to excel, but it also means that Jordan requires greater sensitivity, courage, and support from his caregivers. This is especially true in his early months and years as he develops the skills to manage his arousal system and settle at the level of arousal that fits the situation.

Spirited infants are defined by their highly reactive arousal systems. That is why spirited babies, unlike their low-key counterparts, need extra amounts of attention, touch, and assistance to calm themselves.

Through our support, spirited babies are given the opportunity to rehearse and practice the process of regulating.

. . . .

Spirited infants are defined by their highly reactive arousal systems. That is why spirited babies, unlike their low-key counterparts, need extra amounts of attention, touch, and assistance to calm themselves.

. . . .

THE SENSITIVE, RESPONSIVENESS APPROACH TO THE SPIRITED BABY

Understanding the arousal system helps explain why the right response for the spirited baby often runs contrary to traditionally recommended practices, especially those that encourage ignoring a baby's crying or not responding quickly. Rather than creating a "bad habit," our warm responses change the wiring of their brains. New neural connections form. The babies gradually gain the strength and finesse to smoothly downshift and accelerate their finely tuned engines as needed. Working with their arousal system instead of against it changes everything.

TYPICALLY, BABIES WITH every kind of genetic makeup are lumped together in the advice from the doctors, psychologists, and parenting experts who say:

"This is how to get your child to nap."

"This is how to deal with crying."

"This is how you get your baby to sleep at night."

However, their caveat—their truth in advertising—is the little phrase you'll find tucked into the introductions to their books or talks:

"THIS DOES NOT WORK FOR EVERY BABY."

No explanation is offered, and no effective alternative strategies are provided. Yet, as far back as the second century, Galen, a Greek physician, surgeon, and philosopher, argued, "Children differ from one another from the earliest days." These differences cannot be discounted. One size does not fit all.

Unlike experts and methods that ignore, minimize, or even disparage the unique needs and gifts of spirited babies, *Raising Your Spirited Baby* addresses them head-on with a new set of principles:

- Awareness and sensitivity to the baby's cues—whenever possible "catching" and calming the baby before the arousal system accelerates to an overload level.

- Immediate responsiveness to the baby—providing what *this* baby needs in ways that calm and comfort the baby and the parents.
- Support and caring for everyone—baby, parents, the whole family.
- And gradually bringing the baby into the family's system— using simple, sensitive techniques to meet the baby's needs while simultaneously gently nudging the baby into the rhythm and routine of the family.

These are the hallmarks of the Spirited Baby Method—a clear, shame-free, guilt-free approach for parents of babies from birth to eighteen months of age.

IS THIS BOOK REALLY FOR ME?

While not every baby is spirited, many babies will have some spirited qualities and every parent experiences *spirited baby moments*. To help you see how you're managing and handling the stress, the Parent Self-Assessment is a quick shortcut. If you score 8 and above, be assured that you are among friends and you'll get the help and support you need. If your score is lower, you belong here, too! All the insights and practices in this book will help you be the sensitive, responsive parent you want to be while supporting *you* on your parenting journey.

Parent Self-Assessment
Mark one box ☑ per question.

1. Manageability: How often do you feel your baby is more difficult to manage than other babies?

Almost Never   1   2   3   4   5   **Almost Always**

| *About what I expected* | ☐ ☐ ☐ ☐ ☐ | *I'm shocked at how difficult it is* |
| *Feels like my work is easier than other parents'* | | *Feels like I'm working harder than other parents* |

2. Crying: How often does your baby's crying cause you stress?

Almost Never   1   2   3   4   5   **Almost Always**

I usually can figure out why my baby is crying	☐ ☐ ☐ ☐ ☐	*I often don't know why my baby is crying*
I often can tell myself my baby is okay		*I frequently worry I'm doing something wrong*
Cries about the amount I expected		*Seems to cry more than other babies*

3. Support: How often do you feel alone and unsupported?

Almost Never   1   2   3   4   5   **Almost Always**

I find it easy to ask for help	☐ ☐ ☐ ☐ ☐	*I find it hard to ask for help*
I have friends in a similar situation		*I feel like the "different" person with my friends*
I have support in my community		*I do not have support in my community*
Others can calm my baby		*I feel like I'm the only one who can calm my baby*

4. Sleep: How often does your baby's lack of sleep cause you stress?

Almost Never   1   2   3   4   5   **Almost Always**

My baby's sleep cues are easy to read	☐ ☐ ☐ ☐ ☐	*I struggle to read my baby's sleep cues*
I can nap		*I do not take naps*
I return to sleep after my baby wakes		*I lie awake waiting for my baby to wake again*
I'm tired, but hanging in there		*I'm exhausted*

$\longrightarrow$

5. Feeding: How often does feeding your baby cause you stress?

Almost Never	1	2	3	4	5	Almost Always
Feedings are going smoothly *I feel like my baby is getting enough to eat* *My baby's hunger cues are easy to read*	□	□	□	□	□	*Feedings are a struggle* *I worry my baby is not getting enough to eat* *I can't figure out my baby's hunger cues*

Your score ________

5–7 Low stress

8–16 Moderate stress

17–25 High stress

WHAT IS *TYPICAL* SPIRITED AND WHEN SHOULD I WORRY?

The Parent Self-Assessment not only shows you where the stresses are but also gives you a window into what's *typical.* The reactions and behaviors of spirited babies all fall squarely within the range of normal human behavior. Being spirited—as a baby, child, or adult—is not a disorder. All answers to this assessment are typical and all situations have solutions.

Yet, spirited babies can react with such intensity you may fear something is wrong, especially when you compare your child with babies who are not spirited. Many parents of spirited babies worry that their child is not only different but perhaps facing psychological or medical issues. If you have concerns, such as your baby not gaining weight at the expected rate, demonstrating delays in reaching developmental milestones, failing to make eye contact, or not responding to your voice and actions, you will want to consult with your pediatrician.

If your child does have any types of delays or differences—which are separate from your baby's arousal system—the approach to parenting in *Raising Your Spirited Baby* will still put you on a wonderful path to supporting your child, yourself, and your family. But additional therapeutic aid may be needed to address the concerns that are outside typical behaviors or responses.

The vast majority of spirited infants, though, are *not* more likely to have early signs of autism, ADHD, or other challenges that keep parents up at night. When given the sensitive and responsive care they need, spirited babies will develop normally, happily, and according to the expected milestones. In fact, they often excel.

THE SPIRITED BABY METHOD

Four central questions anchor the framework for the Spirited Baby Method:

1. **What is my baby telling me?** This question is all about listening to your baby and addresses: What is my baby showing me about his present level of arousal? What comforts him? How does he communicate his needs? How intense, sensitive, alert,

and active is my baby compared with others? What do I learn when I listen to my baby?

2. **What do I need to stay calm—so I can calm my baby?** This question is all about listening to oneself and addresses: What messages am I hearing? Do they calm me or cause me stress? How do they make me feel and how can I reframe them? How can I feel more empowered and confident? How can I build my support team so I do not have to do this alone?

3. **How can I meet my basic needs now?** This question gets to the basic foundations each parent and family needs. It addresses: How do I bring predictability into my day when my baby is so unpredictable? How do I make certain I eat and sleep? How, if I am parenting with a partner, do we keep that partnership strong?

4. **What is the Gentle NUDGE to success?** This question focuses on what actions parents can take to gradually strengthen their baby's self-regulation skills, without ever pushing the infant to a point of distress as cry-it-out methods do. It asks parents to identify and break into teeny, tiny steps the skills their baby needs to develop, and focuses on gently practicing those skills. The Gentle NUDGE acronym helps parents remember the steps.

   1. Note what your baby can do now.

   2. Understand your ultimate goal.

3. Determine the teeny, tiny steps to reach the goal.

4. Gently practice.

5. Ease back your support as your baby becomes more proficient.

Together, these four questions create the framework of the Spirited Baby Method, an approach that wraps its arms around both parent and baby as it addresses the key issues of naps, nighttime sleep, feeding, and going out with this little dynamo.

KEEP A JOURNAL TO CELEBRATE SUCCESS AND RECORD PROGRESS

As you learn about and implement the Spirited Baby Method, I am going to encourage you to keep a journal, whether it's a physical notebook or your favorite app. In it you can record your own feelings, trials, and successes as well as your growing insights about your baby. As the chapters unfold, you'll be guided to collect the most effective calming strategies for you and your baby and to track your baby's unique cues, behaviors, and milestones around naps, nighttime sleeping, feedings, and outings. I'll offer prompts throughout the book and reflection questions at the end of every chapter to assist you.

Then on those days when you feel like you are failing, you can look back and see the progress you and your baby are making. There, right in front of you, will be concrete examples of how your baby is learning and growing and becoming part of your family.

MOVING FORWARD
WITH CONFIDENCE AND HOPE

When you live with a spirited baby, the challenges are real and the potential unlimited. While there is no fairy-tale magic to make this journey easy, there is a path with proven strategies to make it better—much better. Perhaps, most important, there is a vision of hope to inspire you, as veteran parents share their tales of their spirited babies and how they learned to survive and thrive. Yes, the one with the piercing cry really can grow up to be the soloist at her high school spring concert.

So, grab your water bottle, put on your trail running shoes, and let's go.

CHEAT SHEET: WELCOME TO THE JOYS AND STRUGGLES WHEN YOUR BABY IS *MORE*

1. *Remember, you are not failing at anything.* You did not make your baby spirited. You are not doing something wrong. Spirited babies arrive in this world wired to be spirited. It is part of their genetic makeup.

2. *Remind yourself of your baby's innate arousal system, which needs extra support to slow down.* When you provide that support, you ensure that rather than creating a bad habit, your baby will excel.

3. *Recognize your "outsider" feelings—and that you're not alone!* Worldwide it is estimated that spirited infants make up 20 to 25 percent of all full-term babies. That is one million infants born every year in the United States alone.

4. *Take the Parent Self-Assessment to check your stress levels and challenges.* Whether your baby is full-on spirited or somewhere else on the arousal scale, being aware of and sensitive to your own needs will help you meet your baby's.

REFLECTION QUESTIONS FOR YOUR JOURNAL

- How are you feeling right now? Take a few minutes to write down your biggest worries, hopes, and dreams. You don't need to make any changes right now, just let yourself take a breath and know that helping hands are here for you.

- What is one thing (or more!) you find challenging about your baby's behavior?

- What is one thing (or more!) you love about your baby?

PART ONE

The Spirited
Baby Method

Chapter 2

What Is My Baby Telling Me?

*Tuning In to Our Infants' Unique
Needs and Temperaments*

*"Allow yourself to fall in love with your baby's huge
personality. Do not crush it. Instead learn to manage
it. When you do, wonderful things happen."*
—Patti, mother of three

Like a race car engine—high-tech, sensitive to the touch, and powerful—the arousal system of the spirited infant is challenging to brake without skidding out of control. Helping your baby manage that powerful engine is critical to his well-being. But how do you calm your baby's arousal system when his responses are so confounding? A mere bump in the road, a sneeze, or literally anything can put your baby's arousal system into overdrive.

Fortunately, there is a pattern to your baby's responses that you can learn to see and predict. This pattern is called *temperament*. Like our arousal systems and our preferences for extroversion or introversion, temperament is biologically determined. It significantly influences how an infant responds to the world.

WHAT IS TEMPERAMENT?

As physicians and researchers, Stella Chess and Alexander Thomas were fascinated by the differences in their own biological and adopted children. In 1956 they began a decades-long and now famous longitudinal study looking at individual differences in children. Along with other researchers, they identified nine traits that we still use today to describe temperament. More recently, researcher Mary Rothbart has defined temperament as "constitutional differences in activity, reactivity, and self-regulation, which are genetically based but may be modified by experiences and later development." While other theorists like to add their own variations to the definition, there's a general consensus that temperament traits:

- are genetically based.
- appear early in life.
- can be observed in various settings.
- reflect individual differences in the energy of responses (low to high, mild to intense, slow to quick).
- are relatively stable over time but can be modified by different life situations and experiences.

That may sound a bit confusing, but the reality is that you see differences in temperament all around you on a daily basis. Have you noticed how babies vary widely in how loudly they cry or how alert they are? Those are temperamental differences in action. The same is true when every sound, smell, sight, or touch alerts one baby while another sleeps through it all. Reactions to new people differ from eager curiosity to shrieks of alarm. Activity levels range from quiet to constant motion. While some babies feed serenely, others are busily patting, grasping, and pinching while little legs pummel Mom or Dad's belly. The cause of these differences is not a deep desire to make their parents crazy. The reason is a variation in temperament.

WHY UNDERSTANDING TEMPERAMENT MATTERS

Temperament traits help answer the question of *why* your baby responds to the world as she does. Suddenly, you are no longer caught off guard. You can predict what will upset your baby, how she will react, and in what situations she will be most vulnerable. When you understand your baby's temperament traits, subtle as they may be at first, you can better anticipate and prepare for the situations that trigger her arousal system. You're able to answer the essential question, "What is my baby telling me she needs?"

. . . .

Temperament traits help answer the question of *why* your baby responds to the world as she does. . . . You can predict what will upset your baby, how she will respond, and in what situations she will be most vulnerable.

. . . .

This newfound knowledge will exponentially increase your ability to select effective strategies to calm her. Your baby will let you know with smiles, contentment, and improved sleep that this is *exactly* what she needs. The sense of empowerment is a lifesaver if you, like so many parents I work with, have been feeling incapable, confused, and lost.

Kendis was one of those parents. Breastfeeding had been perplexing. Her friends made it look so easy. Their babies fed contentedly under any condition. But when Kendis attempted to follow their example, five-month-old Winn arched and wagged his head back and forth to scope out what was happening around him. Kendis struggled to keep him from wiggling out of her arms.

Winn settled to nurse only when Kendis cleared the couch of every toy left there by his three-year-old sister, Addy, and blocked his view of the surroundings by tucking him under a light blanket draped over her shoulder as she fed him. But Kendis's friends questioned her tactics, insinuating she was too finicky. Even her mom was concerned she might smother Winn under the blanket, though it never covered his nose and mouth and he could easily bat it away.

Kendis listened to these voices around her and tried nursing again without clearing the clutter or using the blanket. But the day he painfully stretched her nipple in his quest to follow someone walking by she realized it was time to stop trying to follow their suggestions. They were *not* working!

Kendis contacted me and I had her complete a temperament profile for Winn. It confirmed how alert he was. Unlike her friend's baby, who did not notice the buzzing housefly six feet away, Winn followed its every move. He noticed shadows, sunlight patterns on the floor, and even scrutinized Kendis's face after she cut her hair. It was as though he was saying, *Something is different. I have to figure this out.*

The temperament profile explained what Kendis had intuitively known. Winn was more alert. The steps she had taken to declutter and help him calm before nursing were the fine-tuning strategies he needed. Without those changes in his environment,

Winn was constantly overaroused. He was so aware and excited about his world that he would fail to eat sufficiently, push past his window for sleep, and end up in a frenzy. Buoyed by her new knowledge, Kendis found herself becoming clear and confident about what her baby was telling her. Over time, she could assuredly reply to the questioning of her friends and family, "This is working for us."

Like Kendis, you can get a picture of your baby's temperament so you can work with it to help your baby thrive.

YOUR BABY'S TEMPERAMENT PROFILE—GETTING A SNAPSHOT

Your responses to the Infant Temperament Profile that follows will give you immediate insights into your baby's temperament. Each trait can be placed on a continuum from a mild to strong reaction.

Some traits are easier to identify than others, especially at the youngest ages. Shrieking cries make intensity a temperament trait recognizable from birth forward. Your baby's cries may have made her a standout in the hospital nursery. Energy level, too, is often apparent early on, sometimes even in utero. Jessica, a mom in one of my groups, confided, "Jake wrestled around in the womb so fiercely we decided on the middle name Bernard, which means *bear*!"

No matter how tiny your newborn is or how "advanced" your skilled toddler, the signs of your baby's temperament are there and will become more pronounced as your child matures and your relationship with each other deepens.

As you complete the temperament profile, keep in mind that

there is no perfect profile. There are positive and negative aspects to all the temperament traits. There are spirited babies that score high on all the traits and others who are, miraculously, good sleepers but, when awake, are indeed in high gear. It's the overall picture that matters.

Know, too, that often temperament is thought to be synonymous with personality. But it is not. Personality is a combination of temperament, life experiences, and skill development. I like to think of temperament as the core around which our personality forms. My own daughter was extremely cautious in new situations as a child. Exposure to new people, places, or foods could trigger her arousal system. Today, as an adult, she has hiked in Patagonia, sailed in Croatia, walked solo the El Camino trail through Europe, and loves backcountry skiing. Once when I asked her if she still felt uncomfortable in new situations, she said, "Yes," but added, "I know what to do to make it better."

Your actions influence how your baby's temperament traits are expressed. Through your guidance and support your baby learns to celebrate who he is and develop the skills necessary to flourish. A picture of your baby's temperament profile is a tool that allows you to understand your baby's responses to the world and select strategies that fit his temperament.

. . . .

Often temperament is thought to be synonymous with personality. But it is not. Personality is a combination of temperament, life experiences, and skill development. I like to think of temperament as the core around which our personality forms.

. . . .

Infant Temperament Profile

As you review the traits, think about your baby's typical, most natural reactions. What responses have you come to expect? Remember, there isn't a "perfect" temperament. There are positive and negative aspects of all the temperament traits.

Mark one box ☑ per question.

1. Intensity: How strong are your baby's emotional reactions?

Mild Reaction	1 2 3 4 5	Intense Reaction
It is almost a surprise when she/he gets upset	☐ ☐ ☐ ☐ ☐	Shifts from happy to shrieking in seconds
Cries seem quieter than other babies'		Cries seem louder than other babies'
Easily soothed		Challenging to calm

2. Sensitivity: How aware is your baby of slight noises, emotions, and differences in temperature, taste, and touch?

Low	1 2 3 4 5	High
Sleeps through noisy routines	☐ ☐ ☐ ☐ ☐	Must have quiet to sleep
Does not need to be held to sleep		Sleeps if held, but wakes if laid down
Does not seem to notice soiled diaper		Immediately fusses when diaper is soiled

3. Alertness: Do others remark about how alert he/she seems to be?

Low	1 2 3 4 5	High
Not bothered by crowds	☐ ☐ ☐ ☐ ☐	Requires extra soothing after being in a crowd
Feeds well anywhere		Stops feeding if there is commotion nearby
Not bothered by light		Must have dark to sleep
Sleeps anywhere		Stays awake in unfamiliar places or crowds

$\longrightarrow$

4. Regularity: Are your baby's eating, sleeping, and elimination times predictable?

	Predictable	1	2	3	4	5	Unpredictable
Is hungry at regular intervals		☐	☐	☐	☐	☐	Is hungry at different times each day
Naptimes are predictable							Naptimes keep changing
Morning wake time is predictable							Morning wake time varies

5. Activity Level: Is your baby always on the move and busy, or quiet and still? Does he/she seem to need movement?

	Quiet	1	2	3	4	5	Active
Stays in one place when sleeping		☐	☐	☐	☐	☐	Active even during sleep
Will sit quietly for an extended period							Always on the move
Lies quietly while being dressed							Kicks, squirms, waves, thrusts while being dressed

6. First Reaction: What is your baby's first reaction to new people, activities, or places?

	Jumps In	1	2	3	4	5	Cautious First Reaction
Approaches new things easily		☐	☐	☐	☐	☐	Is distressed by new things
Calm when approached by new people							Gets upset when approached by new people
Enjoys new places							May fuss in new places

7. Persistence: How easily can your baby be distracted or stopped?

	Easily Stops	1	2	3	4	5	Persists
When hungry can be distracted for a few minutes		☐	☐	☐	☐	☐	When hungry needs to eat NOW!
Does not fuss if a toy is taken from him/her							Wails if a toy is taken from him/her
Can be redirected							Not easily redirected

8. Adaptability: How easily does your baby transition from one activity, place, or person to another?

	Shifts Quickly	1	2	3	4	5	Shifts Slowly	
Easily starts and stops a feeding		☐	☐	☐	☐	☐		Cries or fusses when a feeding ends or begins
Falls asleep quickly								Struggles to fall asleep
Is calm when picked up for diapering								Fusses when picked up for diapering
If awakened, he/she is quiet or happy								If awakened, he/she is upset

9. Seriousness (Mood): How much of the time is your baby happy and content, compared with serious or fussy?

	Usually Positive	1	2	3	4	5	More Serious	
Typically in a good mood		☐	☐	☐	☐	☐		Seems thoughtful and sober
Happy even though does not sleep								An old soul in a baby's body

Scoring _____

9–18 Low-key baby

19–28 Spunky baby

29–45 Spirited baby

Now you have a profile of your baby's temperament. Do not be surprised if you have a score of 1 or 2 mixed in with the 4s and 5s. Every baby is unique. Remember, the key is the overall picture. Your snapshot allows you to suddenly hear, see, and even feel what your baby is experiencing, and understand WHY! You can give her traits a name and predict that she will react more intensely, move faster, or give you that "old soul contemplating look" or "future scientist quizzical frown" instead of a smile.

And you can revisit your baby's profile over time. Since she is continually growing and developing, multiple snapshots of your baby's profile will help you discern her true temperament pattern versus a temporary stage of development. This evolving knowledge will enhance your ability to know and respond to your baby's cues. Know, too, that despite sharing parents and siblings, even twins may have very different temperament profiles.

EMBRACING YOUR BABY'S PROFILE . . . EVEN IF IT'S CHALLENGING

Before we go on, I want to address the reality that your baby's temperament profile may be disconcerting to you. While the information provides knowledge you can use, it can also awaken—or confirm—concerns you've been trying to keep at bay. Your baby's temperament profile may reveal a child that's not the one you dreamed of having. Rob, the father of Nathan, a spirited infant who is now a college student, described his reaction.

"When you worked with us to understand Nathan's temperament, my heart felt ripped open. He was just like me! My worst nightmare was a living reality. I had been teased for being too sensitive. And I was so active as a kid that adults strapped me in chairs to force me to sit still. I did not want him to experience similar persecution. I fought the techniques you were teaching us. However, over time I saw how much they helped. As Nathan moved out of babyhood, I began to see his intelligence and compassion. I recognized the energy and curiosity that drove him. It forced me to look at myself. I realized my sensitivity and energy are essential for my work and make me good at it. Something shifted. I stopped worrying and gave myself permission to embrace my son."

If you, like Rob, initially feel resistant to your baby's temperament profile, allow yourself to grieve that baby of your dreams. Then embrace your child with the beluga-size lungs. Use the temperament profile to trust what he is telling you he needs to thrive. Courageously select the strategies that fit his temperament—the strategies that are right for him.

Whether your baby "scored" low-key, spunky, or spirited, here's a quick summary to help you identify, understand, and work with his temperament.

WHEN YOUR BABY IS LOW-KEY

I'm so mellow my needs can easily be overlooked.

Babies who are low-key are mellow. They are easily calmed by their caregivers and do not seem to become upset by things that may disturb other babies.

Their eating and sleeping habits tend to be predictable. If they miss a nap, or a feeding is delayed, their reaction is mild. They easily adapt to changes in the routine, or from one situation/person to another.

Low-key babies are typically happy and flexible.

What your low-key baby is telling you

- Establish regular diaper check times during the day. I may not signal a soiled diaper.
- Be careful not to skip my naps; even though I may seem fine without them, I can become overtired.
- Take time to note my subtle hunger cues, so that a feeding is not missed.
- At the first sign of satiation, stop feeding me. I may not persist in signaling you, *I'm full.*
- When I do become upset, know that something is up. Potentially I'm ill.
- I may merely whimper when experiencing an ear infection or other illness. Notice my subtle cues.
- Provide me interaction and appropriate stimulation, as I may remain content in a "container" and not signal my needs.
- Be thoughtful about where you take me. I'm so adaptable you may not realize this situation is too noisy, crowded, or overstimulating for me.
- Invite me to take over feeding and dressing tasks. Otherwise I may be happy to allow you to do it for me long after I am capable of doing it myself.
- Celebrate the joy of caring for me.

WHEN YOUR BABY IS SPUNKY

I'm relatively mellow, but I do have my "temperament triggers."

Spunky babies are a mix of traits. More intense than their low-key peers, and less intense than their spirited peers, they may still have one or two traits scored at 4 or 5.

They may generally be in a positive mood, but cautious in new situations. Their feeding and sleeping habits may be predictable but they can become overwhelmed in a crowd. Note the traits you scored as a 4 or 5. If your baby is highly sensitive, know that bright lights, noises, smells, and certain sensations may upset her. If she is cautious in new situations, plan to work with her to help her feel more comfortable.

Spunky babies are delightful little puzzles.

What your spunky baby is telling you

- Pay attention to the things that upset me.
- When I'm upset hold me and help me calm.
- If I get upset in a crowd, please take me to a quiet place. I need a break.
- Give me time to shift from one thing to another.
- I like exercise time! Keep me safe by childproofing the environment.

WHEN YOUR BABY IS SPIRITED

I need you to help me calm. Please respond quickly, before I become too upset.

Spirited babies are intense. Every reaction, whether happy or sad, is strong and powerful. Their arousal systems are more reactive. They need help calming. They experience every sound, smell, sensation, taste, and emotion at a deeper level.

A mere click of a closing door may awaken them. Their eating and sleeping patterns are unpredictable. They are alert, tuning in to their environment like a sentry, never missing a thing. They may seem to crave stimulation yet become overwhelmed.

They are busy and on the move, and keeping them safe is a constant challenge. Yet, they may be highly cautious in new situations, leading others to describe them as shy. They aren't, but they are checking things out before they are ready to participate.

If you feel like you are working harder than your peers whose babies are not spirited, you are correct. But life with spirit also can be filled with incredible joy.

What your spirited baby is telling you

- I like stimulation, but I also need you to help me take a break before I get overstimulated.
- I need quiet, serene spaces for feeding and sleeping.
- Touch calms me. That's why I like to be held so much.
- My cues are more important than the clock. Please feed me and put me to sleep when I need it. In time, I can adapt to our family's routine.
- I need to move. Childproof to keep me safe.
- When you rock, bounce, and sway me, you calm me.
- Give me time to warm up to a new situation.
- Don't surprise me. Talk to me. Let me know what is going to happen and when you will be picking me up. Wait until I am looking at you.
- Move slowly. Rushing upsets me.
- Take care of yourself. I sync with your stress level.
- Let me "do" things when I ask. I may be small, but I am more capable than you may imagine.

STRATEGIES FOR THE FIVE CORE TRAITS—INTENSITY, SENSITIVITY, ALERTNESS, REGULARITY, AND ACTIVITY LEVEL

Like Kendis, who found the best way for Winn to feed, you, too, can use your baby's temperament profile to discover "this is what works for us." There are specific techniques that will fit you, your environment, and your baby's unique temperament. Let's take an in-depth look at each of the five core traits that are most common among highly aroused, spirited babies.

Intensity . . .

Your baby who is wired to be intense is telling you, *Watch and listen, I will show you when I need your help to calm.*

Intensity describes the degree of energy in every response. High intensity reflects the turbocharged arousal system and is the most universal characteristic of spirited infants. They experience emotions and sensations like a splash of cold water to the face—sharp, penetrating, shocking. The secret to supporting them is catching their signs of distress before their systems flood. The earlier you notice the subtle changes in their movements, vocalization, and other signals, the easier you can settle them. Luckily, those signals are not random. There is a pattern you can follow. A simple exercise, the Baby-size Stress Test, can allow you to decipher that pattern.

Intensity describes the degree of energy in every response. High intensity reflects the turbocharged arousal system and is the most universal characteristic of spirited infants.

The Baby-size Stress Test

1. Select a time your baby is rested, dry, fed, has had a good burp, and is feeling content. If another adult is available, ask them to video this exercise so you can review it again later.

2. Take your baby into a dimly lit room. (In a brighter, busier room the baby's ever-changing cues are more difficult to distinguish.)

3. Turn off your phone so you are not distracted.

4. Place your baby on a blanket on the floor.

5. Sit down next to your baby, ready to detect every nuance of her body. Note how she turns to you, cooing and smiling. Go ahead, smile and converse with her. Watch her arms and legs smoothly cycling. If she reaches out to you, take her hand, let her hold your finger. If she is crawling, thank her for the toy she brings you. Stay tuned in, do not allow your attention to shift away from her. This is the green zone of calm energy.

Observing the green zone: In the green zone, your baby's arousal system is indicating all is well. She is safe. Her needs are met; all systems are in balance. You will know she is in this zone by her quiet, alert demeanor. She can focus on you and effectively control her limbs. Her heart and breathing rates are slow and steady. In this green zone of calm energy, she feeds well, interacts with you, plays contentedly, and easily falls asleep.

6. Note when your baby turns her gaze away from you, swinging her head to the side as though she has lost interest. She has not. This is a signal she is struggling to remain in a balanced calm state. This is the yellow zone of elevated arousal.

Observing the yellow zone: The signals of the yellow zone can be subtle at first and easy to miss. Your baby continues to be happy, but her vocalization takes on an edge, a line forms between her brows. These are signs she is slipping out of the green zone of calm energy and entering the yellow zone of elevated arousal. A natural inclination is to draw her attention back to you by talking louder, shaking a toy, or even rotating her head toward you. Hold on. She is signaling she is becoming overwhelmed, struggling to remain calm.

7. Today, because you are learning about her cues, continue watching. (I feel guilty every time I do this, but the knowledge gleaned is invaluable. I ask the babies for forgiveness.) Do not try to regain your baby's attention, nor calm her. Instead, observe how her movements change. Short, sharp, jerky kicks replace the smooth thrusts. She pulls up her knees. Then lets loose a wail. This is the red zone of overarousal.

Observing the red zone: The red zone is "catchy." Often, you sense it before you ever see or hear your baby accelerating. A familiar tinge of panic strikes. You hope you are wrong, but you know in your heart you are not. Your baby stiffens. Her back arches, thrusting toward you as though pleading, *Pick me up, now!* If she is crawling, she comes to you, or suddenly collapses. Her cries erupt like a screeching frenzy of high-pitched notes on a scratchy violin. She has plunged deep into the red zone.

You do not want to go into the red zone. Neither does your baby. Fortunately, you do not have to. By closely observing your baby's cues, you'll see she is informing you what zone she is in at the moment. Monitor carefully; she can shift from fine to falling apart in seconds. The higher the spirited infant's arousal system ramps up before you respond the greater the challenge to slow it down. Catch her in the yellow zone, and you'll discover that calming her is speedier compared with what you may have experienced in the past.

The chart of Cues for the 3 Zones of Arousal that follows includes the most common signals parents have experienced with their babies. No two babies are alike, so note the cues that fit your baby, revisit this cue chart over time, and add unique cues that are specific to your baby and how you communicate with each other.

CUES FOR THE 3 ZONES OF AROUSAL

Select those that fit your baby. Add to the list your baby's unique cues.

GREEN ZONE *When babies are in the green zone of calm energy, they typically . . .*	YELLOW ZONE *When babies are in the yellow zone— and beginning to dysregulate—they typically . . .*	RED ZONE *When babies are in the red zone of tense energy and full dysregulation, they typically . . .*
Look at you	Turn away	Cry
Engage in play	Lose interest in or become frustrated with toy/book	Arch their back
Are peaceful	Begin to fuss a little	Move in a sharp jerky manner
Are happy	Seek contact with you	Tightly fist their hands

GREEN ZONE When babies are in the green zone of calm energy, they typically . . .	YELLOW ZONE When babies are in the yellow zone—and beginning to dysregulate—they typically . . .	RED ZONE When babies are in the red zone of tense energy and full dysregulation, they typically . . .
Move smoothly, as though stroking the air	Accelerate movements or start kicking as though starting a motorcycle	Stiffen their entire body
Giggle	Form a line between their brows	Become red in the face
Are bright-eyed	Frown	Pull up their knees
Mimic your movements and vocalization	Purse lips	Bring hands to the midline in a self-protective manner
Breathe quietly and slowly	Grimace	Open their eyes wide
Are aware of things, but calm	Start blinking	Flare their nostrils
Interact with others	Push toys, or other people, away	Scrunch up their entire face
Smile	Pull a blanket over their head	Scream
Hoot	Burrow into your neck	Throw things
Explore	Become restless	Want to be held, then bite you, or push away from you
	Become irritable	Become hyper and frenzied
	Pucker an eyebrow	Collapse
	Start to hum or make a revving-up sound	Become overwhelmed

GREEN ZONE When babies are in the green zone of calm energy, they typically . . .	YELLOW ZONE When babies are in the yellow zone— and beginning to dysregulate—they typically . . .	RED ZONE When babies are in the red zone of tense energy and full dysregulation, they typically . . .
	Lose the sparkle in their eyes—eyes go flat	Are super-needy
	Want to nurse	
	Go for a lovie	

There is magic in catching the cues of spirited infants before they reach the red zone. Suddenly the frequency and duration of the emotional hijackings drop precipitously. Smiles replace screams.

As your expertise in reading your baby's signals increases, you'll realize that with those sounds, gestures, and physical changes your baby is telling you about the state of his arousal system. Green zone: *All is well.* Yellow zone: *I'm struggling. Please help.* Red zone: *I'm overloaded. I need major assistance to calm down.*

What he is *not* saying is *I'm angry at you,* or *You are blowing it here.*

No, he's telling you about what is happening inside his body. It's not personal. It's biology. He needs you and your body to help him bring all systems back into balance.

As you become more aware of your baby's green, yellow, and red zones, take note of your own. Just like your baby, you, too, are constantly moving through these zones as you regulate your own arousal level.

As you become more aware of your baby's green, yellow, and red zones, take note of your own. Just like your baby, you, too, are constantly moving through these zones as you regulate your own arousal level.

Sensitivity . . .

Your baby who is wired to be more sensitive is telling you, *I need your comforting touch.*

In one of my classes, Vera, the mother of seven, nodded in recognition when she reviewed the signs of keen sensitivity. Smiling at Hannah, who was lying in her arms, she remarked, "Her hardwiring is more sensitive. Our house is noisy. Everyone is at home in the evening, running up and down the stairs, grumbling about homework, yelling from one room to another. She picks up everyone's emotions and melts down almost instantly. I thought I was a pro but Hannah has brought me to this class."

Fortunately, the temperament profile helped Vera understand Hannah's sensitivity. In the process she also realized the trait of sensitivity can be a great asset. In fact, it was her highly sensitive older child who noticed when Vera was upset or needed help. "It's as though he has a sixth sense for it," she told me.

If you selected a 4 or a 5 for sensitivity, you can predict that your baby experiences every sound, smell, sensation, taste, emotion, and sight deeply, as though she has a thinner boundary than other babies' separating her from the hubbub of the world. A footfall on the third step—the one that squeaks—awakens her. If another baby whimpers she shudders and bursts into tears. Feedings are preferred at night in the dark and quiet. A wet or soiled diaper requires an immediate change, but then she screams when the cool air strikes her body.

Researchers have documented that highly sensitive babies experience pain more acutely, which explains why sensitive babies truly suffer from teething. For an infant brain wired for survival, every sensation must be reviewed and filed—*threat or no big deal?* Keeping your baby close and reassured while she sorts it all out helps her remain calm.

All infants need touch, but sensitive babies crave it. Spirited infants seek touch to such a high level that parents have told me, "If she could, I think she would crawl back into the womb."

. . . .

All infants need touch, but sensitive babies crave it. Spirited infants seek touch to such a high level that parents have told me, "If she could, I think she would crawl back into the womb."

. . . .

There is a reason for this. When you hold your baby close, his brain tells him, *I'm safe. Despite all the strange noises and sensations in this new world, all is well. My caregiver will protect me.*

Touch brings your baby into the green zone of calm energy. His heart and pulse rates slow. Blood can easily circulate in the digestive system instead of rushing to the muscles. The result is improved digestion, elimination, and respiratory function. Touch even strengthens the immune system, leading to higher levels of antibodies in the baby's system.

In other cultures, like the Kalahari of southern Africa, it is typical for infants to be carried 90 percent of the day. In the United States, in the first few months, infants are carried on average a mere two to three hours a day, and less for older infants. Yet studies conducted in Uganda demonstrated that babies carried in an upright position are quicker to walk and faster to develop in other areas as well. That's not all. The vertical position also promotes normal growth of the head and helps develop strong back and neck muscles.

According to researcher Dr. Maria Blois, premature infants placed in an upright position on their mother's chest demonstrated improved respiratory patterns, more regular than in an incubator. Episodes of sleep apnea—temporary cessation of breathing and slowing of the heart rate—were also reduced.

Keep this in mind when your arms are aching, and you need your hands free. Find a carrier that is comfortable for you and your baby. Keep his body close to yours. Wrap your arms around him. He needs to experience the sensation of your steady heart and pulse rates to regulate his own. Let your body warm his. Gradually, through this tandem practice, he will learn how to calm himself.

Stephanie, the mother of a thriving spirited preschooler (and a great sleeper, by the way), laughed as she remembered how her daughter Teagan had to be plastered to her chest. "Teagan could not calm her body without that strong physical connection. For her, touch was such a powerful tool."

When you provide your spirited baby with the touch he needs, others may criticize you for making your baby dependent upon you. Quite the contrary. Frequent, sensitive touch for young babies results in a reduction in fearfulness and stress hormone levels and less frequent crying.

Babies who receive the touch they need don't become more dependent. They become more *independent*. As their motor skills develop, you will find their arousal system is in the green zone of calm energy, telling them, *All is well. Let's go explore!* (We will address later when and how to ease back our support for our slow-to-adapt little ones, who may need a Gentle NUDGE to venture out.)

> Babies who receive the touch they need don't become more dependent. They become more *independent* . . . their arousal system is the green zone of calm energy, telling them, *All is well. Let's go explore!*

Next time your baby fusses until he is held, know he is telling you, *Your touch calms me. Please keep me close.* And because he is temperamentally sensitive, he will need that closeness longer than his not-so-sensitive peers. He's a snuggler! But there is also an interesting dichotomy with these sensitive spirited babies. While too much sensory stimulation can overwhelm them, they also seem to seek information, activities, and interaction.

Alertness . . .

Your baby who is wired to be more alert is telling you, *I need you to help me take a break.*

The highly alert baby tunes into her environment like a sentinel scanning for information. Little to no stimulation causes her to stop what she is doing and react. She stares at your bright orange running shoes as though studying the design. If you move the furniture in her room, she may be so engrossed in observing the differences that she struggles to fall asleep that night. At two months, when Grandma visits, she never sleeps. She's too captivated by the strange voice.

German researcher Mechthild Papousek discovered that spirited infants train their parents to increase stimulation even though they are almost always overstimulated. It is easy to be fooled by their gusto. *Show me more things! Bounce me higher, faster! Tickle me, laugh with me!* They respond with a resplendent smile or hearty chuckle. But in reality, babies who are high on the scale of alertness whip themselves into a frenzy of overstimulation.

Do not fall for their antics. While increased stimulation may temporarily interrupt their fussiness, these tactics do not have a lasting calming effect and may just delay the meltdown to come. Alert, spirited infants need parents to find the balance, providing the right amount of stimulation and knowing when to help their baby take a break.

> Babies who are high on the scale of alertness whip themselves into a frenzy of overstimulation. Do not fall for their antics. . . . They need parents to find the balance, providing the right amount of stimulation and knowing when to help their baby take a break.

Sabrina recognized this in her son:

"Two weeks after talking with you I had a totally different child. I thought about how alert he is and the need to help him stay calm. I developed a system of immediate responses to him. I had always been very responsive and never just left him to cry, but I stepped it up a notch. He always woke happy. If he was happy, we would do LOTS of things. He loved seeing stuff, doing things, being in the middle of chaos and noise and light, people, animals, novel things, new places, or outside. You get the idea. Anyway, at the first sign of a fuss or discontentment I would take him to my room. Turn off all the lights, no music, not even the tiniest bit of input other than that of nursing. He would fall asleep then wake happy, ready to play again. For months and months, he needed four to five little naps a day. Complete breaks from stimulation were mandatory."

She continues, "We morphed from hours and hours of screaming every day to the world's happiest child. It was magical. He remains a high-needs kiddo, requiring a LOT of rest and quiet and a LOT of stimulation. But he's so freaking cool."

If you have selected a 4 or 5 on the alertness scale, research confirms your baby uses more eye movements and spends more time considering alternatives. However, he may get locked in—literally unable to look away, plunging him into a state of overexcitability. Thus, the dichotomy of his alertness trait, which loves stimulating situations, and his sensitivity trait leads him to fall apart.

When you, like Sabrina, recognize that your baby is alert, you can provide the stimulation your baby needs and at the same time watch for the yellow zone cues of arousal. When you see them, stop or step away to give your baby the time and space to calm. That sensitive response will help your baby remain regulated.

Regularity . . .

Your baby who is wired to be irregular is telling you,
My cues are more important than the clock.

"Why isn't there any predictability to when my baby will eat or sleep?" Kelly lamented to me. "My friend could set a clock by her baby's naps, but not mine."

If you selected a 4 or a 5 on the regularity scale—and most spirited infants are irregular—you can predict that your baby will not be predictable. Patterns of eating and sleeping will initially be nonexistent. You can gently build predictability, but it's essential to recognize that regularity is not your baby's natural domain. These babies have eating and non-eating days. Nap days and non-nap days. Holding this baby off until a previously determined "correct" time to eat or sleep will bite you in the backside. When pushed into the red zone of overarousal she accelerates to the point of not being able to eat or fall asleep.

Irregular babies, with their freewheeling body clock, are our future firefighters, hospital workers, pilots, military personnel, police officers, rock stars, and even entrepreneurs, able to function with lots of moving parts and constantly shifting work hours. But living with irregular babies in the first eighteen months of life can be a challenge, especially when others push you to enforce a rigid schedule.

Believe your baby. Even if she recently ate or slept but is telling you she needs to do so again, respond accordingly. Do not second-guess her.

In chapter 5 I'll introduce the Gentle NUDGE, showing you how to gradually—without tears—bring your baby into the rhythm of your family's daily routine. But in the meantime, one of the most helpful approaches to a highly irregular baby is to make sure you take care of yourself and get *your* basic needs met.

If your baby's unpredictable eating, sleeping, and sociability are driving you crazy, you can turn to chapter 4, "How Can I Meet My Basic Needs Now?," for some immediate help.

Activity level . . .

Your baby who is wired to be active is telling you,
I need to move. Repetitive motion calms me.

Six foot five inches tall, legs like tree trunks, Carl packed the room with his physical presence. Even when sitting, this former college basketball player wiggled and jiggled in place, contorting a paper clip between thumb and forefinger, and rocking back and forth on the back legs of his chair. Kyle, his seven-month-old son, matched his rhythm, lurching back and forth on hands and knees before collapsing, unable to coordinate all his limbs.

High-energy spirited babies have been known to leap out of their cribs at nine months of age, and proudly ascend to the top of the refrigerator before their second birthday.

If you selected a 4 or a 5 for activity level on the temperament profile, you can foresee your baby's need to move. Protect her by childproofing your environment, using safety straps, not placing her on a bed or counter from which she may fall, and padding hard edges as your baby starts scooting and cruising.

It is also important to recognize that repetitive motion is very relaxing and settling for highly active spirited babies. Whether rocking, walking, bouncing, swinging, or swaying, repetitive motion has a calming effect. Science demonstrates repetitive movement calms by eliciting the relaxation response. Like meditation, continuous action lowers heart rate, blood pressure, and muscle tension.

Remember, though, spirited infants seek stimulation even when they are overstimulated. Frequently they signal a desire for FAST walking, BIG bounces, or VIGOROUS rocking. Initially, match the speed with their energy level, but then slow down. Gradually ease into a relaxed pace that is calming to both of you. Over time, reduce the length of each session.

The Five Core Temperament Traits and the Four "Bonus" Traits

The five core temperament traits—intensity, sensitivity, alertness, regularity, and activity level—are the most apparent and significant ones for newborn-to-eighteen-month-old babies and the best place to start. When you're ready, explore the four "bonus" traits—first reaction, persistence, adaptability, and seriousness.

STRATEGIES FOR THE "BONUS" TEMPERAMENT TRAITS— FIRST REACTION, PERSISTENCE, ADAPTABILITY, SERIOUSNESS

My experience working with spirited infants tells me that the five core temperament traits—intensity, sensitivity, alertness, regularity, and activity level—are the most apparent and significant for newborn-to-eighteen-month-old babies. Together, the strategies to support these traits form a reliable soothing/calming tool kit. Add them to those you have already discovered work for your baby. If you're ready to take in a bit more information, look at the strategies for the four "bonus" traits—first reaction, persistence, adaptability, and seriousness. These traits play a significant role as your baby grows and develops.

First reaction . . .

Your baby who is wired with a cautious first reaction is telling you, *Try again. My first reaction may not be my final decision.*

As you interact with your spirited baby you may find that no matter whether it is a new pacifier, caregiver, food, place, or calming strategy, your baby's first reaction is a vehement rejection. Do not assume she hates it or the technique is ineffective. Frequently that first negative reaction is just an initial response. Often, with time and exposure, your baby will come to enjoy this new thing.

Recognize that initial negative first reaction for what it is—a first reaction, not a final decision.

For example, if your baby initially spits out the pacifier you offer, instead of throwing it away, try again. Don't force it, simply provide more opportunities to consider it. After the second or third introduction, or maybe the twenty-fifth attempt, you may find her eagerly sucking.

If you selected a 4 or a 5 on the temperament profile you can expect that your baby will draw back and fret when exposed to new things. Respect your baby's cautious first reaction but do not avoid new things or situations altogether. Repeated short, calm exposures make it better. Slowly but surely you will see her become more comfortable.

> Respecting a baby's cautious first reaction is important. Never forcing is essential. But practice and regular exposure make it better.

Persistence . . .

Your baby who is wired to be persistent is telling you,
I need you to listen to me and respond to my needs.
Please do not ignore me.

Many spirited infants are temperamentally wired to be persistent. Seventeen-month-old Sam loved his older brother Mathew's little cars. Worried that Sam might choke on the small components, his dad, Tyler, offered a ball, dinosaurs, and big trucks, but Sam kept coming back for the cars. Even a firm no fell on deaf ears. Frustrated, Tyler picked up the cars, placed them on top of the counter, and walked out of the room. Sam threw a fit, and then all drew quiet.

Underestimating the little dynamo, Tyler assumed Sam had given up. But moments later big brother Mathew could be heard shrieking, "No, Sam, no!" Dashing back into the kitchen Tyler found Sam standing on top of the counter, gleefully holding the cars. The open oven door was a dead giveaway as to how he had gotten there.

Determined and strong, persistent babies know what they want. If a sound or texture is bothering them, there is nothing that will appease them until it is removed. If they wish to be held, you will find yourself holding them. Advice to ignore or distract them is worthless. They do not give up easily, and, as Sam proved, are willing to go to great heights to achieve their goals!

Fortunately we do not have to be adversaries duking it out with our persistent spirited infants. No need for winners or losers. Instead of having daily skirmishes, we can recognize that our babies, like Sam, are already demonstrating their drive and goal orientation. A predictor of future success, their persistence is not something to get rid of or break. Your temperamentally persistent baby is telling you: *I need to be heard and attended to.*

Next time a recommended strategy suggests ignoring your baby's distress, ignore the advice, not your baby. Instead, seek to understand what she is telling you she needs. Then work together. If she wants to climb, help her find a safe place to do so. If she needs to be held, hold her. If the car seat straps are driving her wild, stop, take her out, and give her a reprieve.

Paying attention to your persistent baby is not giving in. Your tenacious little one is learning you can be trusted to listen and work with her. She will reciprocate in kind. Rather than fighting with you, she will cooperate with you. In the years to come, you will help her develop creative problem-solving skills, to come up with solutions that work for everyone.

. . . .

Paying attention to your persistent baby is not giving in. Your tenacious little one is learning you can be trusted to listen and work with her.

. . . .

Adaptability . . .

Your baby who is wired to be slow to adapt is telling you, *Please slow down. Talk to me. Let me know what is going to happen.*

Ever wonder why your baby fusses when you scoop her up to change her diaper? Why she cries every time you take her in or out of her car seat? Or why she fights falling asleep? The widely varying factors in each of these scenarios can make it challenging to identify what is setting off your baby's arousal system. But look carefully, and you'll realize the common factor is a transition—a shift from one state, place, or condition to another.

If you selected a 4 or a 5 for adaptability, you might have discovered one of the major reasons your baby "redlines" out of the blue and wrestles with sleep. To successfully negotiate all the shifts and stops and starts that occur during the day, she is telling you, *I need you to slow down and explain what's happening so I can remain calm.*

Every time you pick up your baby, lay her down, move from one room to another, hand her off to another caregiver, stop play, start play, change her diaper, place her in a car seat, stop a feeding, start a feeding, dress her, prepare her for sleep, or any other shift, she must regulate her arousal system. Unexpected transitions, surprises, or rushes trigger her arousal system, activating a flood of physiological reactions so powerful they overwhelm her ability to remain calm. She falls apart and you are left wondering what just happened.

Avoid innocently sending your baby into the red zone, by explaining and preparing her for the change. Before picking up your baby bend down to her level. Wait for her gaze to shift to you. Tell her what you are going to do. For example, "I am going to pick you up." Hold your hands, palms open, in front of her, ready to lift her. Wait, do not pick her up yet. If she is able, allow her to reach out to you. If she is merely weeks old, gently caress her cheek, allowing her to turn to you. Now pick her up.

> Unexpected transitions startle spirited babies, triggering their arousal systems. . . . Avoid innocently sending your baby into the red zone, by explaining and preparing for the change.

Converse with her. "I am going to dress you. It's cold today. I've selected a soft, warm, long-sleeved onesie for you." Allow her to have a look before continuing, "I'm going to pull your arm into the sleeve now. Yes, this is your arm." Or, "I'm going to change your diaper. Let's lift your legs. Wow, you can lift your legs all by yourself!"

True, others may question your sanity, talking to a baby in this manner. But you will discover your baby very quickly begins to "help" you, lifting her arm or legs, pulling off a sock, doing more and more as she is able. Everyday activities become delightful points of connection, rich in conversation.

By slowing down, talking to your baby, involving her as you move through your daily routine, you focus your attention on her and what is happening in that moment. Doing so engenders empathy for what she is experiencing. Compassion leads to connection. Connection calms.

After learning about this type of care, Brian, a dad of a baby girl, tried it. "My perspective on diapering changed completely," he reported to me. "It is no longer a dreaded chore, but our time together. We are making the most of it."

And then he laughed before admitting, "We practice her soccer kicks. A few good thrusts before we finish up. I'm pretty certain she'll be a forward."

There may be very few warm, happy moments to enjoy when you have a spirited infant who cries frequently. By turning those daily caregiving functions into *our time*, you increase the frequency of those rewarding points of connection. True, your spirited little one might still cry, but she will quiet faster. When you don't "lose" your baby at every transition, your days will be calmer. Calmer days lead to more peaceful nights.

Slow down. Stop rushing. Talk to your baby about what you are going to do. That smile, even from your more serious and analytical little one, will be priceless.

Seriousness (mood) . . .

Your baby whose mood is wired toward being serious and analytical is telling you, *I'm happy. I'm just a little more reserved about demonstrating it.*

Sometimes with infants it is difficult to discern whether their mood is a result of temperament or due to what's previously been happening. For example, is the baby fussing because of overstimulation, is she communicating her dislike, or is it something else? Even in infancy, some individuals demonstrate a more serious and analytical tendency.

If you selected a 4 or a 5 for mood, you can predict that your baby will be more serious. Know that while your baby may not be effusive in her greeting of you, she is nonetheless excited to see you. And while she is generally content with life, she will make you aware of a few tweaks that could make it slightly better. We need those analysts! Treasure her selective smiles, appreciate the little "old wise soul" who has come to live with you, and look forward to one day being asked by her five-year-old self questions like "How do people in the artic breathe if there are no trees to make oxygen?" Or, "Is God spirited? Listen to that thunder, God must be spirited!"

USING YOUR BABY'S TEMPERAMENT TRAITS AS A GUIDE

Identifying your baby's genetically wired temperament traits helps you to answer the question "What is my baby telling me?" This knowledge guides you in selecting the best responses at any moment. Review the summary of the nine traits to see which ones fit your baby and what she may be telling you. Record your findings in your journal.

SNAPSHOT OF THE NINE PERSONALITY TRAITS FOR BABIES

When your baby is intense . . .	*Respond quickly. Don't wait until he's too upset to calm.*
When your baby is sensitive . . .	*Provide touch. Never worry that holding your baby will create a bad habit.*
When your baby is alert . . .	*Note stimulation levels and know when to help her take a break.*

When your baby is irregular . . .	*Focus on cues, not the clock. Take steps to meet your own basic needs for sleep and food.*
When your baby is active . . .	*Think safety and know repetitive movement calms.*
When your baby has a cautious first reaction . . .	*Do not force, but try again. A first response may not be a final decision.*
When your baby is persistent . . .	*Listen to your baby and work together to meet her needs.*
When your baby is slow to adapt . . .	*Slow down. Talk to your baby. Tell her what is going to happen.*
When your baby is serious . . .	*Know your baby is happy, just a bit reserved in expressing it.*

Your baby *is* more and the right response embraces that truth. It is important work, requiring thought, energy, stamina, patience, and lots of empathy. That is why in the next chapter we focus on you—your needs and how to build your support team. You do not have to do this alone. Your emotions, stress, hopes, and needs are just as important as your child's.

Identifying your baby's genetically wired temperament traits helps you to answer the question "What is my baby telling me?" This knowledge guides you in selecting the best responses at any moment and leads to the sensitive care that underlies secure attachment.

CHEAT SHEET: WHAT IS YOUR BABY TELLING YOU?

1. *Complete the Infant Temperament Profile for your baby.* Assess and reassess your baby's temperament. Some traits might become more pronounced as your baby reaches new developmental milestones.

2. *Identify your baby's green, yellow, and red zone cues by using the Cues for the 3 Zones of Arousal chart.* Find a quiet half hour and do the Baby-size Stress Test. When you recognize your baby's green, yellow, and red zones of arousal, everything changes.

3. *Practice listening to what your baby is telling you.* Focusing on the nine temperament traits helps you to identify your baby's cues and decipher what she is telling you she needs.

REFLECTION QUESTIONS FOR YOUR JOURNAL

- Which of the nine temperament traits are most apparent with my baby?

- What are the most visible cues that my baby is in the green zone? The yellow zone? The red zone?

- Are there certain messages my baby is sending me that I have sensed but have perhaps ignored, thinking that was the right thing to do?

Chapter 3

What Do I Need to Stay Calm So I Can Calm My Baby?

Untangling Our Emotions, Reframing Our Experiences, and Getting Support

> *"If you start thinking negatively, like, 'She's driving me crazy,' you'll get frustrated. But if you think, 'She isn't settling because she's smart and her mind is working very fast,' it's easier to stay calm. Well, maybe not in the middle of the night when she's screaming and your partner is sleeping, but most of the time it helps."*
> —Teri, mother of three

It is not a figment of your imagination: You are working harder as the parent of a spirited infant. German researchers Mechthild Papousek, Michael Schieche, and Harald Wurmser document that the cues of spirited babies are more subtle and difficult to read. These babies truly can shift from fine to furious like an atom shooting through space. It is not easy to provide the warm, sensitive responses they need. In my experience with thousands of parents and babies, doing so requires regulation of your own arousal system.

If you are upset, neural static fogs your brain. A fogged brain misses cues and results in responses that tend to be too late and out of sync with your baby. That is why it is so important to give yourself permission to be compassionate to yourself. *Taking care of you is taking care of your baby.*

. . . .

If you are upset, neural static fogs your brain. A fogged brain misses cues and results in responses that tend to be too late and out of sync with your baby. That is why it is so important to give yourself permission to be compassionate to yourself.

. . . .

But how do you remain calm when exhaustion and worry threaten to take you down? Do you ask for help or struggle to manage this responsibility on your own? Do you search the internet for the right answer or respond from your heart? How do you find the strength to ignore what others insist worked for them but does not feel right for you, your baby, or your family?

The weight of fears and personal stress triggers can be crushing. But denying them prevents you from dealing with them. On the one hand you know you are not supposed to feel envious, but on the other, how do you help it when you see friends at a neighborhood gathering and their babies sleep in a stroller the entire time? If they complain, it requires every ounce of self-control not to yell, "You think you have it bad, but you have no idea!"

And then there is the embarrassing awareness that you have what feels like the worst kid in the group. Theirs are quiet. Yours fusses. Theirs sleep. Yours remains awake. That makes you worry. Do these parents know something you don't?

Not even veteran parents escape the upheaval. Kristen, the mom of three, told me, "I knew it was going to be a lot of work. I've been through life with an infant before. But I definitely did not imagine this."

Like Kristen's, your love is enormous—and so are the demands on you. The disconnect between what we expect before the birth of a spirited baby and the reality we find ourselves in adds enormously to the stress. It's as though someone gathered up our dreams and expectations, stuck a stick of dynamite in the bundle, and lit the fuse. Even if we were somewhat mentally prepared, it is still a shock.

UNTANGLING OUR EMOTIONS: THE CHALLENGES ARE REAL

In a social-media-filtered life where everything around you appears to be perfect, it is tempting to push yourself harder and slam shut the door so no one else finds out what's going on. But doing so has a physiological impact.

Powering through your distress without addressing it pushes your arousal system into the red zone of threat and tension. Your heart rate accelerates. You can't think clearly. And if that isn't troubling enough, your baby synchronizes to your stress. The amount of crying and fussing escalates. The baby's sleep fragments into twenty-minute catnaps. The turmoil snowballs.

It does not have to be this way. Amid the mayhem you have permission to stop and ask: "What helps me stay calm so I can calm my baby?"

Taking care of yourself is not being selfish or self-centered. When you calm your body, your baby calms as well. The question of course is how do we do it? I've been asking this question for decades. What I discovered is that the hardiest parents tell themselves two powerful messages that they return to over and over again:

1. I can reframe and ultimately transform how I feel and think about this experience.

2. I do not have to do it alone. I can ask for and get help.

If you can develop and then hold on to these two powerful statements, you will discover a well of optimism you didn't know you had and a wealth of possibilities that will support you in ways you never imagined possible.

> Taking care of you is taking care of your baby. When you bring your body back into a state of calm energy, your baby calms as well.

WHAT AM I TELLING MYSELF? REFRAMING OUR BELIEFS AND SELF-TALK

What we tell ourselves about an experience changes that experience. It is not merely looking at the bright side or taking a grim view, but instead *redefining* the experience.

I was struck by this fact when my daughter moved to Europe for a job. Upon her arrival with four stuffed bags, a backpack, a bicycle, and downhill skis, she grabbed a cab and headed to the apartment she'd rented online. When she arrived, she found the key that had been left for her, opened the lobby door, and hauled all her baggage up the stairs to the fourth floor, only to discover the key did not unlock the door to her flat. She called the rental agency. No one answered. She searched for another key—found none. That is when she texted me to tell me what was happening. I wrote back, "It's okay to cry." She replied, "Nah, I'm in a safe place. The sun is shining. It's 70 degrees. This is just an inconvenience. I'll get a hotel tonight."

Whatever the stresses we're facing—whether we are locked out of our apartment or the new parents of a spirited baby—we can choose how we perceive and thus handle the experience.

There is actual science to explain how this process works. Lessons from neuroscience and psychology research conducted by Nikki Johnson and Catherine McMahon tell us when it comes to life with spirit, resilient parents manage to transform their perceptions from those in which everything is wrong to messages that explain, depersonalize, and redefine the situation. This change in perception has a physiological impact. It shifts the arousal system from the red zone of threat and tension to the green zone of calm energy.

In my spirited baby classes for parents we bring this experience to life. Recently, I kicked off a class by passing out blank cards, inviting parents to answer the question:

"On the bad, awful, terrible days, what am I telling myself?"

I promised the parents anonymity. It took only a few minutes for everyone to complete the cards. I collected, shuffled, and passed them out, asking each parent to read one card.

Kristen, her hair still wet from a quickie shower, started us off:

- "I'm trapped. I don't have help. It's only me."

The others followed:

- "I do not know what to do."
- "I miss my mom. I'm so alone."
- "UGH, just go the F**K to sleep!"
- "Why me?"
- "I want my old life back."
- "I have the worst kid in the group."
- "I can never do enough."

As they read, I wrote the messages on the whiteboard, and then asked the group to read the list aloud. They refused. It was Jenna who broke the tension when she blurted, "I can't. I'm going to cry." Her comment triggered a visceral, collective reaction and an outpouring from the group.

The negative messages we tell ourselves are raw and oppressive. Our chests tighten, anxiety rises, our hearts pound. They shove us headlong into the red zone of overarousal. The impulse to flee rises in us, as does the question "What was I thinking when I had this kid?"

No one wants to feel this way. Fortunately, we don't have to. We can make a conscious decision to alter how we think and feel about our experience as parents. This does not mean we deny our emotions. We still perceive them—the prickles of resentment, fear, and apprehension—and we accept them. We acknowledge we are human. We recognize this is a tough journey. But accepting our emotions does not mean we must give them control. It is within our power to choose what we will tell ourselves about them and how we will act.

> The negative messages we tell ourselves are raw and oppressive. . . . They shove us headlong into the red zone of overarousal. The impulse to flee rises in us. . . . No one wants to feel this way. Fortunately, we don't have to. We can choose to transform those messages.

Turning back to the parents in the class, I asked them to transform the "bad day" self-talk into "good day" self-talk. We looked for words that redefined the experience to empower us and inspire hope. Here is what they came up with.

BAD-DAY AND GOOD-DAY SELF-TALK

Old Bad-Day Self-Talk	Transformed Good-Day Self-Talk
"I feel trapped."	"Must be time to call a friend to take her."
"I do not know what to do."	"I can figure this out."
"I miss my mom."	"My mom is not physically with me, but I feel her presence in my life."
"UGH, just go the F**K to sleep!"	"My baby is still learning how to consolidate sleep. In the meantime, I can figure out how to get more sleep for myself."

Old Bad-Day Self-Talk	Transformed Good-Day Self-Talk
"Why me?"	"It's not about me and I'm not alone. A lot of other parents are dealing with spirited babies even if we don't tell each other."
"I want my old life back."	"In the big picture I would never send her back."
"I have the worst kid in the group."	"Yep. That's my kid, the passionate, curious, busy one."
"I can never do enough."	"I've accomplished the most important thing I needed to do today."

This time they agreed to read the transformed messages with me. Once again, a physiological response occurred. But this one was different. Our breathing slowed and our bodies relaxed. Buoyed by the sense of hope and possibilities, we were even able to laugh at the craziness of our lives.

Will this sense of well-being be permanent? No. Our bodies constantly cycle through the zones of arousal throughout the day. We are still emotional. But when those dark moments and messages arise, our words and thoughts can calm us. Now we have a tool in hand—a tool that moves us in the right direction. This is especially helpful when we are temperamentally more sensitive and serious and must work a bit harder to create that positive vision and self-talk.

EIGHT MESSAGES TO REFRAME OUR EXPERIENCE AND IDENTIFY OUR STRENGTHS

While conducting my research and interviewing parents, I found there are eight overarching messages that the hardiest parents turn to, like mantras, to help them reframe and transform their experience of parenting a highly aroused spirited baby.

1. I am a problem solver.

Carla, a strong, athletic woman with muscled arms to kill for, was desperate to stop her daughter's crying. She'd frantically flit from one strategy to the next, her own intensity rising ever higher. "I thought something was desperately wrong and I had to stop it," she explained.

What Carla told herself about her daughter's crying changed the day a friend said to her, "This is not a life and death situation. Take a deep breath and go through the things she might require. Crying is just her way of telling you she needs something."

It wasn't a quick turnaround, but gradually Carla found herself able to look at her daughter and say, "Oh, that's her gassy look. She's red in the face and arching her back. I can figure this out. I don't have to bounce her for two seconds and then try to clumsily nurse. I can slow down and give this time to work. I can figure it out."

When you, like Carla, step back and ever-so-slightly depersonalize the situation, you give yourself time to pause and think more clearly. Instead of getting upset, your focus shifts to exploring and analyzing potential reasons for your baby's distress. You become a problem solver capable of tuning in to what your baby is telling you.

You tell yourself: "There's a problem. I know I'm not causing it, let's see what's wrong. I can figure this out."

Sometimes this shift is as simple as switching one word—"*what if*" to "*even if.*"

For example, "What if my baby screams the entire time we are in the car?" generates anxiety. Instead, thinking, *Even if* my baby cries the whole way, reminds us that even if this dreaded event occurs it will not be the end of the world. As important, if this eventuality does occur, it is a problem that can be solved.

. . . .

Instead of worrying about *"what* if," think in terms of *"even* if."

. . . .

2. I can find *my* way to let my responses fit what my baby is telling me.

The night before Greta contacted me, Oliver's shrieks jolted her awake, just as they had for months. "Tears sprang into my eyes," she told me. "I wanted to scream, 'No! No! No! This is a nightmare!'"

I asked her how she responded.

"I waited to see if he self-soothed, like everyone insists I should do," she tells me. "But he didn't stop, and then he got so upset he stayed awake for the next hour."

"How did you want to respond to him?" I inquired.

"I wanted to go to him," she replied.

"What stopped you?"

"The internet."

"The internet?" I questioned.

"Yes, I can't stop myself. I search *crying, shrieking, sleep training*, and *fussy baby*, trying to figure out the right thing to do. I don't want to make a mess of being a mom, but the advice said I should not go to him and instead let him 'self-regulate.'"

The drive to find the right answer for your baby can take you to dozens of websites, articles, and "experts." But all too often, the information is misguided, not appropriate to your situation, or contradictory. Instead of being helpful the messages lead you to second-guess yourself—and upset you.

Hardy, sensitive parents, however, find their way. Instead of trying to follow *someone else's* right way, they sort through the advice and decide if it matches what their baby is telling them he needs. They do not give away their decision-making power to others.

Jenny, the mom of four-month-old Tommy, explained it well: "One book stated that the baby should never be nursed to sleep. That's not an option for us right now. Maybe it works for someone's baby, but not ours—at least not yet."

Like Jenny, it is important for you to trust your intuition and select the strategies that fit your baby. Researchers exploring how strong, healthy attachment relationships form between parent and child explain that when parents' responses fit the cues and pacing of their baby, the development of the baby's self-regulatory capacities are enhanced.

You can find *your* way by becoming a critical thinker. Before implementing a recommended strategy, analyze it. Any strategy that insists it is the *only* way to go is not considering temperamental and developmental differences. One size does *not* fit all. Many well-accepted techniques are not effective with spirited infants because they fail to consider the babies' stage of development, rocket-powered arousal system, and sensitive, intense temperament.

> One size does *not* fit all. Many well-accepted tech-
> niques are not effective with spirited infants be-
> cause they fail to consider the babies' stage of
> development, rocket-powered arousal system, and
> sensitive, intense temperament.

A strategic framework can help you to evaluate those blithely offered strategies and decide whether they fit your baby and your family's values. First, you will automatically rule out unsafe practices. Then find the "good stuff" that fits your child and reject the rest. You can create your own framework, but let me suggest four questions you can ask yourself before implementing any strategy:

1. Does this strategy fit what my baby is telling me?

2. Does this strategy calm my baby or lead to greater distress?

3. If I were my baby, would I want my mom or dad to treat me this way?

4. Does it feel right to me?

When you know why you are doing what you are doing, you'll find you are confident with "your way." You'll no longer frantically flit from one strategy to another. The sense that you do not know what to do is replaced with a trust in your baby and your own judgment.

3. I can decide what is most important.

Parents commonly report being plagued by a sense that they are never good enough or doing enough. Kylie, a mother of five, spoke to this issue: "Tuesday night, our schedule completely got thrown off. I ended up feeding the kids chicken nuggets for dinner and only eating snacks myself. The next morning, I vowed not to repeat that again. But then my three-year-old did not nap and by late afternoon was struggling. She asked to watch a cartoon. The baby had found an entire bag of crackers and was happily chomping them down. I had to decide, good meal or good parenting? Grab fifteen minutes to get a frozen lasagna in the oven, toss a salad, and set the table, or do something productive with my three-year-old and stop the baby from eating too many crackers? I decided that the highest priority and greatest need was a decent meal for the entire family. I chose making dinner. Despite the fact I may not have been a 'good parent' for those fifteen minutes, I could tell myself, 'I accomplished the most important thing.'"

A conscious decision to prioritize the needs of the moment allows you to tell yourself:

"This is good enough."

"This can wait."

"I've accomplished the most important thing."

4. I can maintain a sense of humor.

During one particularly lively spirited-baby class, first-time dad Nick surprised us with his sense of humor. Nick was quiet and observant, and no one could predict what he might say. When I asked the group, "How do you reframe your perceptions?" he chuckled.

"It was two A.M., my spirited daughter had woken again, but this time she let loose with one of those super-poops that oozed out of the diaper, slid up her back, and completely covered every piece of bedding around her." He shook his head. "It was either scream or laugh."

Nick managed to find absurdity in the moment. "Oh my God," he declared. "She's the poop fountain, just like the Play-Doh Fun Factory."

The concept of finding humor in the darkest moments may seem ludicrous, but laughter reduces stress hormones, triggers feel-good hormones, and improves one's sense of well-being.

You are working hard. When the dog is barking, the baby crying, and the older children screaming, rather than yelling, try laughing. Let out a deep-from-the-belly hoot at the madness of it all. Smile, even if you must fake it. The mere act changes the blood flow in your face and lightens your mood—and the load. Tell yourself, "My life is so crazy, I could write a stand-up comedy script from it!"

Laughter and giggles relax muscles, strengthen your immune system, relieve pain, and increase personal satisfaction and mood. If you struggle to find humor in the moment—download it. Find a great comedy or listen to your favorite stand-up comic. Whatever it takes, bring laughter into your day.

. . . .

Laughter and giggles relax muscles, strengthen your immune system, relieve pain, and increase personal satisfaction and mood.

. . . .

5. I can turn to my spiritual beliefs and tools.

Surprising us once again, this time with his seriousness, Nick described feeling demoralized, wondering why he was being punished by the Universe. "I started to pray," he told us. Then his eyes sparkled as he assured us, "Well, not like, 'O Lord, please make this screaming baby shut up.'" He paused for effect, his timing perfect as he sobered again. "But just, 'Okay, I have a large burden. I'm going to send it out and lay it down tonight. This is what I want help with so that I do not have to carry it alone.'"

If spirituality holds a place in your life, use it.

Like spirituality, mindfulness and gratitude practices are also research-proven tools that lift our spirits and calm our body. Tiffany described a transformation in her thinking the day she was holding her son for his nap—again!

"I was pissed. I kept asking myself, 'Why me?' My pity party began. Then, as I sighed deeply, I inhaled, catching his scent. That wonderful baby aroma. I kissed the sweet spot on the top of his head. It was then I noticed his fingers wound around mine, each tipped with a perfect tiny nail. His cheek soft and smooth rested on my chest. Suddenly his perfection filled me, and I thought, 'He is a spitfire, lucky me.'"

If spirituality holds a place in your life, use it.

Pause to absorb the essence of your baby in this moment. Take note of the early morning light, pink and orange streaking across the sky as the sun rises—a gift from Mother Nature you would have failed to receive if not for your little one who woke at 5:30 A.M.

6. I expect development to take time.
I can respect my baby's pace.

Development takes time. Sometimes it is difficult to imagine you will ever get a full night's sleep again or that this baby will not need to feed ten times a day. It's tempting to push, especially if your baby is not yet doing what your friend's baby is doing. Jason, a tech expert who was used to researching a problem and solving it, spoke to this dilemma:

"We kept thinking there was a magic answer. We searched online, took advice from everyone, and tried to implement it all, believing we could somehow make her sleep through the night. But that just left us frustrated and angry. Finally, we simply said to each other, 'That's it! We're done. She's going to do it when she's ready.' In the meantime, we decided to switch gears and do what we needed to in order to get as much sleep as possible, even if that meant other stuff didn't get done. We said to ourselves, 'It's not going to be like this forever.'"

Take the pressure off yourself and your baby. Everything does not have to happen today. This is temporary. This, too, shall pass. When the time is right for your baby, you can gently nudge her forward. I'll even show you how in chapter 5, "What Is the Gentle NUDGE to Success?"

7. I don't need to romanticize the past.

On the days you are missing your old life, allow yourself to stop and think about your past lives as a student, single adult, career person, paired without children. Remember when you had your own apartment and were free to do anything you wanted? The place where you also frequently spent nights crying because you were alone? Each life stage has its high points *and* challenges.

The birth of a spirited infant is the beginning of a new, different life. It, too, will have its trials and joys. Look forward. Time spent romanticizing the past robs you of the possibilities of today. Focus on your successes and the good moments.

8. It's okay to ask for help.

Parents who thrive utilize the twin strengths of transforming how they feel about this experience and recognizing they can reach out to others for help. They do not have to carry the load alone. Even if it's scary, they realize there is relief in sharing their experience and that by doing so they will find other people who will understand and support them.

Caroline explained, "On the bad days, I call my mom. She takes him for an hour. That break allows me to calm down. When I return, I'm happy to see him again."

The willingness to reach out allows us to tell ourselves, "I am not alone." The trouble is, it is not always easy to open the door or ask, "Will you help me?" But when you ask another adult to take care of your baby, you give them an opportunity to fall in love with your baby, too.

CONQUERING OUR FEARS OF REACHING OUT: YOU ARE NOT ALONE

True, others cannot change your reality. Raising this baby remains your responsibility. However, friends and family members can love and support you during this arduous time. From their sustenance you can draw strength and compassion for yourself. Their love calms you.

So how do you allow yourself to unlock the door, pick up the phone, or simply say yes when someone offers assistance?

Often our own super-charged emotions are our biggest road-blocks. To break through them we must identify which emotions are getting in our way and give them a name. Once we do, they lose their power and we feel free to open our door to those willing to help us.

The emotions and fears that follow are the ones parents describe to me most frequently. You may have others that are unique to who you are and where you are in your life's journey.

Feeling incompetent

When I asked the members of a spirited-infant group what stopped them from seeking assistance, Casey, a single mom and avid outdoor adventurer, jump-started the conversation. "I'm a pretty independent person. I like to do things my own way. I'm not one to ask for help. Asking for help feels like giving up to me. I don't give up."

Before continuing she sighed, forehead wrinkling in thought. "I suppose I could think about it like rock climbing. You always have a partner to belay you. Someone keeping tension on the safety rope when you are climbing in tricky situations." Then, her voice rising and chin jutting out, she declared, "But some people go solo." Pausing, as though convincing herself, she added, "It just seems so much easier to accept assistance climbing a mountain than caring for this baby. How could twelve pounds of humanity be so challenging?"

If your internal beliefs about asking for help threaten to keep your door closed, try listening to podcasts or watching videos of great achievers. Whatever their field of endeavor, from sports to scientific invention to leadership, they always emphasize the importance of their support team.

Fear my baby will be viewed as a "problem"

When Jesse paused to think about what was really in the way of asking for help, she realized it was fear. "When someone asks if they can watch my baby, I can't bring myself to say yes. He's so much louder and fussier than other babies. If he lets loose, he may freak them out. My neighbor and my friend from work have offered, but I keep turning them down." Then she sighed and added, "But I could really use the break."

Guilt

Kelsey, dressed in heels and poised at the edge of her chair, ready for the dash back to the office after class, added, "Guilt. I'm gone every day. How can I ask someone to watch him in the evening or on the weekend to give me a break?"

Tiffany turned to Kelsey. "I feel guilty, too, but not because I'm gone. I am home. I chose to quit my job. How can I ask someone to help me? This is my job."

All too often these emotions and the dozens of others that could be added to the list lead to misunderstandings, self-doubt, silence, and isolation. No one wants to feel exposed or that others will think something is wrong with their baby. But the demanding journey with a spirited infant requires the help of others. That is why it is so important to recognize that reaching out to build your personal support team is not a sign of weakness but rather an indication of resourcefulness.

FINDING YOUR PEOPLE AND CREATING A CIRCLE OF SUPPORT

In his book *The Oregon Trail* Rinker Buck writes, "The initial trailblazers of the Oregon Trail did not possess the specific hard skills required for cutting a wagon road west. Their only real endowments were their soft skills such as a willingness to accept the help of strangers, stubborn practicality, and the ability to live with uncertainty."

Together these trailblazers traveled two thousand uncharted miles, lowering wagons down cliffs with ropes, fording rivers, and lifting wheels over boulder fields one rock at a time. Teamwork made a grueling journey possible. And if that is not enough of an incentive to open your door, quality-of-life research has identified a strong support system as a key to longer, happier lives.

The arrival of a spirited infant provides an opportunity to gather together. It is not a time to attempt to go solo. The crucial factor in feeling comfortable letting people in is finding the right people. Comrades who empathize, listen, and don't judge allow you to feel comfortable seeking their assistance and support.

The crucial factor in feeling comfortable letting people in is finding the right people. Comrades who empathize, listen, and don't judge allow you to feel comfortable seeking their assistance and support.

Sweep broadly to find your people.

Often the first people we hope to turn to are family, but our circle of support can be much wider. This is especially true if no family members live nearby or if they do but are unable to help. Look for the honorary aunties, uncles, and "bonus" grandparents in your community. These are individuals you can count on to answer your call, listen, or show up minutes later on your doorstep. They come in many different shapes and forms. I call them *your people*.

Even if you have recently moved to a new city or country and are feeling very much alone, you can find them. Search in your neighborhood, place of employment, community programs, or houses of worship. Don't rule out single friends or retirees. They often have more flexible schedules and can be surprisingly supportive.

You can also request an invitation to the private Spirited Child Facebook group, where thousands of parents share their stories, support, and effective strategies: https://www.facebook.com /groups/2348651727/. While group members won't be able to give you physical support, they can provide loads of emotional support and helpful tips. Perhaps, most important, this community is available anytime.

During these high-stress months, you can also take a hard look at your financial resources. For the short term, hiring someone to help with baby care, child care for older children, or housecleaning may be well worth the dollars spent.

Look for the nonjudgmental listener.

There is comfort in good fellowship, reassurance and liberation in shared experiences. Look for individuals who let you honestly share your experiences and can empathize with how overwhelming life with a spirited infant can be.

What is it about these friends that makes them so supportive? Tiffany explained: "I craved people to tell my story to and who could share theirs. I found that person in a friend who had a spirited baby four weeks before me. I could ask her questions. 'What should I do next? What do you think of this? Has this happened to you?' She listened, commiserated, and offered great ideas but most importantly she let me talk. Just knowing that someone else was in the same boat, going through the same things, made me feel like my baby was not weird. It was good therapy."

Sometimes, to find companions for this journey with a spirited infant you must be willing to be a bit vulnerable and persistent. Ferreting out cohorts begins by honestly sharing your story. Silence robs you of allies who sigh with relief, exclaiming, "That is my experience, too!" You do not have to walk this path alone, but you do have to speak up.

Unfriend the downers.

There can be a troubling realization in this quest for support. A few pre-baby friendships will likely crash and burn in the process. People you thought were good friends may hit you with snarky comments, look at you blank-eyed, or, worse, blame your turmoil on hormones or "new parent syndrome."

Some people come into our lives for a point in time, others stay with us for a lifetime. Distinguish those friends who truly are friends. Notice how you feel *after* interactions and activities with them. Is your mood uplifted? Do you find yourself calmer, more relaxed? Has your sense of confidence and competence somehow grown? Are you more forgiving of yourself? Enjoying your baby more?

If instead you are irritated and drained, it is time to make some changes. Limit or temporarily stop your interactions with the individuals who rile you up and spike your blood pressure. They are shoving you into the red zone. You don't need that.

Instead, surround yourself with individuals who listen, do not judge you, and as a result leave you feeling energized, capable, and content. They do not even need to live near you. Phone calls, text messages, social media check-ins, and the like are powerful, uplifting tools.

Once you find your people, start small.

Invite that willing neighbor to hold your baby while she naps and you work in another room. Once that feels comfortable let her watch the baby for an hour while you run an errand. (Whoever would have thought of an unencumbered trip to the store as a treat?) These short breaks can make the difference between a day spent in the red zone and one in the green zone of calm energy. Unlike weary parents, these helpers arrive with a calm and patient presence. They are not exhausted by the everyday care of an infant.

Be proactive. Create a note on your phone or a list in your journal. When a need arises, write it down. Be specific. Then when a friend asks, "What can I do?" you will be prepared. Maybe it's a request to come over for an hour so you can take a nap or to pick up a container of soup from your favorite deli.

You can also consider creating small, low-risk *rituals of connection*. Similar to the positive feelings we get when we plan and anticipate a vacation, setting up and anticipating small moments of connection is uplifting. Your ritual of connection can be as simple as a good-morning email, text, or phone call. Or it could be the willingness of others to host Sunday night dinners. If cooking is not their thing, someone in your circle might be able to babysit every other Wednesday evening while you have an early night out. This is nirvana!

Small rituals allow you to anticipate and enjoy the support before, during, and after the rituals, and as a result extend your green zone of calm energy.

Teach others the words you wish to hear.

Words can be just as supportive as actions. It was in my Spirited Child Facebook group that a parent stated, "It would be wonderful to have a list of words you need to hear. One you could hand to other people and say: 'Read this! These are the words I would like to hear from you.'"

I took note of this recommendation and started a list, arranging the phrases into categories.

EXAMPLE WORDS OF UNDERSTANDING

Words of respect	I believe in you. I trust that you know your baby better than anyone else. You will figure this out. You make good decisions.
Words of support	You're doing a great job. You make a great parent. I'm proud of you. You stayed so calm. I see how hard you are working. What can I do to help? The strategies I see you using are effective. Trust your intuition. You've got this. Trust your baby. She will show you what she needs.

Words celebrating your child	I love watching her antics. She is so alert. This child does not miss a thing. He is wonderfully energetic and coordinated. She is so curious. Because of her I have learned to notice sights, sounds, and sensations I completely missed before. His behavior is normal. It reminds me of _____, whom we all love. Caring for him is challenging but he is awesome.
Words of hope	One day when she has grown up and moved away you will look back and laugh about this crazy time. I can only imagine the incredible adult he will become.
Words of understanding	I understand now that disrupting his routine is hard on him. I can see that too much stimulation upsets him. She really does sleep better if it's dark and quiet and she is in her own space. I understand why you want to take her home for naps. Holding her for naps is lovely and what she needs. It is not spoiling her. I can recognize now that crowds sometimes overwhelm him. We will adjust our plans to fit the baby's nap/ feeding.

What you will *never* hear from your people, those who truly support you, are phrases such as these:

Words that trigger the red zone	My kids never . . . Your brother's [my] kids were sleeping through the night at six weeks. You are creating a bad habit. It's your fault he acts that way. You are always making up excuses for him. Stop being so overprotective.

Find your people, whomever they may be. It is not only acceptable to ask for help; social connection is crucial for your well-being and vital to life.

Caring for your infant begins with being caring and compassionate toward yourself. Remember you can transform how you think and feel about this experience. Allow yourself to look in the mirror and confidently state, "I'm a good parent. In fact, I'm a *really* good parent! I am an amazing parent and this kid is darn lucky he got me!" And then turn to your partner and your broader community to build a support team that keeps you on your feet.

Reaching out and building your support team is not a cause for tears that you could not handle it on your own. Your ability to seek resources confirms that you are a wise, problem-solving family. Like the Oregon trailblazers, you have the soft skills to not only survive but thrive on this challenging and exhilarating journey.

> Caring for your infant begins with being caring and compassionate toward yourself. . . . Allow yourself to look in the mirror and confidently state, "I'm a good parent. In fact, I'm a *really* good parent! I am an amazing parent and this kid is darn lucky he got me!"

RECOGNIZE AND TREAT POSTPARTUM DEPRESSION AND ANXIETY

What if you are doing your best to care for yourself but you still feel hopeless and unable to see an end to this? That's what happened to Kari. Kari pulled her knees up to her chest, hugging them tight against her as she described the "dark days."

"It wasn't supposed to be this hard," she said, glancing away from me as she drew upon the memories.

"I wanted this baby, but after eight months of no sleep I hit the wall. It felt like what I had hoped for and looked forward to being had become a nightmare." Turning back to look directly at me, she splayed her hands out in front of her, pausing to glance at them before dropping them in her lap as though in surrender.

"How are you supposed to love a baby who cries all the time and keeps you awake at night? A baby who you try to nurse and comfort over and over again but gain only a short reprieve before it begins again?" She did not pause for me to reply.

"I knew I should ask for help. I am a competent woman. I have handled major responsibilities at work. How could it be so hard to get out the door with an infant seat and diaper bag? It was humiliating. My friends, or should I say my former friends, seemed to have disappeared. Even when I tried to tell them how hard it was, or that I was not sleeping, they simply said, 'That's too bad,' but failed to offer help. I know it's very hard to believe, but one even said, 'You wanted this baby. What's wrong with you?'"

. . . .

"I knew I should ask for help. I am a competent woman. I have handled major responsibilities at work. How could it be so hard to get out the door with an infant seat and diaper bag? It was humili-ating."

—Kari

. . . .

"It got to the point that when I drove past the hospital, I found myself thinking, 'I can pull over and admit myself.' Do they allow that? Could I walk in and say, 'Please just give me a bed. Let me sleep.' Or, 'Someone save me?' But I didn't know how to have someone else save me or even help me. I couldn't plan. I was just surviving. I kept thinking, 'One more day, really, how tough can it be?' And then I realized I was having thoughts I never imagined I would experience. I understood how parents throw crying babies against the wall. Thank God, I had not hurt mine yet, but I got scared. Should I be alone with her? Is it safe for either of us?"

Before the birth of her daughter, Kari had never experienced depression or anxiety, yet after her daughter was born, she became one of the one in seven women who experience significant symp-toms of *perinatal mood disorder*, the official title used by profession-als, more commonly known as *postpartum depression*, or *anxiety* or *mood disorders*.

The symptoms can vary widely from one person to another and are not limited to just mothers—depression and anxiety after the birth of a child also affect one in ten men. One individual may experience the classic signs of deep sadness, exhaustion, an inabil-ity to get out of bed in the morning or even shower. But those are not the only symptoms. Some of the symptoms, such as brain fog, light-headedness, headaches, and rage, may surprise you.

Review the symptoms below. Check any that fit your experience.

- ❏ **Sadness**—Those things that normally bring you joy become mere actions to move through.
- ❏ **Anger/rage**—Everything makes you angry. People around you are doing things that irritate you at a level never experienced before. You do not want to be mad, but you cannot help it. You would love to pick a fight, so you have an excuse to scream or even hit something.
- ❏ **Brain fog**—You are forgetting things. Thank God for the key fob or you would never find your car in the parking lot. Words are not coming to mind, leaving you to wonder if you are experiencing early onset dementia. You find yourself driving down a street and suddenly realize you have no idea where you are.
- ❏ **Numbness**—It is as though you are a bystander to your own life. You see yourself going through the motions but feel nothing.
- ❏ **Insomnia**—Even when you have the opportunity to sleep, you cannot fall asleep. If you do fall asleep and then wake, you cannot return to sleep, instead lying there just waiting for the baby to awaken again.
- ❏ **Physical symptoms**—You find yourself plagued with headaches, nausea, or body aches. At times you may struggle to breathe, your heart races, and you are certain you are having a heart attack. Light-headedness leaves you feeling dizzy and off-balance.

- ❐ **Hyperattentiveness**—Startling with every sound or movement your baby makes keeps you in a constant state of alertness. You insist everyone wash their hands before touching her or follow other exact "procedures," fearing that without their doing so something bad will happen to your baby.

- ❐ **Scary thoughts**—Suddenly you are experiencing thoughts you do not want to have but despite efforts to block them you find they continue to creep into your mind. Haunting *what if* questions keep coming to mind. Feelings of panic swamp you as though you were living within an unending nightmare. Is your baby safe with you? Are you safe with yourself? Can you trust others or are they out to get you?

If you recognize these symptoms as your own, you may be suffering from a perinatal mood or anxiety disorder. Reaching out to seek treatment is a sign of strength. You can call your primary care doctor, your gynecologist, your baby's pediatrician, or a therapist, whomever you are most comfortable talking with, to get the help and support you deserve. You can also call the Postpartum Support International HelpLine (1-800-944-4773) or go to their website, www.postpartum.net.

This is what Kari did.

"I contacted a counselor recommended by a friend. The counselor orchestrated a family meeting, insisting, 'Kari cannot go another night without sleep.' It was such a relief to have someone else speak for me.

"My family was receptive as was my church community, who rallied around me. They came to hold my baby, bring meals, clean, do laundry, drive the baby around so she would sleep in the car, and most importantly to spend the night. The first two weeks I had to leave my own home to sleep. I could not sleep there. My husband cared for our daughter with help from the others. Yes, nursing was impacted, but my baby needed a mom first and this mom had to sleep. I learned that I was hypersensitive to her every sound and movement. It took me three months before I could nap in my own home.

"I also had to overcome my ideas about medication. Depression and anxiety reflect chemical imbalances in the body. Sometimes medication is the only way to get back into balance. I told myself I would not have to be on meds forever, but for now it was the boost that was going to get me over the fence."

After two weeks, Kari started sleeping, but it was a full three months before she completely recovered. It took much longer than she ever expected, but she got there.

Kari turned, and then taking a deep breath as the memories flooded her, she touched my arm and said, "Please write about my story. Let other moms and dads know they are not crazy. This is a physical malady, a hormone imbalance. Help is available. It can be better. Much better."

If you are identifying with Kari's story, do not hesitate to act. Make an appointment with your doctor today. Never forget: Calming you *is* calming your baby. When those tough moments threaten to take you down, stop. Take a deep breath. Ask yourself, "What do I need to stay calm so I can calm my baby?" Then do it.

CHEAT SHEET: HOW CAN YOU CALM YOURSELF SO YOU CAN CALM YOUR BABY?

1. *Remember, caring for your spirited infant begins with caring for yourself.* In a culture that encourages you to power through, your distress can push your arousal system into the red zone, making it more difficult for you to think, react, and accurately read and respond to your baby's cues.

2. *Practice reframing your beliefs and self-talk about your spirited baby.* Simple changes in language can influence how you think, feel, and respond to what's happening.

3. *Use the "eight messages" to reinforce your strengths as a parent.* You can return to them over and over, like mantras, to calm yourself. Use these or others like them:

   - I am a problem solver.
   - I can choose to respond in a way that fits my baby.
   - I can decide what is important.
   - I can maintain a sense of humor.
   - I can turn to my spiritual beliefs.
   - I can respect my baby's pace.
   - I don't need to romanticize the past.
   - I can ask for help.

4. *Find your people and start small to create a circle of support.* It is not only acceptable to ask for help; it is vital for your well-being. It's also a sign of your strength, not weakness.

5. *If you are feeling overwhelmed, anxious, or depressed, make an appointment with your doctor or a counselor today.* You can also call the Postpartum Support International HelpLine (1-800-944-4773), or go to their website, www.postpartum.net. Do not wait.

REFLECTION QUESTIONS FOR YOUR JOURNAL

- Which one of the eight messages is my favorite go-to statement when I need to feel stronger and more confident?

- What did I do today to connect with my people?

- What do I need from my support team?

- What did I do, say, or think today that helped me calm myself?

Chapter 4

How Can I Meet My Basic Needs Now?

Creating a Foundational Routine That Supports and Restores Us Even in the Midst of Chaos

"Journal, journal on the wall, where
is my spirit, my soul, my all?
I need some quiet, a time to be.
Days filled with smiles, giggles, and tears.
But somewhere please, just a moment for me."
—Lexi, mother of two

There was a recent uproar on social media. The cause of the ire: a photo of a mom nursing her baby while sitting on the toilet. "YUCK!" one person responded. "DISGUSTING," another roared. "Incredibly unsanitary," one more added. Yet the fifteen parents in my spirited-infant group all nodded in agreement. "We totally get it."

How did taking care of bodily functions without another person wailing in the background become a luxury? How could anyone ever prepare for a reality in which achieving basic necessities like pouring a glass of water, eating, dressing, much less showering, or, heaven forbid, lovemaking, requires painstaking strategizing? I mean, really. Whoever imagined thinking, "Maybe if I put him in his swing and turn on the vacuum, I can get a five-minute shower? This is torture."

These situations are familiar to all parents of newborns and young children, but when that baby is spirited, life can feel like a constant emergency. We don't know what the day (or night) is going to bring. We don't feel like we can make plans, accomplish basic tasks, or spend time with our partner or other significant adults in our lives.

In the short term, we manage. Most of us are vaguely prepared for typical sleepless first weeks with a newborn. But when that short period becomes a way of life, the impact on our relationships and our emotional and physical well-being is profound. As we saw in chapter 3, "What Do I Need to Stay Calm So I Can Calm My Baby?," our lack of control and routine can literally make us feel crazy. We miss our old life. We desperately need sleep and decent food. We crave a sense of rhythm and predictability to our day. We need to be held. Yet all too often we feel powerless to fix the situation.

That's why it is so important to ask ourselves the question that shifts everything: "How can I meet my basic needs now?" It is essential to put aside our naysaying and doubts and then experiment with the small actions that will build routines to support us and our families, now and throughout our lives.

....

We desperately need sleep and decent food. We
crave a sense of rhythm and predictability to our
day. We need to be held. Yet all too often we feel
powerless to fix the situation.

....

THE CONCEPT OF MINIMAL
DAILY REQUIREMENTS

I have been introducing parents to the concept of Minimal Daily
Requirements for years. It is based on the groundbreaking work
of Abraham Maslow's hierarchy of needs for maintaining homeostasis. Homeostasis is the principle by which our body oper-
ates optimally. Maslow proposed a model that he represented as
building blocks in the shape of a pyramid. At the very bottom
of the triangle lies our physiological needs—our basic needs for
food, water, sleep, and shelter. (Some versions also include sex.)
Stacked above our basic needs is the need for safety, then belong-
ing, followed by esteem, and, finally, at the top of the pyramid,
self-actualization.

During our lifetimes, we continuously move through these levels, sometimes striving to meet our basic physiological needs and
at other times, when those needs are met, moving upward in the
pyramid to accomplish higher-level goals of personal development
and meaning. The one consistent factor is that each of the lower
levels of needs must be satisfied before we can move up to higher
levels of the hierarchy. When our basic, lower-level needs are not
met, we feel anxious and tense.

The addition of a baby to the family system literally demolishes all existing daily rhythms, roles, and routines we have in place. Our most basic needs, like sleeping and self-care, are in jeopardy, and we are stressed when we don't know how we are going to fulfill them. Like an astronaut suddenly untethered and floating helplessly in outer space, we find ourselves flying off into the stratosphere of pandemonium, madly attempting to meet the needs of our little spirited comet but failing to meet our own. Though it may seem impossible, you *can* take back some control over your life—while still giving your baby all the love, acceptance, and care she needs. Doing so requires stopping to ask how you can meet *your* basic needs *now*.

That question alone focuses your mind and begins the process of creating a routine that calms, fortifies, and restores you. This foundation, which supports and grounds you on your toughest days, may be the most profoundly helpful step you can take as a parent.

By developing a predictable, rhythmic routine that meets *your* needs, you create a center of gravity that gently draws your baby into your family system.

Of course, the challenge is how to create that routine when you are dealing with a baby whose sleep and eating habits are unpredictable. The answer lies in your body's built-in internal clock.

Though it may seem impossible, you *can* take back some control over your life—while still giving your baby all the love, acceptance, and care she needs. Doing so requires stopping to ask how you can meet *your* basic needs *now*.

UNDERSTANDING CIRCADIAN RHYTHMS AND ROUTINES— YOURS AND YOUR BABY'S

Within every human is a body clock, officially called the circadian rhythm. Its job is to tell the body's cells when to sleep, wake, fuel, raise and lower body temperature, and release important hormones like melatonin, the sleep hormone.

The circadian clock runs on a cycle closer to twenty-five hours than twenty-four. In order to bring your circadian rhythm into alignment with a twenty-four-hour day, you must set it with cues from the environment and your daily routine. Those cues can include such things as consistent wake, sleep, meal, and exercise times and exposure to morning light. When you have a spirited baby who one day wakes at 5:00 A.M. and the next at 7:00 A.M. it's as if on Monday you wake up in New York City, immediately jet to Denver, and wake there on Tuesday. Your body is in a constant state of jet lag, your body clock confused, unable to determine when to be awake and when to sleep. As a result, it tells you to be alert at the wrong time, leaving you wide awake when you want to be sleeping. Such an erratic schedule is even more detrimental to your well-being than sleep deprivation.

> An erratic schedule is even more detrimental to your well-being than sleep deprivation.

Unfortunately, you're flying solo here with your inner clock needing to operate for your baby as well. At birth, your baby's circadian rhythm is not yet developed. No clock is in place to coordinate his systems and inform his body and brain that nighttime is for sleeping and daytime is for refueling and play. Your baby's fickle schedule is, in fact, physiologically based. Researchers do not yet agree on the age that the circadian rhythm appears, but estimates range from two weeks to nine months of age.

Researchers do agree, however, on two important factors:

First, there are striking differences between young infants in the appearance and stability of their circadian rhythm.

Second, the circadian rhythm is strongly influenced by the external environment, including the timing of exposure to bright light and social cues.

This is where you and your actions come into play. You can proactively lay a foundation that will support you, your baby, and the whole family. By establishing a daily routine to cue *your* body clock, three things occur:

1. You reduce the sense of "jet lag" and the havoc it plays on your body and brain.

2. You drastically increase the odds of meeting your own basic needs for sleep, food, water, and—if you play it right—even sex.

3. You boost the development of your baby's body clock, which will gradually result in improved nighttime sleep.

You can establish that routine, keeping in mind what *you* need in order to meet your basic requirements and the things you can control. Your baby will ever-so-slowly catch your rhythm and will respond to your improved well-being. Will things be perfect? No. But a foundation of healthy routines guarantees small pockets of calm you can look forward to.

If you are co-parenting with a partner, you'll want to bring that person into the process, too. When both of you have your basic physiological needs met on a more consistent basis, you will have the energy to work together, calm one another, and reignite intimacy.

Create a rhythm that allows you to meet your basic daily requirements.

The word *routine* may be a trigger for you—a straitjacket stifling spontaneity in your life.

Let's reframe that thought and think about routines not as rigid schedules but as reliable pockets of predictability. These pockets of predictability, when spaced throughout your day, are like coming upon an oasis in the desert. They allow you to pause, center, and restore yourself.

I'm going to introduce you to nine potential pockets of predictability. As you read through them, you do not need to attempt to implement all nine. I'm simply giving you a broad framework of proven routines and daily rhythms. You can choose to try just one.

The creation of a plan also does not mean you must stick to it every single day. Life is messy. The baby will get sick. You'll get sick. The weather will be awful. A report will be due at work. Something will occur that sends you back into survival mode. That's okay. But when you have a plan, it's a foundation. It's a handhold ready to grab as you pull yourself back on your feet.

The first pocket lies at the beginning of your day, and if I had to recommend one place to start, this would be it.

1. Establish a morning wake time.

This recommendation might come as a big surprise to you. Recently I introduced this topic in a parent group, explaining, "You will select a wake time that allows you to begin the day fifteen to forty-five minutes before your children typically awaken so you start your day focused on *your* needs and without rushing—"

Before I finished my sentence, Angelique blurted, "Absolutely not. I am desperately trying to grab *every* second of sleep I can get. There is *no* way I'm waking myself up even a millisecond before the baby wakes!"

Lucia also voiced her adamant opposition. "Gabriella's wake times are so sporadic; it is not possible for me to get up before her."

But a few weeks later, during our time to share successes, Lucia volunteered, "I realized that waking at the same time as Gabriella left me without a minute for myself. I played catch-up the rest of the day. I also recognized that while I do not like routines, my baby needed one. When I finally committed to implementing a routine for myself, the change in her level of contentment was immediate."

When you have a spirited baby, nights can be like a carnival and early mornings a blur. Yes, I know you are bone tired, but please bear with me. There is purpose behind an established morning wake time. Think for a moment how you feel now, jarred awake by the needs of others. Even if you have grabbed a few extra minutes of sleep, your schedule is erratic, throwing off your circadian rhythm. As a result, you wake groggy and out of sorts.

A consistent wake time for *you* functions like a crucial messenger signaling your body clock to act as your inner alarm: *This is when I need to be awake. Start the clock!* From your wake time onward, the rest of your schedule builds.

Just as important, to my mind, establishing a wake-up time means you create a tiny haven for yourself before the demands of the day begin.

. . . .

"While I do not like routines, my baby needed one . . . the change in her level of contentment was immediate."   —Lucia

. . . .

2. Create and maintain a morning routine that centers you.

Imagine how it would feel to wake, have a few minutes to shower, dress, brew a cup of coffee, write in your journal, meditate, or exercise before you begin meeting the needs of others, including your baby, other children in the family, or your partner. It may be a mere fifteen to twenty minutes. It does not matter what you do, as long as you begin the day by doing something for you. Those moments validate your worthiness and bring you into the green zone of calm energy.

The feeling that you don't have time for even those few moments is just that—a feeling. Without a conscious plan, any job or task—whether it is taking care of children or preparing for a big presentation at work—will take up all the time you give it. That means you need to intentionally give yourself time, too—today. *New York Times* writer Benjamin Spall wrote in a Smarter Living column based on interviews with three hundred high achievers that "the choices we make during the first hour of the morning often determine what the rest of the day will look and feel like."

Ask yourself, "Am I worthy of fifteen minutes of time for me?" If you cannot say yes, please reconsider.

"The choices we make during the first hour of the morning often determine what the rest of the day will look and feel like."

—Benjamin Spall, Smarter Living column, the *New York Times*

I asked the parents in one of my classes, "What is one small thing you could do in the morning to meet one of your basic requirements?"

Lucia and her husband, Mateo, came up with a plan. Lucia, a stay-at-home mom, would wake at 6:00 A.M. Before Mateo left for the day, Lucia would take fifteen minutes to shower and dress, no matter what time baby Gabriella woke. If Gabriella woke before 6:00 A.M., Mateo would give her a bottle that Lucia had pumped, but she got her fifteen minutes. "Now," she said, "I'm not anxious, waiting for her to nap and then rushing to get showered and dressed before she wakes. Instead, while she naps, I have bonus time to accomplish other tasks. If she only naps twenty minutes it's not a disaster. If she naps longer, it's bliss. Lately, as I have been consistent with my morning routine, her awakenings have become more predictable, too."

Zaire and Hanna, both employed full-time, figured out how to center one another. "We get up at five-thirty, before any of the kids are awake. We shower and dress, then Zaire makes everyone breakfast and I pack lunches. We are both doing something for one another, and our family, and we're not exhausted like we are at night."

Stephanie, a single parent, savors a cup of coffee and then begins her day. "It's not much, but it does make a difference."

Start small. Perhaps you simply choose not to immediately turn on electronics, or to listen to music rather than the news. Even a three-minute breathing exercise changes how you feel. Simply breathe in slowly as you count to four and then out, again slowly counting to four. Repeat for ten breaths and build up to three minutes. No stressing about the day and your to-do list. Just breathe. That basic life-giving pause will immediately leave you feeling cooler, calmer, and more collected. Keep expectations low and remind yourself that even if you are not able to grab those few minutes every day, without a plan in place, you'll never have the time.

> Even a three-minute breathing exercise changes how you feel. Simply breathe in and out slowly for ten breaths and build up to three minutes. No stressing about the day and your to-do list. Just breathe.

3. Establish when your family's day begins.

After you have had your time to center yourself, determine a wake time for older children that will allow them to prepare for the day without feeling harried and pressed for time. The routine might include time to wake, cuddle, use the toilet, dress, brush teeth and hair. I recommend all these tasks be completed before leaving the bedroom area, thus eliminating all unnecessary stops and starts, going up and down stairs, entering and leaving rooms. All these shifts are transitions with the potential for power struggles.

If you must wake your older children, they are not getting enough sleep. Move their bedtime fifteen minutes earlier until they wake at the determined morning time on their own. (For more information on how to make that happen, you can refer to my book *Sleepless in America*.)

If your spirited baby is a firstborn, select a target wake time that feels natural to your baby's current wake time and allows you to leave the house in the morning without feeling rushed.

Once you have established your family wake time, let the noise and activity of the day begin. Go ahead and grind your coffee beans, blend your smoothie, turn on lights and appliances. Open the blinds in the room where your baby sleeps or tidy up nearby. You are not picking him up to awaken him, but you are allowing the sounds, smells, and activity of your household to do the job. When your baby does wake, greet him with a smile. Talk about your day. Change his diaper, dress him, sit down for a nice feed, and play. Let him know this is when your family's day begins.

Aki, a father of three, did just that. "When my son woke at six-thirty, I used to try to get him back to sleep, hoping for another hour or two before the day started. But once we established six-thirty as the time our older children needed to begin their day, I stopped trying to put him back to sleep. He loves being part of the morning routine with the older kids."

4. Plan meals and snacks ahead so you don't forget to refuel.

We are a "go-go" culture, boasting how busy we are and how hard we push. We laugh about another skipped meal. But combine this go-go pressure with a baby whose eating habits are impossible to predict, and you can find yourself running on empty.

That is why it is essential to consciously plan your meals and snacks throughout the day. Regularly spaced meals are a protective measure, a pocket of predictability. Consistent mealtimes also set the body clock to signal, *Time to refuel*, so it is best to maintain this schedule seven days a week.

The Ellyn Satter Institute, my favorite source of nutrition information, recommends six mini-meals a day. Each meal includes a little protein, carbohydrate, fruit/vegetable, and fat. Meals are served every two and a half to three hours. That means if breakfast is served at seven, morning snack is consumed between nine-thirty and ten, lunch takes place between noon and twelve-thirty, and so forth. By eating every two and a half to three hours you avoid getting "hangry"—as in so hungry you become angry.

Keep it simple. I recommend that parents establish familiar breakfast and snack menus. Fewer decisions mean less strain on your depleted capacity to think and cope.

Add in a ban on the use of electronics in the morning, and this approach allows you to transform breakfast from a red zone of stressful rushing to a green zone time to calm and connect before separating for the day. You may even choose to make breakfast your daily "family meal."

Simple Breakfast and Snack Options for a Calm and Healthy Family

Select breakfast foods for adults, toddlers, and children that include something everyone enjoys. The key is to keep it simple. Planned menus conserve energy.

For example:
- Every Monday, Wednesday, and Friday serve smoothies filled with fruit, veggies, and protein. Top them off with a bit of granola.
- Every Tuesday and Thursday it might be scrambled eggs with veggies and whole wheat toast.

Midmorning and midafternoon snacks should be healthy—and easy.

For example:

- Nuts, carrot sticks, and pita chips served with soft cheese or hummus.

- Yogurt pouches or cheese sticks with whole wheat crackers and apple slices.

- Almond butter and banana slices on whole wheat bread.

- A Power Muffin made with almond flour, walnuts, carrots, and apples from one of my favorite cookbooks, *Run Fast. Cook Fast. Eat Slow.* by Shalane Flanagan and Elyse Kopecky.

5. Get outside and walk.

Natural light is your friend. Studies demonstrate exposure to morning light makes you feel more energetic, less exhausted, and lifts your mood—all factors to help prevent depression and improve nighttime sleep. Exposure to morning light sets your body clock, and infants exposed to natural light develop their own circadian rhythm earlier than infants not offered this experience.

Throughout the day, expose yourself and your baby to natural light. When you can't be outside, place your feeding chair or your baby's swing by a north-facing window so you are both exposed to natural daylight but not overheated. If possible, get outside.

While you are outside, walk. Regular exercise is one of the most beneficial things you can do for your mental and physical health. Combine exercise and exposure to natural light and you have a double espresso charge to your body clock cues. The stronger the cues, the easier it is to sleep—at the right times.

True, finding time and energy to exercise is challenging, so make it as easy as short walks around the neighborhood or in the local park. Use your baby's need for movement and body contact to your advantage. If he shrieks when you place him in a stroller, put him in a carrier and head out the door.

Baby Carriers and Walking Shoes

The right carrier can make a huge difference in your comfort and stamina. Having the proper fit places 80 percent of the weight on your hips—not your shoulders, neck, or knees. Make certain the waist strap lies snug around the middle of your hip bones. Pull the shoulder straps snug. Snap the cross strap and tug the back straps until the pack sits tight against your body. Check the fit by asking someone to slip a hand between the carrier and your back. No gap means a good fit.

You'll also want to walk "right." According to Danny and Katherine Dreyer, the authors of *ChiWalking*, when wearing a pack, stand tall, press down on your abdomen using your pelvic muscles to tip the bowl of your pelvis up, and tuck your buns. Bring your shoulders up. Lift your head high, as though you are a marionette puppet on a string. Move forward, keeping your steps short and under your body so your hips instead of your knees bear the weight. Select comfortable walking shoes.

Let nature soothe your baby and you. Walk during your baby's "crying time" and you'll notice the cries are not so harsh outside. Smile at the neighbors who begin to greet you as the "baby walker."

Establish a time in your daily schedule to walk. Do not let weather, time of day, or needs of older children stop you. Find a rain cape, bundle up, and invite older children to accompany you on their balance bike, scooter, or in a stroller. Better yet, coordinate with your co-parent so you can walk together. One step at a time, repetitive motion centers you.

6. Take a power nap.

Everyone says, "Sleep when the baby is sleeping." But what if the baby only sleeps for minutes, you are employed full-time, or are also caring for older children? That's where power naps come into play. At most a power nap is twenty to thirty minutes in length. Not a napper, or you don't have twenty minutes? It has been found that a mere six minutes of complete relaxation is restorative. Grab the opportunity for a power nap/complete relaxation wherever and whenever you can. An ideal time might be after lunch, but experiment to see what works for you. Those few minutes will help you get through the evening with more energy and patience. You'll also discover that kink in your neck, weight on your shoulders, headache, or nausea will disappear. Take just six minutes to center and you'll have a pocket of predictability in your day.

Take just six minutes to center and you'll have a pocket of predictability in your day.

7. Establish wind-down cues and limit exposure to artificial light.

An abrupt shift from activity to sleep does not go well for slow-to-adapt spirited babies. Preparation for sleep begins before bedtime by creating signals that the day is winding down. After dinner thoughtfully begin to decrease the intensity and amount of social interactions. Slow activities and motions. Limit stimuli. Put away battery-operated toys. Close the blinds. Avoid roughhousing, tickling, blowing tummy bubbles, and any other alerting activities with your baby. Even more important, limit exposure to artificial lighting.

I live in a northern climate. In the winter, when it's dark at 5:00 P.M. switching on a light is a gift, but it also poses a problem. The body clock is set by exposure to light. Artificial lighting can trick your brain into thinking the evening is midafternoon. Artificial lighting can also delay the development of your baby's circadian rhythm.

After sunset, limit exposure to incandescent, LED, or fluorescent lighting. This does not mean you will be sitting in the dark; just pause before switching on the bright overhead light. Is that amount of light necessary, or would a lower-wattage lamp provide the illumination you need?

While you are at it, check the bathroom. If you are bathing your baby in the evening or changing her diaper in a brightly lit room, consider switching to battery-operated, waterproof candles or another low light source. Red or blue voltage lights are the least disruptive to the body clock.

As you move through your home, don't forget about the kitchen or any other room you and your baby are spending time in during the evening hours. Crazy as it may sound, you may even need to cover the tiny signal lights on smoke detectors and other devices.

Perceptive little ones can lock in on those lights and keep themselves awake.

Big-screen electronics can play havoc, but small electronic screens can be worse, since they are held closer to the eyes. If you are scrolling on your phone, check your mood after a session on social media. Are you centered or irritated and in the red zone? Research tells us the more time we spend on social media, the more symptoms of depression we experience.

Those screens affect your baby as well. While she may not be looking directly at the screen, the light and stimulation from it, even if it is in the background, can activate her arousal system and affect her body clock. Notice your baby's behavior and state of well-being after you have held her in your lap while checking email or playing a game on your laptop. Is she calm? Or is she fussy?

Both the American Academy of Pediatrics and the World Health Organization recommend no screen time for children under two years of age. Think before you hand your phone or iPad over to your baby. A few minutes of entertaining your little one with screen time, especially later in the day, can disrupt his body clock and may cost you dearly when he then struggles to fall asleep at night.

The added benefit of slowing down, dimming lights, and reducing stimulation is that it also calms you. Then, when you begin your baby's sleep routine, you are in the green zone of calm energy. Your baby senses your comfort level. The wind-down cues have prompted his brain to inform him, *All is well. Time for sleep.*

8. Make time for adult interaction.

When your baby falls asleep, take the next twenty to thirty minutes to connect with another adult, whether that person is your co-parent, one of your people from the support team you identified in chapter 3, or a friend. Guard this time as fiercely as you do your morning centering time.

Without time to talk with another adult, you start ruminating, reviewing over and over in your head what's wrong. Tension builds. But if you can expect that every day there will be an opportunity for some adult sharing, venting, laughter, and a reminder of your pre-baby self, tensions ease. With our significant other or co-parent, messages, notes, and emails are also ways to stay connected, but, to the extent possible, try to give yourself a few minutes for real conversation. The point is to consider your relationship as one of your basic needs—not an afterthought or an optional nice-to-have—so you build that time into your small pockets of predictability. (The following section on "Thriving As a Couple" will help you navigate the very real challenges you face as parents of a spirited baby.)

· ·

If you can expect that every day there will be an opportunity for some adult sharing, venting, laughter, and a reminder of your pre-baby self, tensions ease.

· ·

9. Establish a consistent sleep time for you.

The average adult requires 8.25 hours of sleep each night. If you are going to wake at 6:00 A.M. your head needs to be on your pillow by 9:45 P.M. (You can tweak this to fit you—8.25 is an average.) Parents laugh when I tell them this, letting me know it is *not* going to happen. But every night we make choices: Social media or sleep? Work emails or sleep? Favorite video game, show, or sleep? I encourage you to choose sleep.

Imagine if the sleep you need was given the highest priority on your schedule, rather than something to do in your spare time. In Sue Monk Kidd's wonderful novel *The Secret Life of Bees*, August Boatwright advises, "The hardest thing on earth is choosing what matters."

Do not allow demands of work or other responsibilities to commandeer your sleep time. Guard it with your life, or you will shorten your life. Lack of sleep is incredibly detrimental to physical health and well-being. Need to stay up later due to the schedules of older children? Odds are they, too, would benefit from more sleep. A preschooler requires twelve hours of sleep in a twenty-four-hour period. An elementary school–age child needs ten to eleven hours.

And let's be honest. You can predict you will be woken several times during the night. Instead of getting upset, expect it and plan accordingly. If you wake at seven, allow yourself time to care for your baby during the night and still get the sleep you need. Put your head on the pillow at 10:00 P.M. You are a problem solver. A consistent sleep time, combined with a consistent wake time, sets the body clock so your brain knows when to be awake and when to sleep, making it easier to fall asleep quickly.

Putting it all together

A foundational routine provides the pockets of predictability your family requires to meet everyone's basic daily needs. It will make a difference in your very core. If you are feeling lost and don't know where to start building structure and rhythm into your day, the chart that follows shows a few examples. Experiment and adapt these routines to meet your basic needs for sleep and eating while boosting the development of your baby's circadian rhythm. If your baby was born preterm, this process may take a bit longer.

SAMPLE DAILY SCHEDULES

As an average, aim for 8.25 hours of sleep. Adjust to fit you.

Wake time for YOU	5:30	6:00	7:00
Personal centering time	5:30–6:00 shower/ dress/make breakfast and lunches	6:00–6:15 meditation	7:00–7:30 exercise/ shower
Children's wake time	6:00	6:15	7:30
Breakfast	6:30	6:45	8:00
Midmorning mini-meal	9:00	9:15	10:30
Lunch	12:00	12:00	12:30
Power nap/relax	1:00–1:20	12:45–1:05	1:00–1:20
Mid-afternoon mini-meal	3:00	3:00	3:00
Dinner	5:30	6:00	6:00
Begin your sleep routine	8:45	9:15	10:15
Head on the pillow	9:15	9:45	10:45

With the goal of creating a strong, supportive foundation, go back and select the most important "pocket" for you—beginning with a regular morning wake-up time that works for you. Gradually add others. Soon you'll feel more rested and less on edge, despite the fact you are still being awakened several times during the night. That's because you are now in sync with your circadian rhythm. Your body and brain are clicking, and you have created a few reliable routines to regroup and connect.

Just as important, your baby's unpredictability begins to diminish as she progressively slides into the rhythm of *your* daily routine. Her sleep and eating patterns increasingly are in tune with your family's day. Now you have more energy to reestablish roles, responsibilities, and romance.

THRIVING AS A COUPLE—YOUR SHARED MINIMAL DAILY REQUIREMENTS

Recently during a decluttering purge I found this letter tucked in the back of my drawer:

> *I really needed to talk with you tonight. God it seems so long since we have had time for us. It feels as though we are always tired or angry. I can tell this is going to be hard. I called a sitter and she can take the baby on Sunday, but when else will we find time for us? I am drained. I need someone to hold me and tell me I'm loveable. I know that's what you need too. What will we do? I love you, buddy, but did you have to leave the dishes?*

Decades after writing these words, I am delighted to report my husband and I are still married. Happily, in fact, but having a spirited infant can test the most ardent of love relationships.

It is true that not all infants are born to two parents, but if you are a solo parent, this information may still be useful to you as you interact with other significant adults in your life. No matter your circumstances, the arrival of an infant requires redefining responsibilities and roles and reconnecting in new and different ways.

Just as you need to meet your basic requirements for rest, exercise, eating, and social connection, you also need to meet the basic needs of your relationship. You might start small, by scheduling time to connect. Or, at a bare minimum, you may figuratively tap each other on the shoulder to say, "I'm here and we're in this together."

Here are a few principles and nuggets of wisdom that will help maintain and strengthen your relationship and parenting partnership while loving and nurturing your baby.

Expect conflict.

No matter how strong and loving your relationship is, it is normal to experience clashes and frustration when a new family member is added. Conflict does not have to mean your relationship is in danger. It simply indicates that, like any developmental growth spurt, this one will include a process of disintegration before reintegration occurs at a new and higher level. The key is to promise yourselves that you will listen to one another and face the tests together.

Accept that you are individuals with different but valid points of view. Appreciate the strengths and weaknesses you each bring to the process. Together you will address the loss of your old life and the new and potentially richer one you are moving into now. You are a problem-solving team, working together to generate respectful and mutually acceptable resolutions. You are finding *your* way.

Reestablish intimacy.

I had never met Sara and Matt before I arrived at their home. They had responded to my request to meet with families with an infant whose crying and difficulty sleeping disrupted family life. Matt met me at the door. Carefully picking my way through the tornado of toys scattered on the floor, I found a seat next to Sara. Arms drooping, she smiled weakly, continuing to rock baby Emily. We had an hour to talk. As our time wound down, the conversation becoming more comfortable, I asked her how she and Matt dealt with conflict arising from the stress of a spirited infant.

"I don't know if it's a conflict or not," she replied, "but we are not sleeping in the same bed all the time." Groaning, she added, "It's not as if we are going to have sex when we haven't slept in weeks!"

A major source of consternation after the birth of any baby is sex—or lack of it. Exhausted, drained, and potentially "touched out" by the contact needs of this baby, you may find lovemaking far from your mind. The mere thought of additional touch may overwhelm you even though that touch comes from someone you craved before this baby was born.

Mother Nature also contributes to this consternation. She stealthily protects your baby's food supply by sending in hormones screaming to a breastfeeding mother, *Not tonight, honey!*

Of course additional factors, such as a change in body shape, can leave you feeling uncertain about yourself right now. A woman may also experience pain from a difficult delivery or a long recovery period after a surgical delivery. Add the fact that when the opportunity presents itself, all you want to do is sleep, and suddenly this alarming question arises: "Will I ever have a sex drive again?"

Complicating this issue, men report needing physical intimacy to feel loved. Creating a "touchy" situation between partners. (I couldn't resist.)

Enter the value in taking a broader view of intimacy.

When we say we are "intimate" with our partners, it may mean that we are having sexual intercourse. But my *Merriam-Webster* dictionary gives us a more expansive definition. *Intimacy* also infers closeness, togetherness, attachment, affection, friendliness, and a warm, comfortable feeling. In other words, it is not limited to the "act." Foreplay can be as unassuming as your significant other pouring you a cup of coffee, or changing a diaper so you don't have to. Sharing tasks conserves energy and garners warm feelings, stimulating vigor to transform those "touchy situations" into pleasurable delights.

Redefine and clarify roles.

A week after the birth of their son, Ada started sobbing, listing all the things she had wished her partner had helped with that day. It turned out he had no idea she needed help with any of them. After the birth of a spirited infant, help of any kind is no longer optional, it's a *necessity*—even if it hasn't been requested or said out loud.

Here's an exercise I do with the parents and couples in my groups:

1. Together create a list of all the household and child-care duties: feeding the baby, changing diapers, washing dishes, preparing meals, laundry, walking the dog, lawn care, paying bills, servicing the car, cleaning the bathroom, buying groceries—the responsibilities and roles are all up for grabs.

2. Once the list is complete, place a star next to the tasks you enjoy doing.

3. Review the list once more. This time check those tasks you are willing to try.

4. Finally, circle those tasks that disgust you. Then get creative.

When we do this exercise in a class, the voices rise and fall. "I did not know you *liked* doing that!" Megan exclaimed, poking her husband, Michael, in the ribs.

You, too, may be surprised by things your partner, or you, enjoy doing. I like to sweep—go figure! Every time I pick up a broom, I am back on my grandmother's porch sweeping with her.

The following week, everyone presents their successes.

Michael and Megan decided to share housecleaning. But to avoid the "you are not doing it correctly" syndrome, they came up with the solution that they would split the house. The first week of the month they would do a one-hour race-clean: Together they would change beds; Michael would clean the bathrooms and vacuum; Megan would tackle the kitchen and dust. Two weeks later, when they cleaned again, they would switch tasks. The jobs missed or done differently by the other person were addressed the second time around.

Heather and Maddie established weekend diapering duties. Heather took Saturdays. Maddie Sundays. On those days the designated person did all the diapering. No discussion needed.

Allow time to work out the kinks in your system. In the end it does not matter who does what, as long as both of you are involved in caring for your infant.

Share baby care.

Whether it is diapering, feeding, dressing, responding to nighttime wake-ups, or holding the baby for a nap, caregiving tasks allow face-to-face time with your baby. Warm, loving relationships develop when the baby looks you in the eye, turns to your voice, and smiles. Both you and your partner need to be involved.

Makes sense, right? Easy to implement? Maybe not.

When an infant is difficult to soothe, sharing child-care responsibilities becomes more complex. For example, Joel and Kristin decided to take turns getting up in the night with twelve-month-old Katlyn. Katlyn, however, had not been included in the conversation. Katlyn's piercing shrieks reverberated through the house when Joel appeared in her doorway. As though the racket weren't enough, she accented her wails by furiously jumping up and down and throwing every pacifier out of the crib. Interminable minutes of howling ensued before Katlyn finally rested her head on Joel's shoulder and dropped into sleep.

How did Joel have the reserve to continue when others would have given up? "It is not as though I like dealing with a screaming baby," Joel replied, laughing, when I asked him this question. Then turning serious he added, "I wanted Katlyn to want me. I knew to make that happen, I had to work through it. It took a while, but I did calm her. That felt great."

I then asked Kristin how she stopped herself from rushing in to "save" the howling Katlyn. She sighed. "Honestly? It was exhaustion. I wanted help and after talking about it, I also understood Joel wanted to do it."

If you have more know-how with infants, or your baby calms easily for you, be careful not to drive your partner out of the interaction. A spirited infant's earsplitting screams make it difficult to avoid freaking out and fearing that the baby is being damaged by another person's attempt to calm him. But when one parent swoops in to "rescue" the baby, the other parent feels unneeded and incompetent. Pushed out of child-care tasks, this odd parent out loses the opportunity to form a loving relationship with the baby and instead may become jealous of the baby, who is gobbling up the other parent's time and attention. If you cannot bear to watch or listen, step away. Walking away is not abandonment; it is giving your partner and baby an opportunity to fall in love.

> When one parent swoops in to "rescue" the baby, the other parent feels unneeded and incompetent. . . . If you cannot bear to watch or listen, step away. Walking away is not abandonment; it is giving your partner and baby an opportunity to fall in love.

Maddie and Heather also affirmed the importance of sharing caregiving tasks. Maddie breastfed. That left Heather trying to figure out her role. Together they decided she would become chief bather of their son. "This was no easy task," Maddie reported. "Our son hated having his hair washed, screeching and flailing wildly whenever a drop of water touched his scalp."

Heather struggled with it, almost giving up, and Maddie struggled to keep herself from "rescuing" Heather. But one night Maddie came home to find Heather grinning like crazy. "We figured it out!" she hooted. "I put a little washcloth over his eyes while I washed his hair, and he did not scream at all!"

That was a real turning point in their relationship. Eyes glistening, Maddie whispered, "I came so close to robbing them of that moment."

Sharing caregiving fosters not only strong parent-child relationships but also strong couple relationships. When both of you have experienced the frustration of changing a diaper only to have it filled again seconds later, there is empathy for the challenge involved in the job. Empathy creates connection. Connection nurtures love.

. . . .

Sharing caregiving fosters not only strong parent-child relationships but also strong couple relationships.

. . . .

Committing to a task does not mean forever nor does it mean you can never call in your partner for backup when you find your intensity rising. The key is talking so you can support one another, share the load, and both develop a deep relationship with your child.

Create pockets of connection.

Use the pocket of adult interaction time in your daily routine to sit down together and talk. Frequent conversations make it easier to get beyond task assignments to what you are contemplating and dreaming. Conflicts and upsets are addressed before they fester and become a major problem. You can make plans for lovemaking, allowing you to look forward to it and conserve energy accordingly. John Gottman of the Gottman Institute has spent his career identifying reliable patterns of interaction of happily married couples. His findings show that happy, long-term couples with satisfying sex lives do a lot of communicating.

Maybe evening is not the right time for you to make this connection. That is okay. Find another way. For Kevin it was phone calls. "When I am at work," he told me, "I try to check in. I ask, 'How is everything going today? How's the baby?' Most days I get the same message. 'Well, there have been a couple of good times.' But I also get, 'The baby is not sleeping. The baby is driving me crazy.' It is actually helpful to me because I know what to expect before I get home and am better prepared."

Daily points of connection nourish relationships. Consciously grab even the smallest opportunities to connect and center one another. Kiss and hug hello, good-bye, good morning, and good night. Before rolling out of bed, make a morning hug as routine as throwing back the covers. There may not be time or energy for more, but at least you are looking one another in the eyes, touching and coming together. Toss in a sincere "I love you" for good measure. Every little bit counts. Do *not* let a day go by without these pockets of connection and communication. In the middle of the night you do not want to find yourself trying to decide, "Is it your turn or mine?"

Daily points of connection nourish relationships. Consciously grab even the smallest opportunities to connect and center one another. . . . Do *not* let a day go by without these pockets of connection and communication.

Create a "tag" system.

No matter how seasoned, skilled, or patient you are, every parent of a spirited infant experiences "reaching the end of the rope" moments. Face flushing, teeth gritting, you know you will momentarily be screaming louder than your infant. Time to call in your tag team!

In professional wrestling, a tag team is a team of two or more wrestlers who give one another a breathing spell during a match. When attempting to calm a spirited infant, it is important to know you can count on your partner to step in and give you a breather.

Earlier, I told you to avoid rushing in and snatching the baby from your partner. That advice stands. But you also need to know you can "tag" your partner when you feel caught in a "stranglehold." Championship teams tag with finesse. Like a game of hot potato, passing on the baby carries no sense of failure. The other parent, no questions asked, steps in, allowing the first parent to catch his or her breath. No blame, no shame, no argument, but rather a kind gesture clearly communicating, *I have your back. We are in this together. We are a team.*

Choosing to tag your partner for assistance feels very different from someone barging in to take over. But what if you sense things are getting out of hand, yet your partner does not call a tag? If you are concerned, offer a tag with a question—*Tag?* Sometimes adult anger and frustration can rise precipitously. If you are worried the baby may be in danger, step in to assist both your baby and your partner.

Tag teaming is two individuals working together. You calm one another so you can calm your baby.

Show appreciation and respect.

By focusing on what is right instead of what is wrong, you build your partner's confidence. Confidence is a balm that allows us to remain calm. As John Gottman writes in *What Makes Love Last?*, "What makes the difference in the durability of a relationship is the proportion of praise to blame. Couples who say five positive things to each other for every negative one should be OK. If the ratio drops to one in two, they're in trouble."

Accentuating the Positive: Remember to Acknowledge What Your Partner Does Well

Try to avoid taking out your frustration on your partner or taking each other for granted. Zero in on what your partner does well. Your acknowledgment may be as simple as:

"Thank you."
"I appreciate it."
"You are the best."
"That was delicious."
"I love it when you . . ."
"You are so good at . . ."
"I love how the baby giggles when you . . ."
"Oh my gosh, she just turned to your voice!"
"Did you notice how she quieted when you . . ."
"Look, when you stick out your tongue, he mimics you!"

An interesting thing begins to happen when we broaden our definition of intimacy to include appreciation, respect, and friendship. Emotional intimacy begets sexual intimacy. When our concerns have been listened to and addressed, we feel loved and appreciated. Those cuddles on the couch, morning hugs, and simple neck rubs begin to evolve into a massage, then a mutual massage. Suddenly you realize you are not quite that tired and, well, you know what can come next. Soon it becomes apparent that the issue with a low libido is temporary.

> An interesting thing begins to happen when we broaden our definition of intimacy to include appreciation, respect, and friendship. Emotional intimacy begets sexual intimacy.

The process of becoming a smoothly functioning team is ongoing. There will be good days and not so good ones. Allow yourselves to be learners. Continue talking. Build your foundation. Focus on meeting your minimum daily requirements, knowing that lowered stress and more rest means you have the energy for deeper connection.

Journal those moments when your family is "clicking." Write down meaningful insights from this book or quotes that inspire you. Reread your positive entries in those moments when you feel angry and tired. Savor them on the days you can't help wishing for the way you were.

Know when to get professional help.

A strong, healthy partnership is one of the best gifts you can give your baby. (It also really helps when you have left the dishes in the sink. . . .) If, despite your best efforts, you feel as though you are about to lose this relationship on the next curve, it is time to call a certified relationship counselor. Healthy families know when to get help. Just a few sessions can make a world of difference. If your partner refuses to participate, go yourself.

It is possible to be sensitive and responsive to your baby's needs and still address your own needs. Be bold. Be fierce. Plan for your basic daily needs and bring peace to your entire family system. Not only will you feel better, but that solid foundation will gradually draw your baby into the secure, predictable routine of your family.

CHEAT SHEET: HOW CAN YOU MEET YOUR BASIC NEEDS NOW?

1. *Think about Maslow's five-tier model of human needs.* Identify the areas where you are most lacking—sleep (for sure), healthy and regular eating, exercise, social connection, sex and intimacy.

2. *Whether or not you're a "routine" person, remind yourself of the power of circadian rhythms.* Your body's clock supports you and your baby, who may not yet have an established circadian rhythm.

3. *Start a morning wake-up time and routine.* A predictable morning routine grounds you in a state of calm energy and can mean the difference between starting the day in the red zone of overarousal or in the green zone of calm energy.

4. *Plan snacks and meals.* Regularly scheduled meals maintain your energy and set the body clock, helping the brain know when to sleep and when to be awake. Create snack and meal menus to make it easy to have nutritious food at hand and to simplify decision-making and preparation.

5. *Always prioritize sleep.* Sleep is a huge challenge for parents of infants, but it is possible to increase the number of hours by intentionally planning for sleep and protecting those hours like a fierce warrior.

6. *Connect with adults every day, if possible.* Your baby is at the center of your life but he or she is not your whole life. Your basic minimal needs include social interaction and relationships that are important to you.

7. *Redefine roles as a couple, daily responsibilities, and romance.* There are strategies to help you adjust to new responsibilities and the organization of tasks, and at the same time reenergize your relationship.

REFLECTION QUESTIONS FOR YOUR JOURNAL

- What time do I need to wake up to not feel rushed?

- What routine activities center me in the morning?

- What else am I missing in my daily routine that I need to stay centered?

- What steps could I take to begin to sleep more and eat on a regular basis?

- What is one thing I really appreciate about my partner?

- What is one thing I can do to express my love and appreciation for my partner?

Chapter 5

What Is the Gentle NUDGE to Success?

The 5-Step Technique for Calmer, More Joy-Filled Days

*"If you are baking a cake, you do not turn
up the heat to make it bake faster."*
—Danny and Katherine Dreyer in *ChiWalking*

All babies need the loving and attuned attention of their parents and caregivers to help them grow and thrive. But now, having read most of Part One of *Raising Your Spirited Baby*, you understand *why* spirited babies require a heightened level of responsiveness and skill.

The foundational principles for raising a more highly excitable and slower-to-calm baby begin with these three questions, which we can always come back to:

1. What is my baby telling me?

2. What do I need to stay calm so I can calm my baby?

3. How can I meet my basic needs now?

Now, we can add this final foundational question:

4. What is the Gentle NUDGE to success?

Once we bring even a tiny bit of calm, rest, and support into our lives, we can use the steps of the Gentle NUDGE to Success to help our babies gradually learn, and adapt to the world around them. Whatever their stage and current challenges, this flexible, five-step technique focuses on our babies' present skills and gently "nudges" them forward. In recognition of our babies' highly tuned arousal systems, the Gentle NUDGE allows our babies to set the pace, while we provide the support they need, for as long as they need it—which is often longer than for their low-key peers. Then, gradually, we ease back as they become more proficient.

> The Gentle NUDGE allows our babies to set the pace, while we provide the support they need, for as long as they need it—which is often longer than for their low-key peers.

The Gentle NUDGE never pushes our babies to a point of distress. It supports them where they are now and *trusts* that through gentle practice they will gain the skills necessary to fare well within the routines of their families and their social surroundings. The approach builds upon research and practices that have shaped our understanding of effective teaching and learning for nearly a century, in all kinds of settings, cultures, and applications.

. . . .

The Gentle NUDGE never pushes our babies to a point of distress. It supports them where they are now and *trusts* that through gentle practice they will gain the skills necessary to fare well within the routines of their families and their social surroundings.

. . . .

FROM BABY "TRAINING" TO BABY "LEARNING"— THE SCIENCE OF DEVELOPMENTAL GROWTH

Why, you may wonder, do our babies need a NUDGE? It's true, most babies will ultimately sleep, walk, eat solid foods, learn to read, use a toilet, go off to school, and more. But in the 1920s and '30s a Russian psychologist named Lev Vygotsky created the concept Social Development Theory. He proposed that while children are born with basic abilities for development, through social interaction they generate more sophisticated and effective processes for higher functioning.

For example, the first time you give a baby a book, she may pick up the book, mouth it, and pound it on the floor. However, instead of just giving her a book and leaving her to explore it on her own, you might sit with her, show her there are pages inside, and read it. Through this interaction, she learns to turn those pages and that one of the pictures is called a lamb and the lamb says, "Baa!" Her learning is enhanced.

According to Vygotsky's theory, there are three zones of learning:

1. Level one is the upper limit of tasks a child can perform independently. Given a book, the baby mouths and pounds it.

2. Level two is the Zone of Proximal Development (ZPD), what we think of as "stretch" learning and tasks in school and in our own lives—say, with work assignments, a new hobby, or a fitness goal. Occupational therapist Jean Ayres coined a much more user-friendly term for this concept—the Just Right Challenge. It is the level of potential development defined as the upper limit of tasks a child can perform with the assistance of others. For example, with the adult's assistance, the baby expands her learning to include turning the pages of the book, naming the animals, and mimicking the sounds they make.

3. Level three is learning outside of the "proximal zone" of ability. It's a skill that is beyond the Just Right Challenge. The child cannot achieve this skill even with assistance. That's why, despite an adult's efforts to help her, the baby still cannot read the book.

For optimal learning, the key is to focus on the middle level—the Just Right Challenge. It's the step that is not too easy and not too hard for the baby to achieve with a caregiver's help.

The idea of this theory may seem a bit overwhelming and it's certainly not something you think about as you go about your daily tasks of caring for your baby. But, in fact, you are living and implementing this theory every single day.

. . . .

For optimal learning, the key is to focus on the Just Right Challenge. It's the step that is not too easy and not too hard for the baby to achieve with a caregiver's help.

. . . .

For example, long before your baby walks across a room, he's developing the skills to do so, and you are enhancing his learning. It is easy to trust he will one day achieve this amazing feat, unless a medical condition would somehow prevent him from accomplishing it. You expect the process will require time, development, and practice. You know that your four-month-old is incapable of walking. Moreover, you don't torment yourself when he doesn't. Instead you notice what he can do, and naturally nudge him forward.

The expectation is clear that long before he's ever upright on his own two legs, he must develop the muscles and master the skill to control his head. You cradle him carefully until he can, but you still provide him with opportunities to practice lifting his head up on his own.

From there he progresses to lying on his tummy and practicing the Superman pose, chest on the floor, head lifted, arms and legs raised in a full, ready-to-fly position. You regularly place him on a blanket for tummy time and cheer his efforts. One day, he suddenly rolls, surprising himself as much as you. Then, after hours and days of experiments, he gets a knee thrust under him, then the other. He pushes up on his hands, then collapses. Gets back up, rocks in position, and smiles gleefully, delighted with his new view and newfound skill.

You place a toy just out of his reach. He stretches to grasp it; his knees follow his arms, and he crawls to get it. One day, he grabs hold of the couch and attempts to pull himself up. You offer a help-ing hand. Soon he begins to switch between crawling and pulling up to cruise along the furniture. You follow, offering a hand to steady him when he pivots. Then, one day, he lets go and takes those first baby steps across the room.

These spontaneous actions, and many more like them on the part of the caregiver, are behaviors that learning theorists call *scaffolding*. They are the series of building blocks that link one Just Right Challenge to the next. The parent notices what skill the baby has and then supports him in practicing the next step in a sequence of skill development.

In the example of learning to walk, the baby enjoys the tasks every step along the way. There's no sense of failure when he lands on his bottom over and over again. If he begins to fuss, the activ-ity stops and he goes back to an easier skill, such as crawling or cruising—or napping—to take a break. The parent remains calm and confident, knowing that sometime between nine and seven-teen months of age the baby will walk.

Never during this long process of learning to walk does a parent set the baby in a room and say, "Okay, I've been carrying you for months. I've gotten you this far. Now I'm going to leave you here to figure out the rest on your own." It's a ridiculous idea—until it comes to sleep.

SLEEP AS AN EXAMPLE OF A DEVELOPMENTAL SKILL

Sleep, like walking, is a developmental skill that requires the successful mastery of many steps, one building on the other, until a baby can attain the ultimate goal of sleeping through the night. Similar to walking, but little understood, sleeping through the night can be a nine-to-eighteen-month journey.

While carrying your baby in your arms or a carrier is tiring and can be a hassle as your baby grows, it is not nearly as disruptive to your life as interrupted sleep. Maybe that's why we're often desperate for a way to hurry up the process, which only makes the situation worse.

> Similar to walking, but little understood, sleeping through the night can be a nine-to-eighteen-month journey.

It is my belief that this desperation has led parents and experts to turn away from the natural process of scaffolding in favor of methods that are based on "training" instead of "practicing," and "extinction strategies" instead of "learning strategies," treating sleep and other behaviors as habits to be established or broken rather than skills to be learned. There is no consideration for what the baby is presently able to do on her own nor what the appropriate next step may be.

This is why I developed the Gentle NUDGE to Success—not just for sleep but also for feeding, outings, and more. These are all developmental tasks, just like walking, reading, and learning to share. Each one requires a process of building one skill upon another until the goal is achieved.

THE GENTLE NUDGE TO SUCCESS

The Gentle NUDGE technique is a much-needed and loving approach to baby development that fits all infants and young children, but especially those with a highly sensitive arousal system. Based on Vygotsky's core concepts, the Gentle NUDGE:

- Balances the two key components necessary for forming a strong attachment: sensitive responses from the parent or caregiver coupled with a secure base, which encourages exploration and growing independence.
- Begins at the baby's present skill level, and, as the baby demonstrates readiness, gently enhances and stretches the baby's continually evolving skills.
- Helps babies gradually develop the skills necessary to smoothly function within their family's system.

I had been employing the concepts of the NUDGE in my work with spirited children for decades. However, it was only after I completed my dissertation research on the role of temperament in infancy and listened to hundreds of stories of parents in my infant classes that I began formally testing and refining the NUDGE technique. I immediately realized how desperate parents were for an alternative to the commonly recommended "training" strategies, such as interval waiting techniques for sleep, which either left their babies in tears or simply did not work.

The steps of the NUDGE are intuitive, baby- and parent-friendly, and can be applied to all kinds of situations and with babies (and children) of all temperaments, but they are especially

effective with spirited infants, who require more support to regulate their keenly sensitive arousal systems. In Part Two, "The
Spirited Way in Practice," each chapter will apply the five steps
of the Gentle NUDGE to a range of skills including nighttime
sleep, naps, eating, and outings and socializing, showing you the
full range of steps that lead to an ultimate goal.

The 5 Steps of the Gentle NUDGE

1. **N**ote where your baby is now.

2. **U**nderstand your ultimate goal.

3. **D**etermine the teeny, tiny steps that build on one another to achieve
   that goal.

4. **G**ently practice with your baby the next tiny step to move toward that
   goal.

5. **E**ase back your support as your baby becomes more proficient.

The Gentle NUDGE begins with taking NOTE of where your
baby is right now, and gradually moving her forward. Rather than
wasting energy worrying about what she cannot yet do, you focus
on what she *can* do. That attention to her present skill level allows
you to listen to what she is telling you she needs now to thrive.
There is no urgency to push. You can trust her to set the pace.
She in turn senses your confidence and begins to move out into
the world, assured that if she needs you, you will be there with a
helping hand.

. . . .

The Gentle NUDGE begins with taking NOTE of where your baby is now, and gradually moving her forward. Rather than wasting energy worrying about what she cannot yet do, you focus on what she *can* do.

. . . .

Second, the Gentle NUDGE encourages you to UNDER-STAND your ultimate goal.

- What about this skill is important for your baby to acquire?
- Does having this skill benefit the overall well-being of your family?
- How is this goal influenced by your family's culture and social norms?
- Does this skill fit who your baby is and what she is telling you she needs today?

No baby arrives knowing her parents would prefer she sleep in a crib versus sharing a bed with them, or eat with a fork and spoon rather than fingers or chopsticks. Nor that in this family's culture one wipes their bottom with only the left hand—never the right. Nor that she is expected to join in all conversations or, alternately, is expected to remain quiet and listen to the adults. Each learning goal is deeply influenced by our expectations and social norms. You get to decide the goals for your baby and your family.

The process continues when you DETERMINE the small steps—what I call the teeny, tiny steps—that lead to incremental change.

For example, before a baby can put himself to sleep independently, many other skills must be in place—including the ability to fall asleep while feeding; staying asleep when the nipple is removed; falling asleep without a feeding or nipple; falling asleep with just a short period of rocking; and staying asleep when transferred from arms to a sleep surface. The process is peaceful and unhurried. Both the baby and parents gradually build confidence and skill.

Like learning to walk, the exact sequence, pace, and style of learning is unique for each baby. There is not one right way and the steps can be continually adapted to fit everyone's needs and ability levels. You can move faster or slower, and you can take steps that are even teenier or bigger, depending on your baby's readiness and pace.

> The power of the Gentle NUDGE is finding success and growth in smaller steps as you move toward the ultimate goal. The process is peaceful and unhurried. Both the baby and parents gradually build confidence and skill.

Once you have devised a few tiny steps, it's time to GENTLY practice. Though it might seem obvious and natural and you may question the need for this formal step, I have come to recognize just how important practice is with a spirited, highly aroused baby. The infant's reactions can be so intense that he quickly conditions us to not even try to lay him down, remove the nipple, pat reassuringly before offering a nighttime feeding, or try an initially rejected food again. As a result, even when the behaviors are within a baby's zone of proximal development with the "just right" amount of challenge, parents are not encouraging these skills because they worry about their baby's reaction if they try.

As one parent said to me recently, "Once I get her quieted, I am too scared to even attempt to remove the nipple from her mouth because I know if she gets upset, I will just have to start all over again."

But practice generates additional synapses in the brain, creating pathways for new skills to develop. Gently rehearsing the next teeny step prepares your baby for success when he is ready, without triggering overarousal. You select the step and the time when you'll practice. Your baby controls the pace. Just expect that pace will be slightly slower than that of your baby's low-key peers and that your baby will need your assistance longer. This is normal; he will get there.

> Practice generates additional synapses in the brain, creating pathways for new skills to develop. Gently rehearsing the next teeny step prepares your baby for success when he is ready.

If your baby is intense and slow to adapt, you may choose to practice once a day. Or, you may decide it will work best for both of you to practice at every feeding, sleep time, or visit to Grandma's house. Then again, you may choose to practice when there is nothing to lose. For example, rather than practicing the transfer of your baby from your arms to a flat sleeping surface at naptime, when *you* need your baby to sleep, you may choose to practice this movement as a "game" during playtime. You get to decide.

However, the middle of the night is *not* a teachable time. Nor will you want to practice when someone in your family is ill. Practice stops and begins again when everyone is feeling well.

Once your baby is proficient in one setting, expand to another. For example, falling asleep independently in a hotel room poses a greater challenge than doing so in a familiar space at home. Likewise, separating from one parent when left with the other is easier than separating to be left with a new teacher or caregiver.

Gentle practice also means keeping everyone in the green zone. Practice sessions end before the baby becomes distressed. Tomorrow is another day. This is a Gentle NUDGE—not a shove.

> Gentle practice means keeping everyone in the green zone. Practice sessions end before the baby becomes distressed. . . . This is a Gentle NUDGE—not a shove.

Time, energy, and effort are required to gently nudge your baby through the ever-more-complex skills. Any hint of backsliding can raise your anxiety. That's why it is easy to fear cutting back your support.

However, as your baby gains proficiency, it is important to EASE back on your support, recognizing that your baby is now more capable of handling this particular challenge. For example, maybe it's time to wean your baby from his pacifier. You are confident the cold turkey approach everyone is telling you to use will never work. Instead, you incrementally begin reducing the frequency of use. He continues to have his pacifier as a calming support for sleep, but when he wakes, he removes it from his mouth and leaves it in his sleeping space. Or, he may have a pacifier when upset, but to use it, he must sit down and calm. When he's ready to play again, it is put away. No walking around with it in his mouth. The fade-out is gradual as your little one becomes more proficient at calming himself in other ways.

THE GENTLE NUDGE IN ACTION

Kristi, a first-time mom, came to me when her daughter Aria was four months old. Kristi had discovered that contrary to the advice she had researched and heard from other moms, Aria napped better and longer if she was held. But she was so worried that her approach would affect Aria's development that she called me the morning after she discovered my website on one of her middle-of-the-night Google searches.

"I know I shouldn't be doing this," she told me. "But it seems to be what Aria needs, and it works."

During my initial assessment with Kristi, she noted that Aria startled at the slightest sound, woke the second Kristi attempted to shift positions, and cried if a draft from the window touched her skin. I pointed out to Kristi how she had intuitively noted where Aria was in her development, sensing that full-body contact helped Aria regulate her body temperature and calmed her, which was helping her drop into restorative sleep. With Kristi's close physical support, Aria slept well. I introduced Kristi to the five steps of the Gentle NUDGE and explained that she could begin easing back a bit to let Aria practice the next step, which was transferring Aria to a flat surface for her nap.

"When you sense both you and Aria are ready, select one nap of the day to begin practicing a transfer to her bed," I coached.

About a month after my first call with Kristi, Aria began to squirm and fuss a bit while being held. Kristi took this as an indication that Aria might be ready for the next step—napping on a flat surface.

Kristi went through their typical sleep routine of nursing and rocking until Aria was sound asleep. On this day, however, Kristi slowly shifted Aria to lower her into her crib. Aria immediately startled awake. Kristi held Aria for the rest of her nap. But the next morning, they tried the shift again, and continued to do so each day.

Several weeks later, Aria successfully transferred to the crib and slept for twenty minutes. When she stirred, but before she was fully awake and became too upset to return to sleep, Kristi went to her, letting her know she was present. "I'm here," Kristi would say. If Aria did not return to sleep after some soft pats, Kristi picked her up and practice was over. No second attempt was made to return her to the crib. Aria's sleep was more important than repeated practices. If Grandpa was visiting, he loved holding Aria for the remainder of the nap as they continued to practice.

It had been a couple of months since I'd heard from Kristi when she contacted me again in a panic. Aria was still not sleeping through the night in her crib. "We are trying, but I am afraid we are failing," Kristi lamented. "Can you help?"

When she told me this, I asked her to walk me through Aria's current sleeping pattern and then surprised Kristi when I asked, "Are you celebrating?"

"What do you mean?" Kristi fumed. "She's not sleeping through the night in her crib!"

"But," I pointed out, "a few months ago, Aria couldn't nap without being held. Today, based on what you've just told me, she manages a transfer to her crib like a pro, remains asleep for a full two-hour morning nap, sleeps an additional forty-five minutes there in the afternoon, and at night is giving you her longest stretch of three to four hours of sleep. Over half of her sleep is now in her crib. This is wonderful progress!"

"Really?" Kristi questioned.

"Oh, yes," I replied. "This advancement warrants celebration! She is doing fabulously. Let's use the Gentle NUDGE to take her to the next step."

On the designated evening, Kristi nursed and rocked Aria asleep then smoothly placed her in the crib. The plan was for Kristi to follow that step with tiny "supports" to encourage Aria to sleep just a little longer in her crib without ever getting to a point of distress.

Three hours later, at 10:00 P.M., Aria awoke, and Kristi quickly went through the steps of reassuring, then patting, picking up, and feeding, to sleeping, before placing her back in the crib. Ten minutes later, Aria woke again and Kristi patted her bottom, which settled her back to sleep. Five more minutes passed when Aria cried once again. This time Kristi rocked her back to sleep and then placed her in the crib. Finally, a mere three minutes passed—Kristi was watching the clock like a hawk—before Aria awoke again. That's when Kristi stopped the NUDGE and brought Aria back to her co-sleeper attached to Kristi's bed, where she slept until 5:30 A.M. with just a quick feed at three. Sleeping all night in her crib was not yet in Aria's "zone," but that did not mean Kristi could not continue to gently nudge her in that direction.

Ten days after our conversation, I checked back in with Kristi, wondering if Aria had stretched her nighttime sleep in the crib any longer.

"Not yet," Kristi replied. "She continues to return to her co-sleeper around ten or eleven. But the good news is that she's begun to sleep until six forty-five A.M. instead of waking for the day at five-thirty."

Two days later I received a text at 7:00 A.M. from Kristi. "Best present ever! Aria just slept all night in her crib. Woke at 4:00 for a quick snack and went right back into her crib until 6:30 AM!"

Will Aria now sleep all night in her crib from this point forward? I'm sorry, the answer is no. Development is not a linear process. Setbacks are normal. But when the backslides occur, Aria will move through the sequence of steps faster than she did the first time, and she'll continue forward toward ever-more-complex tasks. Thanks to the Gentle NUDGE she will get there. But because progress is incremental, sometimes it is difficult to see.

That's why it is so important to keep a journal and to refer to it often.

. . . .

Development is not a linear process. Setbacks are normal. . . . But because progress is incremental, sometimes it is difficult to see.

. . . .

Like Kristi, you may feel that progress is slower than you would like and be tempted to push harder. But as the authors of *Chi-Walking* write, "If you are baking a cake, you don't turn up the heat to make it bake faster."

For now, record in your journal:

- How are you feeling right now? What is going well and where are *you* struggling the most? Where do you want to see change?
- What can your baby do *now*? Think about the four primary skills every baby needs to develop—napping, nighttime sleeping, eating, and going out.
- What tiny step are you practicing or considering?
- And, most important, where have you had one or two teeny, tiny successes?

Those documented successes will prevent you from interfering with, and even holding back, your baby's natural progression. You and your baby will move forward without all the aggravations created by attempting to accelerate the pace beyond your baby's "zone."

When complications such as illness, time variations, teething, growth spurts, family changes, or stress intrude and create setbacks, you'll know what to do. You'll provide more support right away and then you'll ease back as you follow your baby's pace and cues.

Take a deep breath. Review your journal. Trust that the setback is temporary. Then call in one of your people and take a break. While you do, I'll leave you with a story from one of my own recent learning experiences. Hopefully it will provide you with a bit of lightness and a hearty chuckle in those moments when you need it the most.

Forgive me. I know puppies and babies should never be compared. But my husband and I recently brought a puppy into our home and I enrolled in puppy training classes taught by Nancy, a real "dog whisperer." It proved to be a humbling experience. Children, I am good with. Dogs, I am a learner. Our slow progress frustrated me, and I bemoaned my lack of success and ineptitude. Nancy responded to my grumbles with this note:

"My advice to new dog owners, seasoned dog owners, and want-to-be dog owners is this: Learn how to settle in. Learn that nothing will happen overnight. Learn that if you try to take shortcuts and make it all happen to fit your schedule, or your desires, or your needs, it will come back and bite you in the butt, figuratively and literally!"

I laughed. Nancy is direct! But I couldn't resist including this story because it offers a great example of Just Right learning and gets at a bigger truth: All mammals—puppies and babies alike—take time to develop the abilities and skills to calm and manage themselves, self-regulate, and settle into their environment and family. The process can't be forced. As Nancy pointed out, there are no shortcuts. But we can enhance learning with a Gentle NUDGE and a touch of humor to keep us centered.

CHEAT SHEET: WHAT IS THE GENTLE NUDGE TO SUCCESS?

1. *Remind yourself of the developmental learning model of baby growth.* Even if you feel exhausted, impatient, and frustrated with your baby's pace, notice how your baby is learning, growing, and adapting all the time. Take time to note changes in your journal.

2. *Think about one area where you can apply the Just Right Challenge.* You'll lower your stress and your baby's if you work with your baby's actual, current abilities while focusing on a goal in one area toward which to gradually guide your baby.

3. *Experiment with the five-step Gentle NUDGE.* By recognizing our spirited babies' highly tuned arousal system, it allows our babies to set the pace, while we gently nudge them forward, providing the support they need as long as they need it. To recap, here are the five steps:

    1. **N**ote where your baby is now.
    2. **U**nderstand your ultimate goal.
    3. **D**etermine the teeny, tiny steps that build on one another to achieve that goal.
    4. **G**ently practice with your baby the next tiny step to move toward that goal.
    5. **E**ase back your support as your baby becomes more proficient.

4. *Record progress and celebrate successes.* Note in your journal what your baby can do *now*. What is the tiny step you are currently practicing? What successes have you had? Then, on those days when you feel like you are failing, you can look back and see the progress.

REFLECTION QUESTIONS FOR YOUR JOURNAL

- What can my baby do today that she could not do last week?

- What's the next teeny, tiny step I can practice with my baby?

- When will we practice?

- Is my baby ready for me to ease back on my support in one particular area?

PART TWO:

The Spirited Way in Practice

Chapter 6

Successful Naps

The Importance of Daytime Sleep for Playful Babies and Restful Nighttimes

"To get her to nap I took her on an hour-long car ride, transferred her to the front carrier for another hour, and now she's asleep on top of the running dryer. Yes, we are going nuts."
—Roberto, the father of Ada

Leah returns to the child-care program after her exercise class. She cringes as she nears the door, hoping that Mason has not morphed into a trumpeting wild elephant like he did the previous week. Today, there is silence.

"You have such a chill baby," the attendant remarks.

Leah flashes a smile. "Thank you," she replies, but inside she's thinking, "You have no idea how hard I worked to help him nap before we arrived so he would be chill for you."

Sleep. Precious sleep. It may seem counterintuitive, but that good night's sleep you and your baby crave begins in the morning—not at bedtime. Yet, when daytime sleeping is a struggle, it's tempting for parents to give up, forget the naps, and just let their babies go until they crash. But an essential truth about life with spirit, which Leah discovered the hard way, is that naps are crucial for regulating their super-charged arousal systems.

. . . .

Sleep. Precious sleep. It may seem counter-intuitive, but that good night's sleep you and your baby crave begins in the morning—not at bedtime.

. . . .

It's a continuous, positive cycle. The amount and quality of sleep during the day significantly impacts the quality and duration of your baby's nighttime sleep. An overtired baby also struggles to feed well, enjoyably engage in social situations, or welcome new experiences. Naps keep these highly alert, sensitive, intense babies in the green zone of calm energy.

. . . .

The amount and quality of sleep during the day significantly impacts the quality and duration of your baby's nighttime sleep. . . . Naps keep these highly alert, sensitive, intense babies in the green zone of calm energy.

. . . .

Yet naptime presents unique challenges. These tuned-in little ones don't just sleep anywhere or through anything—or merely close their eyes and conk out—as do many of their low-key peers. Instead they struggle mightily to stay awake even when they are exhausted. These contradictory cues lead us to assume that these babies just don't need as much sleep as other babies, but they do—desperately so.

True, there does exist a short-sleep gene, possessed by individuals capable of fully functioning on far fewer hours of sleep than the general population. However, there are very few true short-sleepers. When we look at babies, many of these supposed short-sleepers are spirited babies, who are too overstimulated to sleep. They are *not* happy. The frequency and intensity of their meltdowns are exhausting. Parents will often say, "I thought he just had a crabby personality," never realizing how tired their "short-sleeper" was.

While we cannot make these temperamentally irregular little ones sleep, we can *help* them sleep. Despite their irregularity, which makes falling into a predictable routine challenging, we do not have to give up and slide into chaos. By implementing the seven steps to successful naps we can catch their often confusing sleep cues and gently nudge them to become great nappers, waking and sleeping in a rhythm that fits our families.

The seven steps are based on the commonalities of naps for spirited infants across cultures and family habits. While there is a science to sleep, there is also a significant element of cultural preference. There is not one right way to nap. The goal is to help each unique baby and family to thrive.

7 Steps to Successful Naps

1. Start with a morning wake time.

2. Identify your baby's sleep cues.

3. Make the first nap a priority.

4. Implement a simple naptime sleep ritual.

5. Honor how your baby sleeps best.

6. Create your daily rhythm.

7. Develop your baby's nap skills with Gentle NUDGEs.

STEP 1. START WITH A MORNING WAKE TIME

One of the most frustrating aspects of spirited babies is their unpredictability. The key to bringing a minimum and much-needed dose of predictability to your lives begins at the very start of your day. Remember the importance of a predictable morning wake time, which we discussed in chapter 4, "How Can I Meet My Basic Needs Now?" It is the key to ever-so-gradually drawing your baby into your family's daily routine and bringing a bit of predictability to your day.

Your baby's naps and daily routines will evolve. But once established, a family wake time is one of the constants you can rely on—it's a pocket of predictability during a highly unpredictable stage of life and one you can strongly influence.

Remember, your goal is not to wake your baby but rather to allow the sounds and activities of you, other family members, and pets to cue your baby to realize that this is when we begin our day. Soon your baby will naturally begin to awaken at this time, too.

On the other hand, if your baby wakes at 4:30 A.M. ready to begin her day, you'll treat the awakening the same as an awakening at 1:00 A.M. It's still time to sleep. If, however, your baby consistently wakes at 6:00 A.M. but you'd prefer she woke at 7:00 A.M., in chapter 7, "Peaceful Nighttime Sleep," I'll show you how to make small adjustments to delay wake times, but you also may need to make adjustments. This is a family system. We influence one another.

This consistent wake time then lets you predict your baby's first nap. As Emily told me, "At ten weeks Adalyn had already begun consistently awakening between six and six-thirty, allowing me to anticipate that around seven-thirty or eight, she would be ready for her first nap."

How long your baby remains awake will change as she grows and develops, but with a predictable morning wake time, you have a solid baseline and a shot at planning your morning—not perfectly but a bit better.

That morning wake time baseline also comes in handy when changes or challenges arise. When it is disrupted you immediately recognize something is up. Second, it gives you a starting point for figuring out what that "something" is, as you can see in the chart on morning wake time disruptors and strategies that follows.

MORNING WAKE TIME DISRUPTORS AND STRATEGIES

Potential Disruptors	Effective Strategies
Light/environmental disruptors	Like all mammals, during spring and summer we need slightly less sleep than we do during fall and winter. If your baby is suddenly waking early, check to be certain no light is coming through the blinds. Spirited babies will awaken at sunrise unless the room is dark. If your baby is being awakened by adults rising early, traffic noise, dogs barking, etc., use a sound machine to block the sound. You can also shift your baby's bedtime 15 minutes later.
Stress	Whether it is a new tooth, change in child care, or increase in parents' stress levels, stress can lead to early awakenings. Add in more soothing, calming activities such as massage, rocking, singing, and water play during the day to quiet your baby's arousal system. Don't forget to take care of *you*, so both you and your baby can sleep.
Morning lark gene	Accept you have a baby who is genetically wired as a morning lark. These babies wake early no matter when they are put to sleep. Move your sleep time earlier so you can get the sleep you need and enjoy the sunrise with your baby.
Growth spurt	New skills can be so exciting your baby can't wait to start the day to practice! If your baby is waking earlier than 5:00 A.M. treat it the same as a middle of the night awakening. Feed him if needed, but do not turn on lights, take him from the sleeping area, or interact. It's still time for sleep! Hopefully, you can convince him to wait until at least 5:30.

Potential Disruptors	Effective Strategies
Disrupted routine, travel, illness	If your own morning wake time has been irregular, return to your predictable wake time. Take your baby outside for exposure to morning light. This will help reset the body clock. Increase your household morning activity to cue "this is when our family wakes." If your baby has been ill, just let her sleep.
Fall/winter longer nights	In the fall and winter we need more sleep. If your baby begins sleeping later in the morning, causing you to feel rushed and disrupting the semblance of the nap routine you've established, move your baby's bedtime 15 minutes earlier. Once your baby is waking 15 minutes earlier, move the bedtime 15 minutes earlier again. Typically, you can shift wake time 15 to 60 minutes earlier in this way.

STEP 2. IDENTIFY YOUR BABY'S SLEEP CUES

Whenever I'm assisting parents in identifying their baby's sleep cues I always ask, "How do you decide your baby is ready for sleep?" Often the responses include "when he cries" or "when he arches." Unfortunately, by the time infants are crying and arching they are already in the red zone of overarousal. They look like they are fighting sleep but the real problem is that we've accidently missed their window for sleep—a window that sometimes is a mere fifteen minutes wide.

I was sitting on the floor observing a zero-to-three-month baby class, led by my friend and colleague Sara Bennett Pearce, a lactation consultant and certified nurse-midwife. Next to me a mom and her baby engaged in deep conversation. The baby focused intently on the mother's face, watching her lips move and cooing in response to her words. Suddenly he glanced toward me. "I think he likes you," the mom said to me.

"That's so sweet, I do like babies," I remarked, "but I think he's telling us he's tired."

"Really?" she replied.

"Yes, he just averted his eyes, letting us know he is fatigued and beginning to feel overstimulated. If you swaddle and rock him, he'll probably fall asleep." She frowned in doubt but wrapped a blanket around him, stood up, snuggled him tightly against her body, and began to sway.

"Wow, I have been completely missing his cues!" she exclaimed.

Was I just lucky that day? Perhaps, but my experience tells me it was not luck; it was all about focusing attention—attention on what the baby is telling us. If you watch closely you will begin to see a pattern of sleep cues for your baby.

The three levels of sleep cues

There are three levels of sleep cues. Level one is the point at which infants zero to nine months of age most easily fall asleep. For children ten months and older, level one cues indicate, *Heads up. I'm getting tired. Stay tuned.* Pay close attention and you will begin to notice even the most understated sleep cues. The momentary glance to the side; a gaze locking on the speck of light; an ear rub, yawn, or line appearing between your baby's brows leaps out at you. You sense the squirm as your baby shifts from smooth to jerky movements. The switch from contentedly paging through a book to thrusting it away becomes as obvious as a flashing light: *Warning, baby is getting tired.* (Soon, wherever you go, you'll notice these signals in other children as well, and wonder if you should point them out to their unsuspecting parents!)

Level two cues are the noteworthy sleep cues for babies typically about ten months and older. Do not wait for the second yawn or eye rub before you begin your naptime sleep routine.

Level three cues are an indication of overtiredness. The window for sleep has been missed. A surge of adrenaline has been released. It now may take from forty-five to ninety minutes for your baby to fall asleep—if he does at all. Every baby's cues are unique. What's most important is identifying your infant's signals. But just in case you would appreciate a little assistance knowing what you might see, hear, or sense, here are a few examples of commonly identified cues—and space for you to add your own.

You will notice there are some similarities between these cues and the yellow and red zones of arousal cues described in chapter 2. The key when you first notice the cues is to recognize that your baby is becoming dysregulated. Then ask yourself, "What does he need to calm?" If it's been awhile since he slept—even a mere forty-five minutes—and he was recently fed and has a dry diaper, it's probably time for a snooze.

THE 3 LEVELS OF SLEEP CUES

Level One	Level Two	Level Three
Red around the eyes	Yawn	Cannot settle, even when held
Slight sagging of cheeks	Begins to be a bit irritable	Nothing is right
Glazed/dull look in the eyes	Rubs eyes or pulls on earlobe	Crying
Momentary slowing of motion	Roots or seeks a comfort object	Arching
Slight drooping of eyelids	Loses coordination, falls	Thrashing
Change in skin color/pallor	Seems bored/seeks stimulating toy	Screaming
Makes a certain sound	If mobile, starts to flit from one thing to another	Unable to feed
Looks away from you	Lays head down	Hyper and frenzied motion
Burrows into your neck	Wants to be held	Falling apart
Locks in on an object or speck of light as though unable to look away	Becomes frustrated but not crying	Stands up/crawls around in crib/ seems unable to lie down
Squirms	Stops jabbering/ becomes quiet	Shakes head back and forth
Movements shift from smooth to jerky	Laughs then starts to fuss	

Sleep cues over time.

Expect that as your baby grows and develops her sleep cues will change. At three months, a glance away may be the critical clue that leads to nap success. A glance away at nine months may be, *I'm getting tired but I'm not quite ready for sleep yet. Wait for the eye rub.* And at thirteen months that eye rub might only indicate a heads-up. Attempt to put him down at this point and thirty-five minutes later he's still walking around his crib. It takes another twenty minutes before he lays his head down on the mattress, indicating that now he's ready to go to sleep. Watch, and continue to learn, as your baby changes. The ability to catch level one and two cues typically allows even spirited babies to fall asleep within thirty-five minutes.

Second-guessing your baby's cues.

When you catch your baby's cues at level one and two, a relatively happy baby will be going to sleep. There's a challenge with putting a happy baby down for sleep, though: Observers may think you are misjudging your child. You may even question yourself. Trust your instincts as you experiment to see what works for your unique child.

A study comparing American and Dutch families conducted by Dr. Sara Harkness, a human development researcher at the University of Connecticut, found that when a baby begins to fuss, American parents interpret the cues as boredom and offer more stimulation. Dutch parents, however, assume the baby is tired and put him to bed. Every day, Dutch infants sleep an average of ninety minutes longer than their American counterparts. Don't let your baby's delight in stimulation trick you into thinking he's bored, when he's actually ready for sleep.

Your awareness of your baby's cues helps you decode what may be causing a nap issue or when naps need to be adjusted as your baby stays awake for longer periods of time. Revisit the sleep cue chart to help you assess your baby's current signals.

SLEEP CUE DISRUPTORS AND STRATEGIES

Potential Disruptors	Effective Strategies
Missed cues	The window for sleep may be a mere 15 minutes wide. Miss it and spirited babies get a second wind, not going down to sleep for 45 to 90 minutes. If your baby was falling asleep within 35 minutes, but now is not, check to be certain you are catching the cues at level one or two.
Change in cues	Your baby used to go down when the slightest tint of red appeared around his eyes. Now he's wide awake. Your baby may have shifted from level one cues to level two. Check the chart. This is especially true if your baby is 9 to 10 months of age.

STEP 3. MAKE THE FIRST NAP A PRIORITY

The process of bringing some predictability to your baby's naps begins with the morning wake time and continues with the first nap of the day. I have families start with the first nap because:

- It's typically the easiest!
- It's the most predictable.
- It helps keep your baby from overarousal for the whole day—imagine that!
- And it's a key building block for establishing a rhythm that will support you and your baby for the entire day.

To the best of your ability, schedule activities around your baby's naps, especially the first one. We'll talk more about naps on the go in chapter 9, but if possible, guard the first one of the day and be where your baby sleeps best.

For babies under six months, whose first nap may occur a mere forty-five to seventy-five minutes after awakening in the morning, things can get tricky. If you have older children, your baby's first cues may appear just as siblings are heading out the door. Or if your baby attends a child-care program, drop-off may lie within that same critical time period. If this is the case, instruct your child-care person to immediately offer your baby an opportunity to nap. At home, try to help your baby fall asleep before the transition of older children. That first morning nap is an important one. While the concept of *overtired* defies all logic, it's real. If your baby completely misses that first nap, her arousal system activates to keep her going, increasing the difficulty of getting her down later.

When morning naps are suddenly disrupted, make a special effort to understand the issues and reinstate the naps. (We'll talk later in this chapter about toddlers dropping to one nap.)

FIRST NAP DISRUPTORS AND STRATEGIES

Potential Disruptors	Effective Strategies
Timing of transitions	Drop-offs at child care or older children going to school may occur just at your baby's window for sleep. Consider moving the transition a few minutes earlier, so your baby is already at child care, or older children have been dropped off, so your baby can be put down for a nap when she hits her window.
Development	Your baby has been napping in the child care room but suddenly starts to remain awake. Rather than assuming she does not need this nap, recognize that she may have reached a new stage of development and is now more tuned in to the world around her. Not wanting to miss a thing, she struggles to fall asleep. Ask that her crib be placed in the quietest, darkest corner and request that caregivers help her relax and shift from alert to sleep. With this support she'll very likely begin napping again.

STEP 4. IMPLEMENT A SIMPLE NAPTIME SLEEP RITUAL

A missing ingredient in many naptime routines is the concept of a naptime "ritual"—which I define as a consistent, familiar, and calming pattern that helps your baby unwind and ends in sleep. Ideally, it will be a simplified version of the ritual you establish for nighttime sleep and one you can use most days. It is also simple enough to share with other people who care for your baby. This small amount of time you commit to a naptime ritual reaps big dividends.

Recently when working with a parent I asked her to describe the steps of her baby's naptime sleep ritual. This is what she was presently doing:

1. Change diaper, put on sleepwear.
2. Feed.
3. Read books.
4. Sing lullabies.
5. Put on sleep sack.
6. Go upstairs.
7. Place in crib.
8. Say, "Sleep tight."
9. Check back to calm.

Unfortunately, it was not working. Together we analyzed each step.

✓ Does this step alert or calm?
✓ Are there any transitions, stops, or starts that alert rather than settle down your baby and could be eliminated?

Redesigning this routine with these questions in mind, it now looks like this:

1. Calm yourself.
2. Change diaper, put on sleepwear.

3. Swaddle with a light blanket to calm.

4. Go to baby's sleeping area.

5. Feed, if needed.

6. Sing lullabies and lightly rub brows.

7. Rock until relaxed.

8. Remove swaddle if baby can roll.

9. Place baby in crib (or wherever your baby sleeps best).

10. Baby quickly falls asleep.

In this plan:

✓ The parent calms herself first.

✓ Once in the sleeping area there is no shifting of rooms.

✓ All clothing and diapering activities are completed at once, since undressing can alert a baby.

✓ The book is eliminated. After feeding and listening to lullabies the baby is beginning to calm; switching to a book may alert her.

✓ Rather than immediately shifting the baby into a sleeping space before she's relaxed, we set her up for success by rocking her until she's calm, then moving her to the crib.

As a simple framework for you to experiment with, these are the basic components of a daytime sleep ritual:

1. Bring yourself into the green zone of calm energy.

2. Plan ahead with a sleeping space and environment for sleep.

3. Find the right soothing/calming activities.

4. Feed your baby, if needed.

5. Place your baby in her sleeping space with a few pats (or rock her to sleep, if that's how your baby sleeps best).

6. Know when to take a break.

7. Adjust for the special case of "purgers."

Bring yourself into the green zone of calm energy.

The mere thought of trying to put your little one down for a nap may stress you out. Unfortunately, our sensitive little ones sense our angst.

Before you pick up your baby, bring yourself into the green zone of calm energy. Try to tune out all the messages in your mind and focus your energy on this moment with your baby. Don't fret about yesterday, last night, or any specific number of hours of sleep you're aiming for. The fact is, the recommended amount of sleep for babies ranges from 9 to 19 hours in a 24-hour period, depending on the age and needs of your baby. That's a vast variation. No need to pressure yourself to ensure your baby falls asleep for each and every nap.

If your infant is in child care, try to select a program with stable, long-term staff so your baby is comfortable with consistent caregivers and can relax in their arms. High staff turnover is stressful for everyone and can push sensitive babies into a state of dysregulation.

Plan ahead with a sleeping space and environment for sleep.

It is commonly suggested that babies learn to nap through noise and in bright light. Trouble is, spirited babies don't. They need you to establish a sleeping space, one that is dark, quiet, and shuts out the world so they can sleep. Yes, this does mean that spirited babies do nap best at home or in their regular daytime child-care space. That's not to say we never go anywhere—we do, and I will discuss that in chapter 9. But spirited babies sleep best in their usual sleeping space.

Begin by eliminating light and visual stimuli, including mobiles if your baby remains awake to watch them. Order blackout shades, placing electric tape on the edges to prevent any light from showing. A mere speck of light can catch the attention of highly alert babies and keep them awake. As one parent told me, "She has big round eyes. We joke she's letting in all that light! If there is any at all, she's not sleeping." Remember, this is the child who one day will bring you to the window to catch the comet flashing through the sky.

If you aren't at your baby's sleeping space when naptime arrives, drape a light blanket over your shoulder and your baby's face, or walk into a dark closet or other dimly lit space, to help her calm for sleep.

Do not forget sound. A whisper, barking dog, click of a door latch, creak of the floor, or fire truck's siren six blocks away may awaken sensitive infants. And then again, they may sleep through vacuuming and siblings screaming. Go figure. Sometimes it does not make sense. But if your baby alerts to the slightest sound, put tape or cloth on the latch, and turn on a sound machine or a continuous lullaby app. Do what is necessary to help your baby shut out the world. If your baby will be in child care, select a program that provides a separate napping room or designated sleep area. This baby is unlikely to nap in the midst of a busy play space.

Quiet is a treasure. If you, too, are highly sensitive to noise, you may find your baby's need for quiet wonderfully restorative.

Find the right soothing/calming activities.

Spirited babies need help winding down. Soothing and calming activities are a must for these little dynamos.

- Highly active babies flail, buck, and kick, even though they are tired. The more they thrash the more dysregulated they become. If this is the case with your baby, wrap a light gauzy blanket around him, tucking his arms and legs tightly against your body. This swaddle blanket provides assistance calming his limbs but can easily be removed before placing the baby in a sleeping space. You can use it even with toddlers.
- Alert babies may need help "shutting out the world." Drape a light blanket over your shoulder and your baby's head and eyes to block all visual stimuli as you calm him for sleep.
- Soft music with a slow, steady beat, like lullabies, does have a calming effect. Sound and wave machines provide continual relaxing sensations.
- Repetitive motion also soothes and calms. If bouncing, rocking, swishing, and swaying back and forth like a

rocking cradle is needed, do it. Rocking has the effect of synchronizing the brain for sleep, thus shortening the time it takes to fall asleep and fostering restful and continual sleep. Rhythmic motion even increases the ability to sleep through sounds and interruptions. Ultimately, as your baby's need for movement lessens, you'll back out of it with a Gentle NUDGE, but for now it's what your baby needs.

- If bouncing rather than rocking is what your baby desires, but the bouncing is painful to your knees, purchase a large exercise ball. Brace it against a wall and while sitting on it, hold your baby and bounce. It will save your knees while you provide the movement he needs. Now calm, and if fed earlier, your baby may fall asleep or be drowsy enough to be placed in his sleeping space.

Feed your baby, if needed.

If your baby has not been fed before naptime or sleeps best if she's fed as she falls asleep, feed her. We can use the Gentle NUDGE approach to ultimately help her fall asleep without feeding, but for now it's what she needs.

Place your baby in her sleeping space.

Slowly and gently, place your baby in the sleeping space with a few pats, as a reassuring send-off to sleep. Or, if your baby falls asleep best in your arms, don't fight it. Hold her until she sleeps. (In the next step for daytime sleep I share some tips on babies who cling or push away to manage their arousal system.)

Know when to take a break.

The entire daytime sleep ritual can take fifteen to thirty-five minutes. If your baby has not fallen asleep within thirty-five minutes of completing the sleep ritual and it is obvious she's not going to sleep, you can stop trying. (If it has been less than thirty-five minutes but you realize you are getting upset, it is also okay to take a break.) Step out of the sleeping area. Allow your baby to play and then try again fifteen to twenty minutes later. If stepping out would be too alerting, stop trying to put your baby to sleep and let him play in the sleeping area. Then try again. Better yet, if there's another adult available, tag them to take over. There's no need for those hour-long wrestling matches that leave you both in tears. Don't be surprised when that new, relaxed adult is able to put your baby down in ten minutes! They're not more skilled, they just haven't been coping with the challenges you've been facing and as a result are calmer. Your baby senses all is well and sleeps.

Accept, too, that occasionally, despite your best efforts, today is not a sleeping day. Non-sleeping days are unpredictable. Sometimes we can figure out why they occur and sometimes they just happen. Do not assume your routine is failing and stop following it. Instead, simply give a long sigh. Place your baby in a safe location. Step away. Get a drink of water. Be mindful of the cool liquid quenching your thirst and soothing your body. Breathe. Recenter yourself. Give it a few minutes, then try again.

If your blood pressure spikes merely thinking about returning to the sleeping area, put on your carrier, place the baby in it, throw

on your coat, and go for a walk. If he falls asleep offer a silent al-
leluia. If he doesn't, well, you've gotten your exercise. It is just not
a sleeping day.

. . . .

Accept, too, that occasionally, despite your best
efforts, today is not a sleeping day. Non-sleeping
days are unpredictable.

. . . .

Adjust for the special case of "purgers."

Unfortunately for some babies, even when you catch their early
sleep cues and go through a calming, wind-down sleep ritual, they
still struggle to fall asleep peacefully. Sometimes that shift is a
grinding of gears. The wails of protest may be ear piercing. If this
is your baby, check that she is not hungry and does not need to
burp or a diaper change. If all is well in these areas, you may be
experiencing what I refer to as the *purging cry*.

Susan Daniels and Michael Piechowski describe in *Living with
Intensity* how highly intelligent gifted children display an elevated
energy level and are more alert and active. Their intensity is also
greater than average. This surplus energy must be discharged—
usually through action.

While we do not know yet if your baby is gifted, many infants come to sleep with a buildup of internal energy that must
be released. That energy is discharged through fierce crying. It's
almost as though they are shouting, *This world is crazy. I cannot
believe all the sensations, energy, and stress. I'm just going to have
a good cry!*

A purge cry is different from the *I've been left here to figure it out on my own* cry of distress. Your baby may shriek loudly but there truly is a sense of discharging rather than distress—a "letting it all hang out" purging of toxins and overstimulation through their tears.

A purge cry occurs even when you are holding your baby. It also continues despite your having purchased a sound machine, given your baby ten pacifiers, lying next to him, rubbing his back, rocking, moving to a different room. You name it, you've tried it, and your baby still cries before falling asleep.

The length of this cleansing period is often predictable. Five, eight, ten minutes max and she's done—every time. Your heart is racing, wondering what is wrong, but suddenly the shrieks shift to a whimper then abruptly stop. She shudders and sighs. Her body slumps against you, relaxed. She drops into sleep. Your heart is still beating wildly, and she's sound asleep!

Take a deep breath. Tell yourself, "I am not doing anything wrong. This is a tough transition for her. She experiences the world so profoundly, it's the only way she can release the tension."

It is important to remember that even when we do our best to meet our babies' needs, there are still times they will cry. An analogy to labor and delivery is apt. A labor nurse can't take away the contractions or the pushing, but they can say to us, "I'm here with you while you do this work." Sometimes babies are doing their work—we cannot fix things for them, but we can stay with them.

With a sleep ritual in place, your baby will know it's time for sleep. If suddenly she's not falling asleep as easily, review your ritual to see if slight adjustments need to be made.

DAYTIME SLEEP RITUAL DISRUPTORS AND STRATEGIES

Potential Disruptor	Effective Strategies
Development	• Your baby has needed a swaddle to unwind for sleep but now can roll over. Without the swaddle, however, he's not sleeping. Instead of a tight swaddle, wrap your baby in a lightweight blanket to quiet his body. Once he's relaxed this blanket can easily be removed. • Rocking calmed your baby, now she's wrestling in your arms. Soothe her until she's relaxed, then lay her in a crib or on her sleeping surface.
Growth spurt	• Your baby is going through a growth spurt. The sleep routine does not seem to be working. Slow down the steps to allow your baby to relax and calm, but do *not* drastically change or stop the routine. This frequently occurs when your baby is 4 to 5 months of age and "wakes up" to the world or hits another key developmental growth spurt such as crawling or walking. Growth spurts typically last one to three weeks. After a spurt your baby is likely to have stronger self-soothing skills. Experiment to see if she is ready for you to simplify, shorten, or eliminate one or more steps you have in place to calm her. For example, you used to rock her until she was asleep, now you can rock until her eyes flutter then lay her down.

Potential Disruptor	Effective Strategies
Missed cues	• Go back and check wake time and cues. If the sleep routine is not working, it may be an issue of an erratic wake time or you're missing cues, and as a result your baby is either not yet ready for sleep or overtired.

STEP 5. HONOR HOW YOUR BABY SLEEPS BEST

During an interview, University of Denver researcher Sarah Watamura told me, "Sleep is a physiological mechanism that has to get aligned. People try to shove babies into a box that doesn't fit and because it doesn't fit, they don't sleep at all."

Babies each come with their unique—and strong—temperaments. When it comes to sleep, their preferred place to sleep is not always the same as what we would like it to be. Work with your baby. His sleep is more important than *where* he sleeps. Ultimately, you will get him in a bed, but it will be a gradual process.

Body huggers–*please hold me.*

Some babies, especially those under nine months of age, often have a strong need for full-body connection. The moment the contact is broken, their eyes open. Note where your baby naps best. If she naps while held, hold her. Do not worry that she will never sleep on a non-human surface. She will. You will not be holding your baby for naps forever. Slowly you will build her capacity to sleep independently, but for now, start where she's a rock star and let her get the sleep she needs.

. . . .

If your baby naps while held, hold her. . . . You will not be holding your baby for naps forever. Slowly you will build her capacity to sleep independently, but for now, start where she's a rock star and let her get the sleep she needs.

. . . .

For body huggers—sometimes known as Velcro babies—your chest is your baby's natural habitat. Before her nap begins, empty your bladder, get a drink of water, have your own mini-meal available, then pick up a good book. Sit in a comfortable chair. Better yet, lie down in your safe sleeping space and take a nap with her. If you have older children, use a front carrier so your hands are free. This is also the time to bring in your support team, those individuals who would love to hold your baby while she sleeps.

When you allow your baby to sleep where she sleeps best, her naps lengthen. If instead you fight to lay her down forty times a day and it's not working, you'll both end up a mess.

Spirited infants have a very strong startle reflex. The moment you attempt to shift them from arms to a sleeping surface they will startle themselves awake. In the Gentle NUDGE section of this chapter I will show you how to transfer successfully. But the ability to make this shift requires time, patience, and teeny, tiny practice sessions. In the meantime, avoid unnecessary transfers. If your baby is sleeping, you may choose to attempt to lay him down, once. That's it. If he startles awake hold him and let him sleep. It is important to recognize this is a transfer issue, not a sleep problem.

Researcher Ron Barr found that babies who are held and carried more cry 43 percent less. The frequency of the crying bouts remains the same as for babies who are held/carried less, but the duration shortens.

Once your baby is asleep, let him sleep. Do not awaken him from his naps—it's a myth that reducing daytime sleep will lead to longer stretches of nighttime sleep.

· ·

Once your baby is asleep, let him sleep. Do not awaken him from his naps—it's a myth that reducing daytime sleep will lead to longer stretches of nighttime sleep.

· ·

Put-downers—*please let me go.*

While most spirited babies are calmed by our touch and presence, there are also highly sensitive babies who tell us, *Whoa, this touch is way too stimulating. Lay me down! And, in fact, your presence is also too stimulating. I want to interact with you when you are around, but I'm so tired! I prefer a few minutes to myself right now.*

You will know you have this baby because instead of calming while you hold her, she's squirming, as though to escape your grasp. Or, she gets more upset when you stand next to her bassinet. But if you lay her down and step away, she lets out a disgruntled yelp, then settles immediately. Don't take it personally. She loves you; your touch and presence are just too exciting right now—not all the time, just right now.

Think about how your baby sleeps best and use that knowledge when you run into a hiccup in the process.

HONOR HOW BABY SLEEPS BEST DISRUPTORS AND STRATEGIES

Potential Disruptor	Effective Strategies
Insisting on naps in a crib	• If your baby startles awake the second you attempt to lay her down, accept that for right now your baby sleeps best when held. • If your baby sleeps for 20 minutes on a non-human surface then wakes, pick her up, help her return to sleep, and hold her as she finishes the nap. But begin the next nap in the crib again. Gradually that 20 minutes will lengthen.
Development	• Your baby may have needed to be held for naps but now is squirming. Try laying her on a sleeping surface once. If she doesn't fall asleep, hold her for the nap, but try again next naptime, or the next day. • Baby can climb out of the crib. This is a safety issue that occurs much earlier for active babies than their quieter peers. Time to move him to a mattress on the floor or a toddler bed. (I recommend a mattress on the floor, big enough for you to sleep comfortably, too.)

There is often criticism of parents who provide extra sleep support, which your spirited baby needs to sleep well. Despite the attachment research that has demonstrated that giving babies what they need now leads to greater independence later, others often question your tactics and insist your baby will become forever dependent upon you. Those who do not understand temperament may accuse you of being rigid, overprotective, or a creator of bad habits. Always remember, this is what your baby needs *now*. We can use the Gentle NUDGE to gradually move her toward more independent sleep.

STEP 6. CREATE YOUR DAILY RHYTHM

Once you have established your family wake time, identified your baby's cues, and are beginning to see some consistency in the timing of your baby's first nap, you can use this information to begin creating a rhythm for the remainder of your day.

Analyze the pattern.

Now is a great time to turn to your journal to track your baby's daytime sleep over several days. Record the time your baby first wakes in the morning and the time of the first nap of the day. When your baby wakes from that nap, note the time. Watch for cues for nap number two. Check the clock when he falls asleep. Again, record it. Continue observing and recording throughout the day as your baby wakes and sleeps.

Over time, as you record your baby's wake and sleep times, a general pattern will begin to evolve. There is no perfect pattern. Babies under five months of age may just take short naps throughout the day, but if you look closely there may be a general pattern to the spacing between them.

For babies six to ten months of age, the first nap often occurs shortly after waking. Then, over the course of the day, awake times gradually lengthen. For example, you may note that about seventy-five to ninety minutes after waking your baby is ready for his first nap. Ninety minutes to two hours after that first nap ends, he's ready for the second. Two or three hours after that one ends, he's ready for the third. This third nap, which often occurs late in the afternoon, is an important one to help your baby make it through the evening without becoming overaroused. When babies are around seven months of age, parents often report a lengthening of naps as well as more consistency in their timing.

By 10 months of age spirited babies are often down to 2 naps a day, one in the morning and one in the early afternoon, but may continue to need those 2 naps until 18 or 19 months, much longer than their low-key peers, who will have switched to one nap per day. This can create an issue in child-care toddler programs that shift all children to one nap at fifteen months or sometimes even younger. If this is the case for your little one, request that the caregiver offer her two naps. Otherwise she may become the "problem napper," when the real issue is she was reduced to one nap too soon and by the time she is offered a nap she's overtired, in the red zone, and can't fall asleep.

At some point around fifteen to nineteen months your baby will stop falling asleep for her early morning nap—on some days but not every day. Initially it will be important to continue to offer her the opportunity for that first early nap. If she falls asleep, let her sleep. If she hasn't fallen asleep after thirty-five to forty minutes of trying, let that nap go. Try again later in the morning.

Once she's skipping that nap four or more days a week she's ready for just one nap a day. This nap often occurs about four hours after awakening, which means she's ready for sleep before lunch at noon. Be certain your baby is fed her lunch before this naptime. By feeding her early, around eleven or eleven-thirty, you won't miss her window, and she will fall asleep easily and will tend to nap longer. If the length of her single nap does not match the length of her two naps combined, bedtime will need to be moved earlier so the total amount of sleep in a twenty-four-hour period remains about the same as when she was taking two naps.

Let me stress: These ranges are just examples. Your baby's rhythmic routine will depend on her individual needs, length of each nap, age, and stage of development. The most important thing is recognizing your baby's needs—no other baby's rhythm matters.

Child-care director Charrisse Jennings, who has provided care for hundreds of infants, explained it to me this way: "Some babies sleep for fifteen minutes, some for two hours. An average is forty-five minutes—but it all depends. If they wake after fifteen or twenty minutes we start over, to see if they'll return to sleep. If they do, we hold them to finish the nap. If the baby does not return to sleep, naptime is over for now. We will watch cues closely and offer another opportunity to sleep when we see the need." (If you are wondering, yes, Charrisse employs a person whose sole job is to hold babies who need that full-body contact to nap. Look for this person when you select your child-care program.)

Using the information you've recorded in your journal, you can begin to create a rhythm to the day. Not a rigid clock-focused schedule, mind you, but rather a general sequence of waking, offering a meal, playing, sleeping. If your baby is uninterested in a feeding, move on to play and offer a feeding later when she indicates hunger. If your baby falls asleep after a feeding, let her sleep. Your baby's cues always trump the sequence of the cycle. But cues from your environment and a rhythmic routine help your temperamentally irregular baby begin to slip into a pattern that allows some predictability.

The great thing about creating a predictable rhythm is that your baby's nap is likely to occur after a feeding and short playtime. Since your baby is not hungry when you see his sleep cues you may be able to snuggle him up and help him transition into sleep. This gives him the opportunity to fall asleep without feeding or having a nipple in his mouth—two critical steps that gradually move him toward independent sleep.

If your baby is hungry or needs to nurse to sleep, go ahead and feed him, but try to see if he will fall asleep simply snuggled in your arms without eating. If he doesn't, try again a few days or weeks later. Gradually, your baby will get there.

However, even with a rhythmic routine, do not expect a cookie-cutter pattern of naps. Infants who are temperamentally persistent, alert, and irregular tend to be less consistent in their sleeping and eating patterns and require more time and practice to fall into a pattern. That means, especially during the first months before their body clock is fully developed, the time, frequency, and length of naps may be different every day. What may be consistent, though, is your baby's morning wake time and that your baby is ready for sleep again much sooner than "average" recommendations. That's what Leah discovered.

Match naps to your baby's needs—not "averages."

The day after her exercise class, where she had been complimented on her son's mellow demeanor, Leah attended a local infant and mommy class. The instructor informed the group that on average, 4-to-8-month-old babies should stay awake 2 to 3 hours between naps.

"You do not want them to get overtired," she stated.

Leah frowned before remarking, "My guy is five months and he can only stay awake seventy-five minutes before he needs to nap. If I push him longer, it's a sure bet he won't nap at all, or he will only nap if I hold him."

All eyes turned toward her.

"You hold him for naps?"

"Yes."

"He only stays awake seventy-five minutes?"

"Yes."

"Maybe you want to push him a little longer," the instructor suggested, despite the fact she had *just* warned the parents not to let their babies get overtired.

Leah walked out of class and hit my number on speed dial.

"I'm feeling big-time mommy judgment," she told me and proceeded to describe what had just occurred.

I forced myself not to blurt, "I detest the word *average*!" All too often *average* is misused, thrown down like a stake in the ground, as though there is some invisible line that says that "up to this point" behavior is normal and "beyond this point" something must be drastically wrong.

Average, however, is merely a mash-up of different babies. For example, if we collected the data from 3 infants and found that the first stayed awake 2 hours between naps, the second only 1 hour, and the third 1.25 hours, then added up those 3 lengths of time, divided that sum by 3, we would end up with an average of 1.41 hours between naps. This is an estimate that does not reflect the true figure for any of the babies. It's merely a guideline, not a given.

Averages are helpful in providing a sense of when to expect certain behaviors to occur, but they merely signify a midpoint. Spirited infants, with their super-charged arousal systems, are rarely if ever average!

I pulled myself together and asked Leah, "Are the other babies sleeping or musing during the group, while Mason is noticing everything?"

"Yes," Leah replied, and added, "He turns toward each voice. A door opens, he startles. His gaze rests on my face, studying how I'm feeling. He frowns when I do. A speck of light? He's got it."

Mason spends the hour visually sprinting around the room while all the other babies stroll. No wonder that after seventy-five minutes he is worn out.

Your baby will show you she is getting the sleep she needs with her demeanor and physical cues. When not demonstrating her sleepy cues, she will be happy and curious. Her eyes will be bright, not red-rimmed. There will be a vibrant glow to her skin tone, rather than a dull, drawn pallor.

. . . .

> Your baby will show you she is getting the sleep she needs with her demeanor and physical cues.

. . . .

You can trust yourself and your baby. No second-guessing needed. Let go of any guilt, frustration, or shame that you are responding "incorrectly" and your baby should be doing something he is not yet doing. This is what your baby needs now.

Once you have a sense of your baby's rhythm you'll recognize when something is off and can take steps to correct it so your baby gets the sleep he needs and you can maintain a bit of predictability in your day.

DAILY RHYTHM DISRUPTORS AND STRATEGIES

Potential Disruptor	Effective Strategies
Disrupted wake and feeding times	• Check your morning wake time, daily routine, and feedings. If the rhythm has been disrupted, do your best to return to a rhythmic routine.
Not napping at child care or napping at child care but not at home	• Work together to coordinate nap and feeding times and a sleep ritual for your baby. If your baby naps at 8:30 A.M. at home, ask that she be put down at 8:30 A.M. at child care. Match sleep routines as much as possible. • Know that as your baby "awakens" to the world she may no longer be able to nap in a busy noisy room, especially if her window for sleep is being missed. Ask if your baby may nap in a quieter area. • If necessary and it's available, consider a different child care with a separately staffed nap room.
Development	• Your baby is growing and developing and may now be able to stay awake longer. Observe cues closely, maintain a journal, and find your baby's new first nap sleep window. If he used to fall asleep after 45 minutes of being awake, check cues at one hour. Move forward in 15-minute increments until you find the new window. If your baby is staying awake longer than 3 hours and is less than a year old, check other culprits, such as disrupted morning wake times, environmental disruptors, etc. • If your baby is 15 to 18 months, he may be moving to one nap. Continue to offer the opportunity for a morning nap until the baby is skipping that nap at least 4 or 5 days a week. Once down to one nap, move bedtime earlier if needed for your baby to get the sleep he needs.

STEP 7. DEVELOP YOUR BABY'S NAP SKILLS WITH GENTLE NUDGES

Despite what you may read, babies' sleep habits are *not* established by four months of age. It's a process that can take eighteen months or longer, but there can be many, many improvements in your baby's sleep and your sanity! Sometimes, though, because it is so difficult to get these babies to sleep, we may fear even attempting to lay them down, remove the nipple, or stop rocking. Then, even when the baby is developmentally ready to be a bit more independent, we are still providing a level of support that is not actually needed. Fortunately, we can use the Gentle NUDGE to gradually practice skills and provide our babies with the opportunity to show us when they are ready—without disrupting sleep or leaving anyone in tears.

. . . .

Despite what you may read, babies' sleep habits
are not established by four months of age. It's a
process that can take eighteen months or longer,
but there can be many, many improvements in
your baby's sleep and your sanity!

. . . .

The Gentle NUDGE to transfer your baby to a sleep surface (bassinette, crib, sleeper)

The Gentle NUDGE method can help you along the way in your baby's sleep journey, particularly the challenge that looms over all the others related to naps—the satisfactory transfer to a non-human sleep surface, which means freedom for you and independent sleeping for baby.

Note where your baby is now. If your baby has a strong startle reflex, she awakens the moment you lean forward to lower her onto a non-human sleeping surface. Loss of full-body contact is like a cannon firing, signaling, *Wake up! You are about to be separated from your caregiver!* That's why this is a gradual process of building trust and confidence so that your baby knows *Even if I'm laid down, I'm safe.*

Understand your ultimate goal. Your goal may be to successfully transfer your baby from your arms to a sleeping place without her startling and waking.

Determine the teeny, tiny steps. There is not one right way to break down the steps to successful naps. Look at what your baby can do now and then think about the next right challenge—the next teeny, tiny step to move her toward success.

TEENY, TINY STEPS TO A SUCCESSFUL TRANSFER

Teeny step 1	Teeny step 2	Teeny step 3
Practice lowering your baby away from your body during playtime. This allows practice but does not disrupt her sleep.	Hold until deeply asleep. Attempt to transfer. If she startles awake, pick her up and hold to finish nap. Practice is over.	Hold until deeply asleep. Transfer. If she awakens, pat and support for a minute or two to see if she'll settle. If not, pick up and hold for nap.

Teeny step 4	Teeny step 5	Teeny step 6
Hold until deeply asleep. Transfer. Pat, watch her return to sleep. If she awakens 10, 15, or 20 minutes later, respond quickly (i.e., pat), but if needed hold for remainder of nap.	Hold until relaxed. Transfer while drowsy. Pat if helpful. Step away if your presence alerts. Give her the opportunity to put herself to sleep. If she does not fall asleep, stop practice, hold until asleep. Transfer once. If she awakens in less than 30 minutes, hold her. If she returns to sleep, continue holding to finish nap.	Hold until relaxed. Starting with one nap, transfer while awake. When baby falls asleep independently and stays asleep for 30 minutes, start transferring while awake for second nap. Then follow with the third nap.

Gently practice. Once you've determined your steps, begin practice. Keep sessions short. You want your baby to be successful. Her sleep is much more important than a battle to make her transfer. If she's overtired when you begin, or skipped an earlier nap, expect that the only way she will sleep today is "on you." Don't worry that this is a step back. Falling asleep when conditions are perfect is an easier skill than falling asleep when stressed by overfatigue, or being in a new and different place.

Ease back. As your baby's ability to control her startle reflex strengthens, gradually ease back your support. If you used a light gauzy blanket to swaddle her, try a transfer without. Practice in different settings. Allow your baby to set the pace as you rehearse the new skills.

The Gentle NUDGE to consolidate naps

Use the elements of the NUDGE to consolidate naps to gradually transition your baby from two to eventually one nap a day.

Note where your baby is now. Perhaps your baby is beginning to skip the early morning nap. Not every day, but sometimes.

Understand your ultimate goal. The most important goal is ensuring your baby gets enough sleep. A second goal is establishing more predictability in naptimes. A third goal is making sure you are getting your basic needs met so you can help your baby. Finally, you'll have a goal around your baby's independence with naps. Look for where a change is most helpful.

Determine the teeny, tiny steps, using the chart on dropping to one nap as a guide.

TEENY, TINY STEPS TO DROPPING TO ONE NAP

Teeny step 1	Teeny step 2	Teeny step 3	Teeny step 4
Offer baby an early morning nap, as you have been doing.	If baby does not fall asleep within 35 minutes of completing the sleep ritual, take a break. Try again 20 to 40 minutes later.	Baby begins skipping the early morning nap 4 to 5 days a week.	Shift baby to one nap about 4 hours after awakening. Watch cues to fine-tune the time. Move bedtime earlier if needed.

Gently practice. Offer the early morning nap. If your baby doesn't fall asleep take a break. Try again later.

<u>Ease back</u>. As your baby begins to consistently skip the first early nap, stop trying. Offer just one nap, about four hours after awakening. Observe cues to establish the new naptime and then allow him to sleep as long as he needs. Don't be alarmed if he sleeps three hours or longer. You do not need to wake him. Since he began the nap around 11:00 A.M. to noon, he will still be ready for sleep early in the evening and can easily sleep ten or more hours at night.

By using the Gentle NUDGE, you can gradually strengthen the skills your baby needs to move toward more independent sleep. If you feel as though you are stuck, trust your baby. She may be taking longer than her peers, but she *will* be successful. Those supportive practice sessions along with patient acceptance of where she is now are just what she needs to move forward. One day, those teeny, tiny steps will snowball, and the new skill will slide into place.

SENSITIVE, ALERT BABIES see, feel, and sense their world at a level not experienced by their low-key peers. As one mom posted in my Spirited Child Facebook group, "My spirited 6-year-old wakes up every morning and asks, 'What exciting things are we going to do today?' After the day's excitement he asks, 'What exciting things are we doing next?' Before he goes to sleep he asks, 'What exciting things will we do tomorrow?'"

Life with spirited babies *is* more exciting. This is also why extra steps are required to help them nap. But the payoff for your effort is big—a happier, better sleeping, contentedly well-feeding baby, *and* a touch of predictability so you can have restorative and productive breaks.

CHEAT SHEET FOR SUCCESSFUL NAPS

1. *Establish your baby's morning wake time.* This is the baseline from which you can begin to bring predictability into your baby's naps and your day.

2. *Watch for your baby's cues.* Learn your baby's sleep cues and remember that naps for spirited babies often are needed closer together than might be expected. Get to know *your* baby's needs and signs.

3. *Strictly protect the first nap of the day and build a rhythmic routine.* A familiar rhythm gives you and your baby a natural heads-up, "typical naptime approaching." You are prepared and can anticipate when your baby will be ready to slow down and slip into sleep.

4. *Establish a simple, consistent naptime ritual.* Like an evening bedtime ritual, a similar daytime routine cues your baby it is time for sleep. Take extra steps to create a sleeping space, reduce stimulation, and help him downshift to sleep.

5. *Allow your baby to sleep where he sleeps best.* Spirited babies often need full-body contact to nap well. Get comfortable. Pull in your support system. Make your baby's sleep more important than how or where he sleeps.

6. *Use the Gentle NUDGE to practice skills.* If you wish to move your baby toward independent napping and sleeping on non-human surfaces, you can get there gradually, without leaving your baby in tears.

REFLECTION QUESTIONS FOR YOUR JOURNAL

- What is my biggest challenge with my baby's napping right now?
- Where does my baby nap best?
- What's my most important goal for naps right now?

Chapter 7

Peaceful Nighttime Sleep

Your Baby's Sleep Is a Family Affair

> *"I've never encountered a subject like infant sleep where so many people have so many opinions and so little data. As a researcher and parent, the gap between what I am being told and what I can see is best for my child leaves me troubled."*
>
> —Sarah Watamura, Ph.D., University of Denver

If at this moment you are feeling exhausted and desperate for sleep, the most important thing I can tell you is that there is hope. No matter how many strategies you have already tried to get more sleep—and to get your baby to sleep through the night—the Spirited Baby Method will provide you with steps to bring you and your family to a better place. I can wholeheartedly tell you that spirited babies can and do become great sleepers. You get there by working with your child's temperament and the needs of your family system.

THE CHALLENGE OF NIGHTTIME SLEEP

When your baby wakes in the night, others may insist that you are doing something wrong. The barrage of negative comments doesn't stop there. "What's the deal with the pacifier?" they inquire with eyebrow raised. Or, "Don't you think you are giving in to her fussing too much?" The weight of the judgment wears you down as much as the lack of sleep itself.

When we're desperate, it is easy to turn to the sleep training models that others insist are the fastest way to teach babies to sleep independently. With variations, these models instruct parents to place their awake baby in a crib and walk out. Then, if it is an "interval waiting technique," the parent returns every 5, 10, or 15 minutes to reassure the baby of their presence, but not to pick up the baby. If, however, it is a cold turkey "cry it out" approach, the parent does not return until the next morning.

No matter which version is implemented, the premise is that the baby will figure out how to self-soothe and sleep. Studies by pediatric psychologists Jodi Mindell and Daniel Lewin have shown that sleep training techniques can be effective in stopping some infants from waking in the night. Yet even these researchers have found that these strategies do not work for about 20 percent of infants. That 20 percent is largely made up of spirited babies, which is why I never recommend sleep training methods.

Even for those babies who seem to demonstrate some improvement in sleep using these techniques, the long-term research does not support sleep training as a miracle cure that, once completed, leads babies to sleep through the night, every night. Sleep training advocates acknowledge that, over the long term, the effect will likely wear off and the training must be repeated.

Spirited babies are not waking because their parents "reward" them by responding. Spirited infants wake because they are in the process of developing their self-regulation skills and because their genetically wired temperament leads them to be more easily aroused. This is verified by the research.

Ruth Feldman, Ph.D., a professor of developmental social neuroscience at Yale Child Study Center, writes, "Regulation must include a developmental perspective. There exists a subset of infants who take longer." And, yes, once again spirited babies make up a significant percentage of this subset.

Researcher Ron Dahl adds, "At any one moment the brain must choose a state of relative vigilance or sleep. The two states are mutually exclusive." When your baby is more alert, intense, and sensitive, switching off the vigilance mode is tough. That is why a baby's temperament and developing self-regulation skills cannot be ignored as you address nighttime sleep. Nor can your own need for sleep be minimized—especially for eighteen months! Yet all too often, your losing sleep is exactly what happens when you try most infant sleep methods.

. . . .

> Spirited babies are not waking because their parents "reward" them by responding. Spirited infants wake because they are in the process of developing their self-regulation skills and because their genetically wired temperament leads them to be more easily aroused.

. . . .

The Spirited Baby Method views nighttime sleep differently. It considers your baby's temperament *and* takes a holistic, family system approach, which shifts the focus from viewing the baby as the problem to looking at how we can help *everyone* get the sleep they need.

Imagine for a moment you are a contestant in a new reality show, *Parents of Spirited Babies*. Winners receive one million dollars. The challenge is to see which *family* can get the most sleep. Each family member's hours of sleep are tallied—not just the baby's. Now, instead of frantically striving to make the baby sleep, in order to win you must think more broadly. Instantly, new solutions occur to you like: Go to bed earlier. If your baby's longest stretch of sleep is from 7:00 P.M. to 1:00 A.M., instead of staying up until 10:00 P.M., go to bed at 8:00 P.M. Then when she wakes at 1:00 A.M. you have already enjoyed five hours of uninterrupted sleep. Reduce other commitments. Turn off electronics that tend to "alert" and disrupt asleep. Ask a friend to spend the night and take first-wake-up duty. Or, change expectations so you stop ruminating about what you are doing wrong when your baby wakes in the night and just go back to sleep. You get the idea.

When your baby's sleep is no longer viewed as the problem, it is easier to accept where she is now and patiently nudge her toward a full night's sleep. But in this process your needs also remain paramount.

With the Spirited Baby Method there are seven steps to successful nighttime sleep—steps you can come back to over and over again as your baby grows and changes.

Two notes before we get started:

1. If you skipped ahead to this chapter, please go back and read Part One of this book. While sleeping may be the most immediate concern for you, the interplay of the relationships and needs of everyone within your family system is thrown into disarray when a new member enters. Part One will provide relief,

knowledge, and support you may be missing and will lay the groundwork for getting the sleep you need.

2. Remember, what transpires during the day significantly influences how your baby sleeps at night. If you skipped chapter 6, "Successful Naps," I encourage you to go back and read it, too. Then use that knowledge—on sleep cues, environmental supports (like blocking out light and sounds), and the fundamentals of sleep routines—as you begin a new approach to nighttime sleep for you and your baby.

. . . .

Remember, what transpires during the day significantly influences how your baby sleeps at night. If you skipped chapter 6, "Successful Naps," I encourage you to go back and read it. Then use that knowledge . . . as you begin a new approach to nighttime sleep for you and your baby.

. . . .

7 Steps to Successful Nighttime Sleep

1. Reframe your view of "normal" infant sleep.

2. Plan ahead for a safe sleeping space.

3. Establish a bedtime based on your baby's "ballpark" needs.

4. Create an evening wind-down routine.

5. Implement a simple nighttime sleep ritual.

6. Respond quickly to awakenings.

7. Develop your baby's nighttime sleep skills with Gentle NUDGEs.

STEP 1. REFRAME YOUR VIEW OF "NORMAL" INFANT SLEEP

Chapter 3, "What Do I Need to Stay Calm So I Can Calm My Baby?," highlights the power of reframing our experience to reduce stress and help us find solutions that will work for us. When your baby does not sleep through the night, the weight of fatigue is multiplied by the stress of worry. Do not disregard your concern. If your baby was born preterm, is experiencing developmental delays, never sleeps longer than an hour or is extremely difficult to console even when held, or has other health issues or concerns, it is essential to consult a pediatrician or a pediatric sleep specialist to rule out health-related problems.

But even when potential medical issues are eliminated and your baby is otherwise healthy and happy but not yet sleeping through the night, you may still ask, "*Should* my baby be sleeping through the night?" And because he's not, "Why am I failing?" University of Washington anthropologist Kathleen O'Connor notes, "The overriding perception that knowledge and advice about sleep is scientifically based obscures the reality of its embeddedness within a socio-cultural and historical context. The reality is that what is considered normal, right, and good sleep varies widely and what we tell ourselves about it matters."

In Scandinavian countries and many other cultures outside of the U.S., parents expect and take for granted babies' frequent awakenings—it is not a source of frustration for them. These parents are roused frequently in the night yet report feeling happier and better rested than parents who believe babies should sleep like little adults, with minimal—or no—awakenings.

Why would this be? The Scandinavian parents expect the first eighteen months of an infant's life to be difficult. When the baby wakes or wishes to be near them, they do not view it as a short-coming. Instead of expending energy questioning if their baby is sleeping correctly, they accept that he is sleeping like a baby.

These parents also recognize that the concept of sleeping through the night is ambiguous. Is it six hours of consecutive sleep? Eight? Twelve? That's never quite clear in the online discussions. As a result, awakenings are not viewed as a negative reflection on themselves. When their baby awakens, they meet his needs and go back to sleep. No time is spent lying awake mulling over what is wrong. (True, they do have generous family leave policies that make this all more manageable!)

But think about it: How frequently does your baby wake, take a few minutes to feed, and then go back to sleep? Yet you do not. You remain wide awake, frustrated, and angry, just waiting for him to wake again. What if instead you told yourself, "This is normal infant sleep. Despite the awakenings I can find ways to grab the sleep I need." As frustration slips away, the joy in the cuddles and touch of a tiny hand on your chest, even at 2:00 A.M., begin to fill you.

The reality that normal infant sleep includes frequent awak-enings is also supported by research. Temple University professor of psychology Dr. Marsha Weinraub and her colleagues followed 1,200 infants and their parents over a period of thirty-six months to answer the question "What is normal infant sleep?" Apply-ing statistical analysis to find different patterns, they identified two subgroups, which they named "sleepers" and "transitional sleepers."

Sleepers were the babies who, around six months of age, began to consolidate longer stretches of nighttime sleep, unless they were ill. The transitional sleepers continued to awaken during the night up to eighteen months of age. However, by eighteen months the two groups were indistinguishable in their sleep patterns.

What causes a baby to be a transitional sleeper? First let me explain what does *not* cause transitional sleepers. Weinraub's team found there was no statistical relationship between transitional sleepers and parent-infant attachment, maternal employment, family income, separation distress, birth weight, birth order, single parenting, or self-regulation skills. Instead, the research pointed to developmental and temperament characteristics that were related to transitional sleep.

The highest percentage of transitional sleepers were breastfed boys with spirited temperament traits. Spirited girls and babies who were formula-fed were also transitional sleepers. If your baby is a transitional sleeper, the gene pool has simply dealt you a hand that requires more skill to play. Biology is biology.

Like any other developmental skill, the ability to sleep for longer stretches will gradually progress, but according to your baby's own time frame. In the meantime, there are no advantages in mental and physical development between sleepers and transitional sleepers, and according to Wendy Middlemiss, Ph.D., in her book *The Science of Mother-Infant Sleep*, "Night awakenings may serve as a protective factor, preventing babies from going into too deep of a sleep from which they cannot awaken."

When you make peace with how your baby sleeps, you will remain calmer and find it easier to respond sensitively to your baby. Both you and your baby will return to sleep faster. If, despite your efforts to reframe your experience, you continue to find yourself awake and ruminating in the middle of the night, make an appointment with your doctor. You may be experiencing undiagnosed anxiety, depression, or a sleep disorder of your own.

If, despite your efforts to reframe your experience, you continue to find yourself awake and ruminating in the middle of the night, make an appointment with your doctor. You may be experiencing undiagnosed anxiety, depression, or a sleep disorder of your own.

STEP 2. PLAN AHEAD
FOR A SAFE SLEEPING PLACE

The American Academy of Pediatrics has specific recommendations for creating a safe sleeping environment for infants.

American Academy of Pediatrics
Sleep Safety Recommendations

- Place the baby on his or her back on a firm sleep surface such as a crib or bassinet with a tight-fitting sheet.

- Avoid use of soft bedding, including crib bumpers, blankets, pillows, and soft toys. The crib should be bare.

- Share a bedroom with parents but not the same sleeping surface, preferably until the baby turns one but at least for the first six months. Room sharing decreases the risk of Sudden Infant Death Syndrome (SIDS) by as much as 50 percent.

- Avoid baby's exposure to smoke, alcohol, and illicit drugs.

These recommendations can and do protect babies from getting squished, trapped, and suffocated in bedding, furniture, or by a sleeping adult. Yet these recommendations are not followed by a significant percentage of the world. Millions of people view the correct sleeping space for a baby as one in which the baby is tucked in bed with Mom. And despite the warning, it is estimated that as many as 75 percent of American parents ultimately bring their baby into their bed, even though they never intended to do it.

I encourage you to plan to bed share, not because I am promoting this choice but because I am a realist. Many intense, sensitive infants need touch to calm. Physical contact with you also helps them to regulate their body temperature and breathing, which is necessary for successful sleep. Despite the academy's recommendations, all too often these babies let you know in a very loud voice that neither a co-sleeper attached to your bed nor a crib is their preferred sleeping space. Without body contact, they do not sleep. The result: Even if you *never ever* expected to bed share, one night you will find yourself so exhausted you cannot continue to hold your baby while sitting or standing.

Aware of the recommendation not to bed share, you may choose instead to go to the couch, a daybed, or a recliner. This is not safe. Infants can easily slip into the crevices of these furniture pieces and suffocate. Instead, I want you to have a safe sleeping space prepared. This is no different from placing your baby in a car seat every time you drive. You have no intention of having an accident and yet—you prepare. Plan for your baby's safety at night.

Begin by assessing your bed-sharing risk. It varies widely. The following list is distilled from multiple resources. If you would like more information on the topic, *Sweet Sleep* by Diane Wiessinger, Diana West, Linda J. Smith, and Teresa Pitman is an excellent guide.

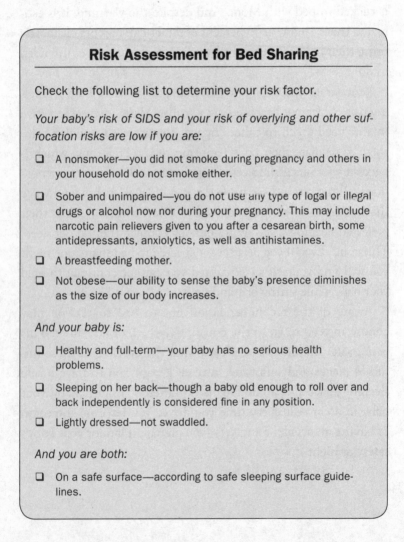

Risk Assessment for Bed Sharing

Check the following list to determine your risk factor.

Your baby's risk of SIDS and your risk of overlying and other suffocation risks are low if you are:

❏ A nonsmoker—you did not smoke during pregnancy and others in your household do not smoke either.

❏ Sober and unimpaired—you do not use any type of legal or illegal drugs or alcohol now nor during your pregnancy. This may include narcotic pain relievers given to you after a cesarean birth, some antidepressants, anxiolytics, as well as antihistamines.

❏ A breastfeeding mother.

❏ Not obese—our ability to sense the baby's presence diminishes as the size of our body increases.

And your baby is:

❏ Healthy and full-term—your baby has no serious health problems.

❏ Sleeping on her back—though a baby old enough to roll over and back independently is considered fine in any position.

❏ Lightly dressed—not swaddled.

And you are both:

❏ On a safe surface—according to safe sleeping surface guidelines.

If your risk factors for bed sharing are low, take the steps to make your sleeping space safe. Then, when the night you hit your limit arrives, you will be prepared to safely sleep with your baby. If your risk factors are high, have a backup plan. Know who you can call for help. Make the decision intentionally—not at 2:00 A.M., when you can't think straight.

Guidelines for a Safe Sleeping Surface

- Your mattress (not a waterbed mattress) is firm and set on the floor or on a low platform in case of falls. You will also want to place it away from walls so that your baby cannot become trapped between the wall and the mattress.

- If you have a footboard or headboard or side rail(s), there are no gaps between it and the mattress.

- You have removed extra pillows, loose bedding, stuffed animals, duvets, quilts, and comforters.

- Bedcovers are light and minimal—think "Japanese futon serene."

- No pet shares your bed.

- All sharp, poking, and pinching hazards have been removed as well as dangling cords, scarves, ribbons, etc., that a baby could become entangled in.

Ultimately, you and your partner, if you are co-parenting, are the only ones who will make the decision to bed share or not. While there are risks to bed sharing that must be considered, researchers have also identified benefits to the baby such as the mother's tendency to extend breastfeeding, protection from cold, and increased sensitivity and responsiveness by bed sharing mothers to their infants. Most important, for parents of sensitive infants who like to feed when it is quiet and dark, bed sharing can allow you to return to sleep quickly when your baby awakens hungry.

Your sleep is critical and sleep deprivation is serious. Last year one out of twenty-five drivers reported falling asleep while driving. Every year an estimated 72,000 crashes, and as many as six thousand fatal automobile accidents, in the United States are the result of sleep-deprived drivers. Do not become one of those statistics.

Ana, a family breadwinner and mother of four, made a conscious decision to bed share with her spirited infant. She told me, "I did not plan to bed share. Our three older children all slept in a co-sleeper and then a crib. But with Tyler that did not work. He had to be next to me, touching me, to sleep. When I put him in bed with me, he slept. I knew I fit the low-risk profile for bed sharing, so my husband and I made the decision to do it. Tyler never did sleep in a crib. He went from our bed to a mattress on our floor, and at age two, to a toddler bed in his own room. Bed sharing was what Tyler needed and it allowed me to get my sleep, too."

Like Ana, you may choose to always bed share, or you may wish to begin the night with your baby sleeping in his crib or co-sleeper. When he awakens and it is apparent that without physical contact he's not going back to sleep, bed sharing, when you have prepared a safe sleeping space, can be a tool in your toolbox, an option to help everyone get the sleep they need.

If you are parenting with a partner, another way to plan ahead for more extended sleep is to decide on a system to take turns getting up with the baby during the night. For example, one person can respond from 9:00 P.M. until 3:00 A.M. while the other one sleeps. Even if you are breastfeeding, your partner can bring the baby to you, so you barely awaken and return to sleep easily. If you are comfortable with it, your partner can also offer your baby a bottle. Some individuals will be upset with me for this suggestion, but you are more likely to stop breastfeeding if you are not sleeping, due to both fatigue and the accompanying lowered levels of breast milk. Again, I'm a realist working within a family system model—that means taking care of *everyone*.

Then from 3:00 A.M. until wake time, the person who was on duty at the beginning of the night sleeps while the "sleeper" takes over. The next night reverse roles so every other night you are each getting six hopefully uninterrupted hours of sleep. Not perfect—but better.

- -

If you are comfortable with it, your partner can also offer your baby a bottle. Some individuals will be upset with me for this suggestion, but you are more likely to stop breastfeeding if you are not sleeping. . . . I'm a realist working within a family system model— that means taking care of everyone.

- -

If you are single parenting or your partner is unable to help, call in a friend or family member. Asking for assistance is not a sign of failure. In many parts of the world helping hands are an expectation. A dad from Malaysia told me, "When a baby is born relatives move in for the first year. It's no big deal when the baby wakes, there are multiple pairs of hands to hold her."

Instead of fighting awakenings, plan for them. Take steps to mitigate how much they alert you and keep everyone safe. Go back to chapter 4, "How Can I Meet My Basic Needs Now?," for more ideas on how to protect your own sleep. Once you've addressed your own needs, you'll have more energy to work with your baby.

STEP 3. ESTABLISH A BEDTIME BASED ON YOUR BABY'S "BALLPARK" NEEDS

In a study conducted by Avi Sadeh, children with regular bedtimes slept approximately one hour longer and woke less frequently than did children with inconsistent bedtimes. (Let me clarify, *bedtime* denotes the time by when all preparations for sleep are complete. As an adult this is when you lay your head on the pillow, not when you begin brushing your teeth.) Your baby's bedtime will shift as she grows and develops, and you'll adjust accordingly, but around twelve to sixteen weeks, you can begin to establish a "ballpark" bedtime. That bedtime will be based on a combination of the clock and your baby's cues. *Cues will always trump the clock.* By establishing a ballpark bedtime you can begin to bring your baby's sleep into the rhythm of your family's and implement a wind-down period to prepare both body and brain for sleep.

> Bedtime will be based on a combination of the clock and your baby's cues. *Cues will always trump the clock.* By establishing a ballpark bedtime . . . you can implement a wind-down period to prepare both body and brain for sleep.

To identify your baby's ballpark bedtime, record in your journal what time your baby wakes for the day, the time and length of each nap, and when she falls asleep at night. Total the number of hours of sleep in each twenty-four-hour period and identify the most frequent daily amount over a one-week period. Say over one week your baby sleeps a total of 15, 15, 15, 17, 12, 15, 14 hours each day. You can drop the outliers—12 and 17—and expect that in general your baby needs about fourteen to fifteen hours of sleep daily. Again, this is an estimate.

Now go back and note the ending time of your baby's last nap. For babies under nine to ten months of age, the "last" nap may finish as late as 6:00 or 6:30 P.M. Track how long after that nap your baby exhibits sleep cues again. This is the "heads-up" signal indicating, *I'm getting tired, but I'm still in the green zone of calm energy.* (See the chart "Cues for the 3 Zones of Arousal" on page 36.)

You can test this ballpark bedtime by estimating a bedtime according to the clock. For example, if your baby napped a total of 4 hours during the day, typically wakes at 6:00 A.M., and seems to need 15 hours of sleep, you can predict his ballpark bedtime is likely to be about 7:00 P.M.

Your baby's preferred time to be laid down for the night may be a mere thirty minutes to three-plus hours after the last nap, depending on age. The younger the infant, the closer together each sleep episode will occur. Parents are often surprised by how early their baby's bedtime is.

Then again, sometimes a genetically wired night owl has come to live with you. This baby is *not* ready for sleep at 6:00 or 7:00 P.M. That's fine, if your family's wake time falls later in the morning. But if your schedule does not allow for sleeping later in the morning and your baby must be woken, you'll need to consistently cue him for an earlier sleep time. Without dependable cues from the environment he will shift to later and later bedtimes, until he's not falling asleep until 11:00 P.M. or later. Due to the need for early awakening in your family, he'll become sleep deprived, resulting in not only a fussy, irritable baby but also one who struggles to sleep.

Kelly told me, "During the first three months we played with the schedule to see what worked. By four months he was in bed by six-thirty and asleep by seven. Sometime around a year to eighteen months we shifted to in-bed at seven and asleep by seven-thirty. During his transition from two naps to one, if he only took one nap, we dropped him back to a six-thirty bedtime but otherwise, we've stuck close to this bedtime for the last four years."

No matter what your baby's sleep time is, honor and *fiercely* protect it. Do not attempt to keep your baby awake until an employed parent returns home, dinner is served, or because you would like more time with her in the evening. Cut your other commitments, not your baby's sleep. Better to let your infant fall asleep when she hits that natural sleep window. Then the time you do have with her is spent with a happy, well-rested baby. Push her past that window for sleep and she can become so dysregulated and hyperaroused that it may be another ninety minutes until she can shift into sleep. In the interim she will not be a happy camper and getting her down will be a wrestling match.

> Cut your other commitments, not your baby's sleep. Better to let your infant fall asleep when she hits that natural sleep window. Then the time you do have with her is spent with a happy, well-rested baby.

A wonderful benefit of identifying your baby's preferred bedtime is that observing it works, and because this works, when it doesn't you know something is up.

Guidelines for Your Baby's
Preferred Ballpark Bedtime

You will know you have identified your baby's preferred bedtime when:

- He falls asleep within 25 to 35 minutes of bedtime.

- Falling asleep does not feel like a brawl.

- He naturally begins to awaken to your family's morning signals.

You will know you have missed your baby's preferred bedtime when:

- She can't settle.

- It is taking 45 minutes or longer for her to fall asleep after bedtime.

- She's arching, crying, and can't feed.

- Nothing is right.

- She's "wild" and can't seem to stop moving.

If you've misjudged your baby's preferred bedtime:

- Tweak bedtimes in 15-minute increments, either earlier or later.

- Your journal can help you identify which direction to move first; 15 minutes earlier is the most likely option to try.

- Make the initial bedtime shift and continue at this time for at least 5 to 7 days. See if your baby goes down more easily. If not, and she still seems tired, move bedtime another 15 minutes earlier. Continue until you hit the window. If, on the other hand, your baby seems relatively content but just isn't sleeping, you can shift the bedtime 15 minutes later.

- Expect that in spring and summer your baby will need slightly less sleep than in fall and winter.

BEDTIME SLEEP DISRUPTORS AND STRATEGIES

Potential Disruptor	Effective Strategies
Child care shifts baby to toddler room and only allows one nap a day.	Move bedtime earlier to allow your toddler the same amount of sleep in a 24-hour period as when she was napping twice a day.
Missed cues	Baby has passed into level three cues and is now overaroused. Additional soothing/calming strategies will be required, as outlined in Step 4 to establish an evening wind-down routine. Catch cues at level one or two in the future. (See the cue chart on page 158.)
Late putting baby down	Expect your baby to take longer to fall asleep. Maintain the sequence of your routine but slow down the soothing strategies to allow more time to calm.
Illness/growth spurt	If your baby has been falling asleep and now is not, he may be getting sick or going through a growth spurt. Maintain the sequence of your routine but slow down the calming strategies to allow more time to settle. If needed, feed more frequently. This is temporary.
Vacation and time change	Springing ahead or falling back for daylight saving time and time zone changes disrupts the body clock and makes it more difficult for your baby to fall asleep—often for 2 to 3 weeks.
Skipped naps	Move bedtime earlier—watch for sleep cues and begin when you see the first one.

Despite the complexities of family life, strive to establish a consistent bedtime. If tonight's soccer game for the nine-year-old disrupted baby's routine, don't give up. Think creatively for ways to protect your baby's bedtime next time. This is a process and not one well supported in our go-go culture. Not every night will be perfect. Aim for your personal best record of consistency. Celebrate progress.

STEP 4. CREATE AN EVENING WIND-DOWN ROUTINE

A consistent bedtime sets your baby's body clock for sleep. But you cannot stop there. Babies who are highly alert, sensitive, and slow to adapt need to wind-down their arousal system *before* that bedtime. During the day they absorb stimulation from their environment and their internal world. Every emotion, sensation, hunger pang, pain, discomfort—you name it, these babies collect it all. That's why sixty minutes *before* bedtime, any vigorous, alerting activities need to stop, replaced by calming activities that cue the day is ending. For example, if baby's bedtime is seven, all alerting activities end by six and wind-down begins.

The challenge is that many recommended pre-bedtime activities that seem to soothe other babies, like baths and reading books, can alert rather than calm your spirited baby. Your baby also proves that the common advice to "wear your baby out" before bedtime with arousing activities like chasing, tickling, or wrestling is disastrous rather than calming. So, too, is the recommendation to eliminate or shorten naps, especially those in the late afternoon or early evening. Your baby desperately needs every minute of those naps to be calm enough to sleep at night. And then there are the little things that you never would have imagined could wind up your baby, like undressing her to diaper or put on pajamas, moving from downstairs to upstairs, gum wiping/tooth brushing, lotion rubbing, turning lights on or off, or shifting from one parent to the other. One small action and suddenly the baby who seemed sleepy seconds before is wide-eyed. What happened?

Many recommended pre-bedtime activities that seem to soothe other babies, like baths and reading books, can alert rather than calm your spirited baby.

Physiologically and temperamentally your baby is wired with that more reactive arousal system. Every stop, start, change, or sensation during this crucial time of the evening has the potential to accelerate your baby's arousal system and push him right past his window for sleep.

Alerting Activities to End

Avoid all alerting activities 30 to 60 minutes before bedtime. These include but are not limited to:

- "Wearing out" activities like tickling and chasing.
- Shortening naps to tire your baby.
- Too many changes or steps in the bedtime routine.

Wind-Down Activities to Try Before Bedtime

Experiment with potential wind-down activities to see what works with your baby, including:

- Preparing your baby's sleeping space.
- Bathing.
- Diapering, changing into pajamas, and gum/teeth cleaning.
- Reading books.
- Massaging/rubbing with lotion.
- Creating quiet floor time to help you catch your baby's sleep cues.
- Calming yourself.

Preparing your baby's sleeping space

As you begin your baby's wind-down, the last thing you want to occur is a sudden exposure to light, the *whoosh* of blinds dropping, or the whir of a sound machine to startle and rev him up again. To prevent that from happening go into your baby's sleeping space *before* his bedtime. Turn off all but the faintest of lights. Lower blinds. Turn on a sound machine, if you're using one. Then, when it's time to shift your baby to that space for the steps of your sleep ritual, it's already prepared.

Bathing

Researchers at the University of Texas at Austin found that a warm bath about one to two hours before bedtime efficiently lowers the body temperature as blood moves from the body core to hands and feet. This decrease in body temperature improves sleep quality and hastens the speed of falling asleep by an average of ten minutes. While many children find baths calming and an excellent cue for sleep, highly sensitive spirited children may become dysregulated if the bath is at the "wrong" time or temperature.

Other unsuspected pitfalls in bath time for highly sensitive little ones are hair washing and water in the ears, which can upset them and trigger their arousal system. And for those who are slow to adapt, the simple transfer in or out of the tub can start a spiral of upset. Observe closely. If your baby is keyed up after bathing, adjust the timing of the bath. Complete it at least one hour before bedtime or consider moving it to mornings or following an afternoon nap.

Diapering, changing into pajamas, and gum/teeth cleaning

Exposure to cool air and touch in sensitive areas like the mouth can upset your baby. Try your best to complete these activities during wind-down, so if your baby does become distressed there is time to calm her before the first sleep cues appear. Of course, if your baby requires a last-minute diaper change, you'll do it, but always be mindful that any activities with the tendency to alert should be completed at least thirty minutes before your baby's ballpark bedtime.

Reading books

It is important to read to your baby but books can also stimulate these bright, persistent little ones who want *more* books. Observe closely. After reading is your baby calmer or excited? If your baby is excited, plan to read during the day or at least an hour before bedtime, at the very beginning of your wind-down activities.

Massage/rubbing with lotion

In a study in the *Journal of Developmental and Behavioral Pediatrics* titled "Massage therapy by mothers enhances the adjustment of circadian rhythms to the nocturnal period in full-term infants," researcher Dr. Sari Goldstein Ferber and colleagues stated, "Massage serves as a strong time cue, enhancing coordination of the developmental circadian system with environmental cues." In India babies are massaged every morning and evening. Massage benefits both your baby and you. Just as your baby's body calms during massage, so does yours. As a result your bond is enhanced, and if you are a breastfeeding mom, milk letdown is promoted.

However, while massage has been proven to help babies sleep better and support the development of the circadian rhythm, it can pose challenges for sensitive babies. The key is finding the right type of touch and time for massage when your baby is naturally in a quiet, alert phase. You'll know you have found the touch that fits your baby because he will be happy, content, and relaxed. Often the "right" touch is firmer than you may expect. Soft tickling touch can be alerting. If massage seems to wake up rather than calm your baby, complete it earlier in the day. But when your baby is relaxed and calm after a massage it can be a perfect wind-down evening activity completed in the thirty-to-sixty-minute window before your baby's bedtime.

Creating quiet floor time to help you catch your baby's sleep cues

It's essential to know when to end your wind-down routine and begin the sleep ritual. A helpful "activity" is quiet floor time. Lay your baby on a blanket on the floor with the lights turned down low as you complete light household tasks like folding laundry or picking up the room as he settles. Keep an eye out for those level one and two sleep cues. Does he swipe at his eyes? Do his cheeks slacken? Does he lay his head down? Is he kicking his legs as though attempting to start a motorcycle? Do you see a yawn? When you observe these cues, he's letting you know he's ready for his final sleep ritual.

Calming yourself

Before you pick up your baby, take deep breaths. Center yourself. Move slowly. Bring yourself into the green zone of calm energy so your baby can synchronize with you. Quiet that nasty voice in your ear that wants to shout, *He'll never go down!* Whether your baby falls asleep is not a reflection of your skill as a parent. It's all about the readiness of his arousal system to call it a day.

Your wind-down plan, which is completed thirty to sixty minutes before your baby's bedtime, may look like this:

WIND-DOWN PLAN EXAMPLE

Prepare baby's sleeping space	Bath and/or books	Pajamas, diapering, gum wiping/ teeth brushing	Quiet floor time	Calm self before picking baby up to begin the sleep ritual

Do you feel the sense of slowing down as you read through these sample steps? This is wind-down. Pediatrician and sleep physician Laurel Wills reminds us, though, that "wind-down is not a linear

decline in arousal, but rather a curvy, up-and-down, settling phe-
nomenon." Allow your baby the time she needs to wind-down so
that her body and brain shift into the green zone of calm energy,
able to switch into sleep.

WIND-DOWN DISRUPTORS AND STRATEGIES

Potential Disruptor	Effective Strategies
Bath	Observe your baby closely. If after bathing your baby is more alert and active, complete bath at least one hour before bedtime, or move it to a different time of the day.
Diapering, putting on pajamas	Exposure to cool air can alert. Obviously if your baby needs a last-minute diaper change, you'll do it, but try to have your baby dressed for sleep before you begin the sleep ritual.
Gum wiping/teeth brushing	If a sensation is uncomfortable, sensitive babies get upset. Complete gum wiping and tooth brushing at least 30 minutes before bedtime.
Reading books	Notice what your baby is like after reading books. Is he aroused by the pictures or the sounds you make? If so, do read to your baby, but stop 30 to 60 minutes before bedtime.
Massage/lotion rub	Massage promotes sleep. Just be certain to massage your baby at the "right" time and with the "correct" touch so it calms rather than alerts. If it does alert, move it to earlier in the day.
Turning on night-lights or a sound machine, lowering blinds	Prepare the sleeping space before you bring your baby into it to avoid potential distractions and alerting sounds.

STEP 5. IMPLEMENT A SIMPLE NIGHTTIME SLEEP RITUAL

The sleep ritual begins at the end of wind-down with the sighting of your baby's first sleep cue. Typically, that first cue appears about thirty minutes before the ballpark bedtime. If your baby feeds slowly, you may start a few minutes earlier. The key to an effective sleep ritual is simplicity. The steps are few, non-alerting, and can be completed in about thirty minutes, just as your baby hits her bedtime and window for sleep. It may look like this:

NIGHTTIME SLEEP RITUAL EXAMPLE A

Go to baby's sleeping space.	Swaddle or wrap your arms around your baby to help settle.	While in baby's sleeping space give final feed of the day.	Sing lullabies, rub brows, shush, sway, bounce, or other calming strategies.	Rock until relaxed. Give pacifier or lovie if desired.	Place in sleeping place.

Or:

NIGHTTIME SLEEP RITUAL EXAMPLE B

Go to baby's sleeping space.	Sing lullabies, rub brows, shush, sway, bounce, or other calming strategies until baby relaxes.	While in baby's sleeping space give final feed of the day.	Continue to rock until you feel baby's body relax.	Place in sleeping space.

You will notice in these sample routines that once you are in the sleeping space, you stay there. Stops, starts, and changes are minimal. Reading books and giving a bath are not included. They were completed during wind-down because both can alert your baby. If, however, you have been reading to or bathing your baby right before sleep and it's calmed her, feel free to include either in your sleep ritual. Our goal is calming the baby; whatever works, use it.

During the wind-down period, you already darkened the room and, if you are using one, turned on the sound machine. You want the space to be as it will be throughout the night. That's because your baby moves through sleep cycles during the night. Initially those sleep cycles are simply stages of active and quiet sleep. But around six months of age your baby will develop hour-long sleep cycles. During a sleep cycle the baby shifts from light to deep sleep and back to light sleep. If everything in the environment is unchanged from when she fell asleep, she is more likely to move into the next sleep cycle. But if something has shifted, the likelihood she'll awaken increases. For example, if a sound machine was on as your baby fell asleep, keep it on throughout the night. If it is turned off after she falls asleep, the quiet may alert her as she rises into light sleep. If you do not want the sound machine to run all night, turn it off as your baby becomes drowsy but is not yet asleep.

When you begin to feed your baby, relax your body and slow your breathing. Remember, your baby synchronizes to your arousal level. Consider placing a light blanket or soft toy against his hand or cheek as you feed him. This may one day become his lovie, a soothing/calming tool he can use as he becomes able to put himself to sleep. If you are breastfeeding and co-parenting, once the feeding is complete you may ask your partner to finish the sleep routine. That way your baby will be comfortable with both of you putting him down for sleep. If initially the shift from one person to another proves to be too alerting, back off, but do try again later as your baby's self-regulation skills strengthen.

Should your baby fall asleep while feeding, no worries. Place her in her sleeping space. This is not a "bad habit." It's what many young babies do. Feeding is hard work. True, the nipple will not be in her mouth as she moves from one sleep cycle to another, but she may surprise you and slip right into the next one, despite the change. If it proves to be a problem, you can use the Gentle NUDGE approach to gradually support her in falling asleep without the nipple in her mouth.

Touch, sound, and movement help babies relax. Whatever calming activities you used at naptime, repeat them now. Rub your baby's brows. Stroke her arms. Rock, glide, bounce, and sing a favorite lullaby. Singing rhythmic lullabies quiets babies just as rocking and holding do.

Sucking is also a very effective soothing and calming tool. Spirited babies, with their tendency toward dysregulation, need to suck. Once your baby is breastfeeding well, and no one is worried about the baby's weight gain, you can decide if you'd like to offer a pacifier. When you do, observe your baby after the initial introduction. Sometimes after taking the pacifier, the baby is not as effective or comfortable in latching on to it due to the differences in sucking techniques for the nipple and the pacifier. If this is the case, wait another week before offering the pacifier again. In the meantime, continue practicing breastfeeding skills. Then offer the pacifier again.

Use the pacifier selectively. Offer it to your baby at sleep time or when your baby is struggling to regulate, but not as your first response to any fussiness.

Ignore advice that insists babies should fall asleep without comfort measures. Find what works for your baby and do it.

The Great Pacifier Debate—and Why Pacifiers Are OKAY!

Ultrasound photos show babies sucking their thumbs in the womb. Interestingly, no one seems too concerned that these in utero thumb-suckers will experience *nipple confusion,* which is typically defined as the inability of the baby to successfully latch on to and nurse at the breast after having sucked a thumb or artificial nipple. Yet nipple confusion is often a source of controversy, especially when it comes to the use of pacifiers and the potential impact on breastfeeding.

I defer to the American Academy of Pediatrics, which rather than discouraging pacifier use states that in the first six months pacifier use at the onset of sleep may be beneficial in reducing the risk of sudden infant death syndrome. The academy recommends parents consider offering pacifiers to infants one month and older (after breastfeeding is well established). Pacifier use has also been shown to decrease the frequency of breastfeeding mothers reaching for formula, assuming their baby's ravenous need for sucking signifies low breast milk supply.

Once your baby relaxes completely in your arms and his breathing begins to slow, lay him in his sleeping space. Be prepared, however, that despite your efforts your baby may shriek. During a spirited baby class Olivia's eyes narrowed as she declared, "The next time someone tells me, 'Just lay him down and he'll go to sleep, or just give him a pacifier or a pat,' I'm going to scream. Obviously, they never had a child like this one!" Kelly, sitting next to Olivia, offered a high five in agreement.

That's the frustrating part of having a spirited baby. Everything related to self-regulation takes longer. Do not lose heart. It's not your lack of technique or finesse. Pick up your baby and hold her until she's completely asleep, then place her in her sleeping space. But the next time, try once to lay her down while she's still awake. One day it will work!

While I've described wind-down routines, sleep rituals, and bedtime as three separate components so you could visualize them more clearly, you'll soon realize they blend into one gradual process leading your baby toward sleep. On a night your baby is taking longer than thirty-five minutes after completion of the sleep ritual to fall asleep, do not assume something is wrong with your routine and switch it up. Instead, presume your baby has reached a new developmental stage, is not feeling well, is experiencing stress, or something else is going on with her. Simply increase the soothing time in your wind-down and sleep ritual until you feel her relax. Or, if you are getting frustrated, take a break then try again a few minutes later, or, better yet, hand her off to another adult if one is available.

Continue to maintain your journal. Record progress. When your baby sleeps in her crib for an hour before needing to co-sleep to finish the night, that *is* progress. Work with your baby—at her pace. Celebrate each little success.

SLEEP RITUAL DISRUPTORS AND STRATEGIES

Potential Disruptor	Effective Strategies
Feeling rushed	When you are late getting home or a visitor is present, instead of skipping steps of your baby's sleep routine, shorten them. Attempting to skip steps alerts your slow-to-adapt baby.

Potential Disruptor	Effective Strategies
Lullaby or other calming strategy is alerting rather than calming your baby	Choose a different soothing strategy or switch the order. Calm, then feed. Once you have established the order that works for your baby, maintain that sequence. If initially your baby requires vigorous rocking, swaying, etc., do so in the beginning but gradually slow the pace and shorten the amount of time.
Erratic or skipped naps	An overtired baby needs more time and support to calm for sleep.
Missing sleep cues	Watch closely for level one and two sleep cues. Move bedtime earlier.

STEP 6. RESPOND QUICKLY TO AWAKENINGS

A frequently heard and often-unquestioned statement is this: *Babies must learn to self-soothe.* The reality is, if a baby has the capacity to self-soothe, he's doing it. The highly sensitive arousal system of spirited babies necessitates a stronger braking system. That's why you don't want to allow your baby's arousal to accelerate in the middle of the night. Move fast. Respond before he gets rolling. This advice is probably counter to everything you have read about developing the baby's self-soothing skills, but those experts have largely failed to consider temperamental differences. Do what you need to do to let everyone go back to sleep as quickly as possible. Don't wait until your baby becomes so upset during the night that it takes an hour or more to return to sleep. The middle of the night is not a teachable time. In *The Science of Mother-Infant Sleep* author Wendy Middlemiss writes, "Meeting the baby's needs before he gets distressed tunes the baby's body and brain up for calmness."

A frequently heard and often-unquestioned statement is this: *Babies must learn to self-soothe.* The reality is, if a baby has the capacity to self-soothe, he's doing it.

Respond by centering yourself first. Let your body language communicate, *I'm coming to help.* Your baby reads you well. She knows if you are upset and will react to your stress.

Once you are calm, start with the least intrusive response. You might say, "I'm here." If it's apparent that this response is inadequate, offer a soft, comforting pat. If that's not enough, gently pick her up. Still not satisfactory, feed her. This is not the time to be fighting over feedings. Move through these steps as quickly as needed to calm your baby. Try to avoid changing your baby's diaper unless it's necessary. Cool air on her skin can alert and irritate her.

As your baby's self-regulation skills grow stronger, you'll begin to hear an *eh, eh, eh* when she first awakens. At this point she still has it together. Wait to see what happens next. Listen carefully. If she quiets, celebrate and return to sleep. If you sense she's winding up, respond.

If the initial cry is a shriek, forget the pause—move fast! An infant's crying does not indicate that she's spoiled or trying to irritate you. It's a signal of her need, and her needs are *intense*.

One slight exception to the immediate response is if you, too, are highly sensitive. Babies are noisy sleepers and even open their eyes while still asleep. As a highly sensitive parent you will hear every snort, sniff, and shift of your baby. If this is true for you, delay long enough to be certain your baby is truly awake. Just like your baby, you are highly vigilant—that's a good thing, as it allows you to be responsive, but give yourself permission to pause a bit.

In the next step, I'll show you how to use Gentle NUDGEs to gradually practice self-soothing skills with your baby during the day—but at night respond quickly, so everyone can go back to sleep.

NIGHTTIME SLEEPING DISRUPTORS AND STRATEGIES

Potential Disruptor	Effective Strategies
Stage of development	A young baby may consume a mere ounce or less of milk at one time. Respond quickly, feed, allow everyone to go back to sleep.
Low iron	Low iron levels, specifically low ferritin levels, can disrupt sleep. Ask your pediatrician to check your baby.
Parental stress	Perceptive babies have a radar for stress. Schedule a few sessions with a certified counselor to reduce your stress levels.

Potential Disruptor	Effective Strategies
Developmental growth spurts	Growth spurts typically last 7 to 10 days. The BIG ones like walking can last 3 weeks. Maintain your sleep routine. Respond quickly, do what's needed to allow everyone to go back to sleep.
Parent traveling	When a parent travels, stress hormones rise the first few nights the parent is gone, then return to normal. Maintain your sleep routine. Add in more soothing/calming activities during the day. Respond quickly to awakenings. Bring in your support team.
Hectic daytime feedings	Sensitive babies often feed during the night, when it's dark and quiet. Find a protected space to feed during the day to increase efficiency of daytime feedings. At night, feed when your baby awakens then return to sleep.
Temperament	Highly active babies need to eat frequently— even at night. Feed and return to sleep.
Disrupted daytime naps	Skipped or sporadic naps will leave your baby overtired by bedtime. Prevent night wakings by taking steps to protect naps during the day.
Erratic bedtimes	The body clock is set by regular sleep times. Strive to increase the consistency of your baby's bedtime.

STEP 7. DEVELOP YOUR BABY'S NIGHTTIME SLEEP SKILLS WITH GENTLE NUDGES

The Gentle NUDGE supports skill building. As Rachel told me, "By using the Gentle NUDGE I learned to listen to my child and guide her without ever forcing her. It worked."

The five steps of the Gentle NUDGE can help you see what *is* working and can lead to easier bedtimes and longer stretches of nighttime sleep. It's a gradual process that occurs over a period of weeks, and occasionally months. But breaking the skill down into teeny, tiny steps allows you to see progress, celebrate each success, and feel comfortable letting your baby set the pace. The Gentle NUDGE begins with an emotion-free assessment of where you are.

<u>Note where your baby is now.</u> Initially it may feel as though your baby has no sleeping skills. Review the following Infant Sleep Skills chart. You may be surprised. This chart is not a formal research tool nor is it in perfect sequence, but it does include a broad collection of sleeping skills necessary for your baby to achieve independent sleep. Keep in mind, though, that the age when independent sleep is expected remains a cultural choice.

When you break this developmental process into steps, you can see your baby's starting point and identify where he is right now. You can then look at the potential next step you'd like to nudge him toward.

INFANT SLEEP SKILLS

Falling Asleep Skills	Independent Sleep Skills	Transition Skills	Returning to Sleep Skills	Consolidation of Sleep Skills
1. Falls asleep while feeding.	**1.** Sleeps on you.	**1.** Stays asleep when nipple is removed from mouth.	**1.** Wakes and returns to sleep with feeding.	**1.** Sleeps for 30 to 60 minutes.
2. Falls asleep while held but not feeding.	**2.** Sleeps on a flat surface for 10 to 20 minutes.	**2.** Transitions from your arms to a sleeping surface without startling awake.	**2.** Wakes and returns to sleep by being held.	**2.** Consolidates sleep for 1 to 2 hours.
3. Falls asleep lying next to you.	**3.** Naps in crib but sleeps with parents at night.	**3.** Stays asleep when you move away.	**3.** Wakes and returns to sleep with pat and shush.	**3.** Consolidates sleep for 2 to 4 hours.
4. Falls asleep being shushed and rocked, but not nursed.	**4.** Sleeps in crib/co-sleeper, wakes and finishes the night with parents.	**4.** Sleeps for 20 minutes after transfer.	**4.** Needs parent to respond immediately but if you do, returns to sleep quickly.	**4.** Consolidates sleep for 4 to 6 hours.

Falling Asleep Skills	Independent Sleep Skills	Transition Skills	Returning to Sleep Skills	Consolidation of Sleep Skills
5. Falls asleep after 20 minutes of rocking.	**5.** Sleeps in crib, wakes once, feeds, returns to crib, finishes night.	**5.** Sleeps for 30 minutes after transfer.	**5.** Parent can pause for 15 seconds before responding and baby does not "lose it."	**5.** Consolidates sleep for 6 hours.
6. Falls asleep after 10 minutes of rocking.	**6.** Sleeps in crib, does not wake, sleeps all night.	**6.** Remains asleep until first night feeding several hours later.	**6.** Parent can pause, and baby is able to calm self sometimes.	**6.** Consolidates sleep for more than 6 hours.
7. Falls asleep independently when put down drowsy.			**7.** Baby wakes and returns to sleep independently.	
8. Puts self to sleep when laid down awake.				

We could add other sleep skills such as:

- Sleeps with or without a swaddle.
- Falls asleep being rocked, but no pacifier.
- Transitions for Dad but not yet for Mom.
- Plays on a flat surface for five minutes without fussing but does not yet sleep there.

Add your own as you notice them.

No matter how young or how unskilled your baby seems, when you break sleep down into a developmental process you can see your baby does have skills. Note where she is now. Then look at the next step you'd like to nudge her toward.

<u>Understand your ultimate goal.</u> Keep in mind that your culture and the media influence your goals. You can choose whether an accepted cultural goal fits your family or not. Do you want your baby to sleep in a crib or do you feel pressured by others to *make* this happen? Not all babies sleep in a crib. Is it important that your baby sleeps six to eight uninterrupted hours, or do you treasure those quiet moments at 2:00 A.M. when the two of you are cuddling and everyone else is asleep? You get to define your goals and choose what is best for your family.

<u>Determine the teeny, tiny steps.</u> Here are a few examples of potential teeny, tiny steps to success for the common goals of helping your baby fall asleep, return to sleep, reduce the frequency of nighttime feedings, sleep in her own space, and delay morning wake-ups. These are just examples. Identify your own teeny, tiny steps depending on your goal. Think *teeny, tiny,* so you can see how far your baby has come!

TEENY, TINY STEPS TO FALLING ASLEEP INDEPENDENTLY

Teeny step 1	Teeny step 2	Teeny step 3	Teeny step 4
Remove nipple when baby is sound asleep.	Remove nipple when baby is drowsy but not completely asleep. Return nipple to mouth if baby starts to become upset. Hold until asleep.	Remove nipple when baby is drowsy. Pause to see if baby will calm without nipple. Hold until asleep.	Remove nipple when baby is drowsy. Transfer to sleeping space. Pat. If alerts, respond quickly. Hold until asleep.

Teeny step 5	Teeny step 6	Teeny step 7	
Remove nipple when baby is drowsy. Transfer to sleeping space. Pat and shush. If alerts, pause to see if baby can calm. Pick up before baby becomes upset.	Remove nipple when baby is drowsy. Transfer to sleeping space. Allow baby settling time. If after 15 minutes baby is not asleep, help to sleep.	Feed. Remove nipple. Rock until calm. Transfer to sleeping space. Baby puts self to sleep.	

TEENY, TINY STEPS TO RETURN TO SLEEP INDEPENDENTLY

Teeny step 1	Teeny step 2	Teeny step 3	Teeny step 4
Respond immediately. Pick up and comfort.	Respond immediately. Comfort with voice. Add soothing, slow, calm pats. Pick up if necessary. Feed if hungry.	Respond immediately. Comfort with voice and pats. Pick up if needed.	Short pause. Respond first with words then pats and pick up if needed.

Teeny step 5	Teeny step 6	Teeny step 7
Slightly longer pause. Baby does not initially become upset. Wait. Starts to fuss. Words to comfort if needed, pats, pick up if needed.	Longer pause. Baby fusses, but not upset. Able to use words alone to comfort.	Baby awakens, talks to self, returns to sleep.

TEENY, TINY STEPS TO REDUCE FREQUENCY OF NIGHTTIME FEEDINGS

Teeny step 1	Teeny step 2	Teeny step 3	Teeny step 4
Feed baby as needed recognizing developmentally this is what baby needs. Creatively meet your own sleep needs as described in chapter 4.	Take extra steps to provide quiet, relaxing feedings during the day.	Baby drops one nighttime feeding. Respond quickly when baby does awaken. Provide feeding. Calm self: Drink ice water to cool your body and take 4 long, deep breaths. Remind yourself this is normal infant behavior. Go back to sleep.	If *before* midnight and shortly after a recent feeding, pause slightly. Respond first with words then pats and pick up. Feed if needed. If *after* midnight, just feed.

Teeny step 5	Teeny step 6	Teeny step 7	
Slightly longer pause at first awakening. Baby does not initially become upset. Wait. Starts to fuss. Words to comfort if needed. Pat, pick up, then feed. Second awakening feed immediately.	Longer pause. Baby fusses, but not upset, nor hungry. You are able to use words or pats to comfort.	Baby awakens, talks to self, returns to sleep.	

TEENY, TINY STEPS TO SLEEP IN OWN SPACE

Teeny step 1	Teeny step 2	Teeny step 3	Teeny step 4
Baby sleeps in co-sleeper in your room until 6 to 12 months of age.	Baby begins night in crib. Sleeps 45 minutes. Feeds. Returns to co-sleeper in your room.	Baby begins night in crib. Sleeps 2 hours. Feeds. Returns to co-sleeper.	Baby begins night in crib. Sleeps 4 hours. Feeds. Returns to crib for 3 hours. Then goes to co-sleeper once awakened again.

Teeny step 5	Teeny step 6	Teeny step 7
Baby begins night in crib. Sleeps 6 hours. Feeds. Returns to crib for remainder of the night.	Baby begins night in crib. Sleeps through the night.	Baby feeds, points to crib. Goes into crib. Falls asleep.

TEENY, TINY STEPS TO LATER MORNING WAKE-UP TIMES

Teeny step 1	Teeny step 2	Teeny step 3	Teeny step 4
Recognize my real goal is more sleep for me. There is a genetic element to early awakenings. Go to bed earlier myself.	Expose baby to morning light to help establish circadian rhythm.	Respond immediately before baby fully awakens. See if with assistance baby will return to sleep.	Shift baby's bedtime slightly later—no more than 15 minutes— so he does not become overtired.

Teeny step 5	Teeny step 6	Teeny step 7	
Once baby is falling asleep at the later bedtime and sleeping 15 minutes later, shift another 15 minutes later.	Accept this is as far as baby can shift.	Parent awakens 15 to 30 minutes before baby so parent can have time to center self.	

<u>Gently practice.</u> Once you have determined the steps you can begin practice sessions. Depending on your baby and your preference, select a time and place, ideally during the day. For example, you may choose naptime to begin removing the nipple before your baby is completely asleep. Try it once. After that, practice is over. But the next day or the next feeding, try it again.

Jill told me, "I love that you call it 'practice.' That word really took the pressure off for me. I stopped feeling anxious about trying to make it work. Even if my spirited twins didn't change after one practice, I still felt like we were working toward better sleep. I remember being stunned when what we were practicing worked—just like you said it would!"

You may also find that another adult in your support system can be especially effective in introducing a new skill. Experiment. For Hanna it was her father-in-law. A patient, nurturing man, he took Colby after his feeding, then rocked and softly talked to him until Colby fell asleep without a nipple in his mouth. And then again, the most effective "nudger" may be you. You get to decide what works best for you and your baby.

<u>Ease back.</u> Pay close attention to your baby's growing skill level. If you're practicing pausing before helping your baby back to sleep, start by pausing for five seconds before responding, then stretch it to ten. Once your baby is keeping it together during a 10-second pause, increase it to 15 to 20 seconds, then a minute, gradually building the length of time before you step in to assist. You want your baby to be successful. Don't test him by pushing it too far.

INDEPENDENT SLEEP DEVELOPMENT DISRUPTORS AND GENTLE NUDGE STRATEGIES

Potential Disruption	Effective Strategies
Worry baby is not making progress	Development is like an iceberg. Two-thirds of it happens beneath the surface. Know that what you are doing is setting your baby up for success. Thanks to practice with you, once the development clicks into place, she'll be ready.
Gentle NUDGE is not working	Go back a step. You may have selected a step your baby is not capable of achieving. Or, break steps down into even teenier ones.
Baby is sick	During illness, do what your baby needs. This is not a time for practice.
Unrealistic expectations	Stay off social media sites. Every baby is different. Love and nurture the one who came to live with you. Allow your baby to set the pace that works for her.
Feeling exhausted	Call in your support team. Take a well-deserved break!

These first eighteen months with a spirited baby are tough. As you think about nighttime sleep remember that your goal is for your entire family to get the most and best sleep possible. There is not one right way. Be creative. While ensuring safety, sleep how and where your family sleeps best. (Remember our fictional Spirited Baby reality show? The million-dollar prize for *total* family sleep is out there.)

Yes, your baby's awakenings do affect your sleep, but so does worrying that you are somehow failing. Expect setbacks. Even as you move forward, the development of sleep skills is like a spiral touching the same points over and over again. One day your baby sleeps for four consecutive hours and your hopes rise precipitously. Soon, he'll sleep through the night, or at least six hours! But suddenly he's back to waking after an hour or two. And if that is not bad enough, he remains awake, cooing and smiling as though this is a lovely time to visit. It's disheartening enough to bring you to tears, and yet that smile is so cute! When progress seems too slow or it feels as though things are backsliding it can be discouraging.

Lucia emailed me after an especially difficult backslide. "She was sleeping in her crib all night, just waking once for a feeding and then returning to her crib for the rest of the night. But at twelve months she started to walk and cut teeth. Then she got sick and it all went downhill."

It's during those times that we remind ourselves how frequently a baby pulls herself up to stand, only to collapse again. The same is true of sleep. Frustrating, yes, but predictable and normal. Stay strong. Though your previous efforts may seem for naught, they were not. It is okay to meet your baby's needs where he is at now, even if that requires returning to strategies you let go of long ago. Maintain your sleep routine. Tweak if necessary. Extend soothing and calming strategies. Your baby temporarily needs a little extra help regulating during this upheaval. Know that if this is a developmental surge, after the crash of the old system, the new, more mature level of development will click into place. The baby who could not put himself back to sleep suddenly can. Record it in your journal. Read through your previous entries and you'll see. It's getting better and better.

CHEAT SHEET FOR SUCCESSFUL NIGHTTIME SLEEP

1. *Rethink and reframe your view of normal infant sleep.* Write your own description.

2. *Be ready for safe bed sharing, no matter what your beliefs and current plans.* Honor the way your baby will sleep best and the way you can meet your own sleep needs. Be ready. Be safe. Do not bed share if you haven't prepared for it.

3. *Identify your baby's "ballpark" bedtime and establish an evening wind-down routine.*

4. *Establish a simple ritual to lead your baby into sleep.* A sleep ritual cues your baby: *This is when our family sleeps.* Include just a few non-alerting steps that can be completed in thirty minutes or less. ,

5. *Use the Gentle NUDGE to practice skills.* Remember that the most important goal is enough sleep for the whole family. Also, don't forget that sleep extinction methods are not scientifically proven to be lasting nor are they effective for most spirited babies. Take it one teeny, tiny step at a time so everyone gets the rest they need in the best way they can.

6. *Focus on how to meet your own sleep needs.* This may be as simple as turning off the electronic gadgets and going to bed.

REFLECTION QUESTIONS FOR YOUR JOURNAL

• How am I defining normal infant sleep?

• What are one or two things I can do right away to increase the amount of sleep I'm getting?

• What is one skill I'd like my baby to develop with a Gentle NUDGE?

Chapter 8

Happy Feeding

Creating Trust and Calm
for Healthy Eaters

*"Do you believe your baby can be trusted to
eat the right amount of food for his body?"*
—Ellyn Satter, nutritionist and
author of *Child of Mine*

When it comes to sleep, our paramount feeling is often exhaustion and a sense that life will never go back to normal. But with feeding, the overriding feeling may be fear. Terror that we will somehow fail to meet the needs of this baby whose life is completely dependent upon us. Worries torment us. Are we doing it right? Is our baby getting enough milk? Is she eating too frequently, too little, too fast? Is she gaining weight properly?

Suddenly our worth and competence as a parent seem to get tied up with our baby's tummy and selective tastes. The responsibility can feel overwhelming for every parent, but add to it a baby who is temperamentally wired to be more intense and sensitive, and the sensory-rich, worry-filled process of feeding takes on a whole new level of complexity.

The temperature, texture, smell, taste, and, as the baby grows, color of food are all potential snags for these keenly sensitive little ones. Thanks to their intensity, hunger is experienced like a sledgehammer to the gut. Attempts to "hold them off" are futile. They need and love to suck in order to soothe themselves, but their constant need to do so may lead caregivers to wonder if they're getting enough. And to make things even more confounding, sometimes, even when these babies are starving, they don't eat, instead shrieking and bouncing off the nipple yet never latching. When a wave of parental worry is added to the mix, complete havoc can break out, disrupting what is supposed to be a natural process.

The reality is that a keen arousal system and intense temperament affect eating as much as sleeping. When in the red zone of overarousal, the brain not only signals *Stay awake!* but also *Don't eat.* The result is that spirited babies can and often do have more difficulty feeding. If your baby is not gaining weight as expected, you will definitely want to check in with your health-care provider or lactation consultant to rule out any potential medical problem, but once that is addressed, take a look at your baby's arousal system as a potential culprit fueling your feeding challenges. By taking steps to bring the baby—and the whole family system—into the green zone of calm energy, your baby's brain can signal, *All is well. Go ahead and eat and stop eating when your body is full.*

The six steps to successful feeding can help you accomplish this goal. The result is a happy, healthy baby who eats just right for her.

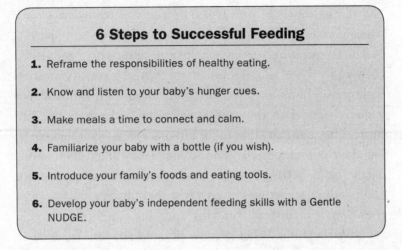

6 Steps to Successful Feeding

1. Reframe the responsibilities of healthy eating.

2. Know and listen to your baby's hunger cues.

3. Make meals a time to connect and calm.

4. Familiarize your baby with a bottle (if you wish).

5. Introduce your family's foods and eating tools.

6. Develop your baby's independent feeding skills with a Gentle NUDGE.

As we move through the steps, I've done my best to focus on the common denominators around feeding issues with spirited babies, no matter where they live. Fingers, forks, or chopsticks; rice, veggies, or beef. The tools and foods may be different, but we all eat.

STEP 1. REFRAME THE RESPONSIBILITIES OF HEALTHY EATING

Your newborn baby is out of the womb but still completely dependent on you to provide her the nutrients she needs to grow and develop. For a parent and baby, this is a symbiotic relationship, an intimate living together of two separate individuals in a mutually beneficial and cooperative relationship. Whether you are using formula or breastfeeding your baby, efficiently and smoothly working together with your baby, as with any well-functioning team, requires defining roles and responsibilities. Without that clarification, conflicts and misreads may occur. That's why, before we talk about your baby's hunger cues, growth rate, introducing a bottle or solid foods, or any other specific feeding questions, we need to define our responsibilities as parents and caregivers.

At one of my parent workshop sessions on feeding, before the parents arrived, I wrote on the whiteboard: *Do you believe your baby can be trusted to eat the right amount of food for his body?* It's a quote from the wise author and nutrition expert Ellyn Satter. The parents glanced at the question as they found their chairs. Even before she settled Alyssa remarked, "I didn't at first, but now I do." And you can, too (unless a medical problem is disrupting this natural process).

In 1937 Arnold Gessell and Frances Ilg conducted a series of experiments in which babies were fed when hungry, were allowed to eat until satiated, and slept when and how much they wished to sleep. The babies thrived.

Building from this research and adding to it with updated studies and years of clinical practice, Ellyn Satter developed her philosophy of child feeding, which she refers to as the *division of responsibilities*. On her website (www.ellynsatterinstitute.org) she writes, "Parents of infants are responsible for the **what** of feeding— whether breast milk or formula. The baby is responsible for everything else—**when, where, how much**, and **how fast**."

. . . .
Ellyn Satter's philosophy of child feeding, which she refers to as the *division of responsibilities*: "Parents of infants are responsible for the *what* of feeding—whether breast milk or formula. The baby is responsible for everything else—*when, where, how much*, and *how fast*."
. . . .

As long as your baby's weight gain is in accordance with the expected growth curve, he can be trusted to eat the right amount of food for his body. No internet site, professional, business, family member, or friend knows better. But it's not easy to trust this baby, less than eighteen months old, when every voice around you seems to be insisting, "Take control!" If your baby is not gaining weight as expected, then a nudge to increase calories will be called for. But if your baby is thriving, you can trust him.

The division of responsibilities slightly changes when your little one is competently and consistently consuming solid foods. At this point the parent's responsibilities broaden to selecting the foods, always including something the child likes, and deciding when (typically every two and a half to three hours) and where to serve the foods. The toddler's job is to decide whether to eat, what to eat of the foods served, and how much. How much is managed by what's in the serving bowls, which have been filled by the parent. If a bowl is empty, the child is offered another option that's on the table. No short-order cooking required. We'll address the introduction and serving of solid foods later in this chapter.

Once responsibilities in the feeding relationship are clearly defined for both you and your baby, anxiety and tension drop dramatically. There's no need to second-guess your baby. Your job is *not* to cajole, bribe, tickle, or push her to eat. Your job is simply to provide the food and trust your baby to decide everything else. When you do so, your child learns to honor her body's cues. She eats when hungry and stops when full. Feedings become stress-free, joyful points of connection. This is the foundation for a life-long healthy relationship with food.

A clear understanding of feeding responsibilities also provides you with a framework to analyze the plethora of feeding advice available. Poor advice presumes that what your baby is telling you is somehow wrong. Rather than recognizing that your baby can be trusted to eat the right amount of food for her body, these purveyors of bad advice somehow know better.

Here are a few examples of **poor** advice that does not respect the division of responsibilities in the feeding relationship:

- Establish a feeding schedule by withholding a feeding until it has been three hours since the last feeding, despite the fact your baby is rooting and fussing.
- Hold your infant's hands to spoon-feed her, so you can get some food in her, even though she is furiously batting away the spoon and pursing her lips.
- Withhold nighttime feeding once your baby reaches a certain age, despite your baby's signals that she's hungry.

Each of these instructions ignores and fails to trust what your baby is telling you she needs. In some ways it is obvious that these messages are wrong and not where you want to go, but your conviction may waver when you are the recipient of comments like "Your baby is tiny; get some food in her any way you can." Or, "Whoa, Mr. Thunder Thighs has the quads of a sumo wrestler, better limit calories on this one." Suddenly you find yourself doubting if your baby really does know what he needs.

When you find yourself vacillating and faced with a barrage of adamant advice givers who insist your baby does *not* know what she needs, scrutinize their recommendations closely. Does the advice feel intrusive? Would you want someone to do this to you? Is your baby healthy and thriving? Does it place trust in your baby's ability to know what she needs? Any advice based on an underlying philosophy that mistrusts your baby's cues, or that feels intrusive and insensitive, is *not* based on attachment research and is not in your baby's best interest.

Decades of attachment research clearly confirm that trusting your baby, listening to your baby's cues, and responding sensitively lead to secure attachment and the development of strong, healthy relationships. Ignoring your baby's cues or responding intrusively disrupts the attachment and feeding process. That's why Katja Rowell, M.D., author of *Born to Eat*, writes, "If a suggested action feels wrong to you, don't do it."

. . . .

Ignoring your baby's cues or responding intrusively disrupts the attachment and feeding process.

. . . .

Solid advice, on the other hand, recommends actions that respect that your baby knows how much food her body needs and is communicating that to you. Examples of **good** advice include:

- If your baby purses her lips, turns her face, or brings her hands up to block her mouth, respect that she is finished.
- If he grabs for the spoon, give him one and let him help or feed himself. At this early age he is getting most of his nutrients from breast milk or formula. No worries about how much he gets in his mouth.
- If she prefers to feed herself with finger foods, let her do it.
- Allow your baby to decide when she is full.

. . . .

Good advice respects that your baby knows what she needs and trusts that she is communicating that to you.

. . . .

But even when the responsibilities are clear, the research and advice sorted, it can still be difficult to trust this little person. Fortunately, your baby's growth chart can provide the backup data.

Growth Charts

During each well-baby checkup an assistant at your doctor's office weighs, measures, and charts your baby's growth. Ask to look at that chart. If you see steady growth on a consistent curve, relax and appreciate how capable your baby is at getting what she needs.

Children come in all shapes and sizes, just as adults do. That's why it does not matter if your baby is in the 5th or the 95th percentile for growth. What is significant is the consistency of her pattern.

At various times you may see periods of catch-up growth that temporarily result in a slight change in your baby's growth curve. Often weight will rise slightly, followed later by a spurt in height. There may be eating days and non-eating days. But overall, the pattern will be there, steady and consistent for your baby.

If, however, your baby's growth suddenly veers off in a different direction it may signify something is not quite right. Before you panic, ask for a remeasure. It's difficult to accurately measure a baby. But if there is a significant alteration in the trajectory of your baby's growth curve, follow up on it.

Samantha found this to be true. At birth her son was in the 65th percentile for weight. But at his one-week checkup he'd dropped to the 55th percentile. She knew that newborns often drop ounces from their birth weight in the first week or two, and her pediatrician wasn't concerned. But the next check put him at the 50th percentile. After feedings he'd been crying, but when Samantha voiced her concern, others still insisted, "There is nothing wrong. Babies cry."

Fortunately, Samantha trusted her baby and her own intuition. She contacted a lactation consultant to learn strategies to build up her milk supply, and in the meantime supplemented with formula. Her "cry" baby stopped crying. Soon he rose to the 90th percentile for weight and has consistently remained there.

Even when your baby's growth curve is constant, if that curve is different from that of your friend's infant it may cause concern. That is what happened to me. A close friend and I both had babies within weeks of one another. My daughter ran along the 95th percentile for height and weight. My friend's son consistently followed the 50th percentile. During their youth my daughter was always significantly larger than my friend's son, never obese but taller and heavier. I fretted, "Is she growing too fast?" My friend worried about her son, "Is he growing too slowly?"

But growth is not a race. It occurs steadily and at the pace that is just right for each child. Today my daughter and my friend's son are adults. My daughter stands at 5 feet 10 inches, and my friend's son at 5 feet 9 inches. Both are athletic, strong, and just right for their body type.

No growth line is superior to another. Each child is simply different. Rest assured your baby knows what she needs even during those times when she shifts from nursing every two to three hours to every hour. She is doing her job, building up your milk supply for her next growth spurt. Relax and enjoy your feeding relationship. She's got this. Her growth chart confirms it.

STEP 2. KNOW AND LISTEN TO YOUR BABY'S HUNGER CUES

Four-year-old Grace breathlessly ran into the kitchen shouting at her mom, "Feed the baby!"

"Feed the baby?" Kristin thought. "I just fed him forty-five minutes ago."

Frowning, she turned to Grace and asked, "Why do you think he needs to eat?"

"He's eating his fist!" Grace insisted. "He's starving!"

Kristin doubted the baby was hungry again but picked him up. Immediately he turned to her breast, rooting like a hunting dog on a scent. He *was* starving. A growth spurt had begun and for the next two days he nursed every hour on the hour, building up her milk supply. Shortly thereafter he rolled from front to back for the first time. Had Kristin ignored her baby's hunger cues and instead rigidly adhered to an every-three-hours feeding schedule, she would have deprived her baby of the calories he craved during his growth spurt.

Whether it is hands in the mouth, rooting at your breast, a little frown, a whimper, turning toward you, smacking sounds, breathing faster, puckering lips, sucking on a fist, waving his head back and forth, opening his mouth, or shifting from a smooth, easy rhythm of sucking a pacifier to a furious staccato, your intense baby has his initial hunger cues. Mobile little ones may walk to the high chair, open the pantry, or point to the fruit bowl on the table. Pay attention. Don't wait until your baby is crying. If he's letting you know he's hungry, feed him.

Zari, the mom of three active boys, told me, "I trusted them and fed them on demand. It was less stressful, and they were happier."

Catch hunger cues.

If you find yourself struggling to catch these early cues, begin recording feedings in your journal. Note the time your baby begins each feeding. As you did for sleep cues, use that information to give yourself a heads-up of when to begin watching for cues. For example, if feedings typically occur about every 2 hours, take your baby into a quiet place about 15 to 20 minutes before the feeding is expected to begin. Observe closely. Watch for that change in activity level: the frown, smacking, or a fist in the mouth. These cues appear briefly and are subtle, but they are there. Once you identify them, they'll pop right out to you.

Even if it has been a shorter amount of time than recommended or expected, believe your baby's cues to feed. He is capable of shifting from sucking on his fist to red-faced howling in seconds. The failure to catch those initial cues, or attempting to hold your baby off, can find you spending the next thirty minutes swishing, swaying, and hushing him in a desperate attempt to calm him down enough to eat.

When your baby frequently shuts down and falls asleep without feeding and is not demonstrating a healthy weight gain, make a concerted effort to catch her cues earlier, when she can still settle and eat.

. . . .

When your baby frequently shuts down and falls asleep without feeding and is not demonstrating a healthy weight gain, make a concerted effort to catch her cues earlier, when she can still settle and eat.

. . . .

HUNGER CUES

Early Hunger Cues	Mid-Level Hunger Cues	Late Hunger Cues
Little sounds such as *mmmm* or *ahhhh*	Rooting for the breast	Crying
Hand to mouth	Furious, staccato sucking on pacifier	Arching
Tongue thrusting	Increased energy and wriggling	Frantic
Frown or line between the brows	Whimper	Waving head back and forth
Lip smack	Faster breathing	Bouncing off the breast, can't feed
		Shutting down and falling asleep without feeding as a coping mechanism

Recognize the need for frequent feedings.

There are many reasons spirited babies may require frequent feedings. One is a high activity level. Long before they can run, high-energy babies are waving, pumping their legs, wiggling, and rolling, burning calories like a competitive athlete. They are also sensitive. Small, frequent feedings feel just right.

Keep in mind that some of the recommendations for how far apart to space feedings were created for efficient hospital schedules, not from observations of what babies need. In fact, when researchers actually observed babies, they found that short intervals between feedings and quick response times were associated with infrequent fretting at two months of age.

It's also possible that frequent feedings are a protective factor to help babies avoid deep, long sleep. At four months of age the risk of SIDS begins to diminish and infants often start to sleep for longer stretches, thus lengthening the time between feedings. The exception to this may be the alert little one who decides that since Mom has returned to employment during the day, he'll fill up during the night when she is available. When the baby can latch on and both Mom and baby quickly return to sleep, this is not an issue. Difficulties arise, however, when the advice that infants of a certain age should not be eating at night disrupts parents' trust in their babies and leads them to try to withhold a feeding. Stress levels skyrocket and no one sleeps.

It's not only during the first year that babies may require frequent feedings. Down the road, during toddlerhood, when your baby is well into solid foods, plan to serve 6 mini-meals a day spaced 2.5 to 3 hours apart. These frequent, small meals, each containing a little bit of protein, carbohydrates, fruit/vegetables, and fat will prevent blood sugar drops. Low sugar levels can trigger meltdowns. A steady stream of nutrients throughout the day will keep your spirited toddler in the zone of calm energy. Calm children eat well.

You can also trust your baby or toddler will awaken if hungry, but sometimes this, too, gets confusing. Immediately after birth parents are typically advised to provide their baby 8 to 12 feedings every 24 hours. The purpose for doing this is to build up the breastfeeding mother's milk supply and ensure the baby regains her birth weight within ten to fourteen days of delivery. Often this means you are waking your baby to feed. What is not clear, however, is whether, once a baby has regained those lost ounces and is demonstrating consistent weight gain when her spontaneous hunger cues are followed, there is still a need to wake her for feedings.

A baby should be awakened when she has medical needs that require more frequent feedings or if she has not yet regained her birth weight. If a feeding regime has been recommended for your baby, Sara Bennett Pearce, lactation consultant and certified nurse-midwife, suggests, "Be certain to ask your pediatrician or lactation consultant when you can stop waking your baby. All too often I see this type of intensive feeding intervention continued long past when it could have stopped."

You may also find with this temperamentally intense baby that long after your breast is drained, he contentedly pats your chest, smiles, and continues to suck. He's calming himself. If his bottle is empty, or your nipples are screaming for relief, introduce him to a pacifier. If he has found his thumb to be a helpful alternative, celebrate. Thumb-sucking babies sleep better because they have a handy calming tool. If your baby is in child care, let your provider know that he needs to suck and that it is acceptable for him to have a pacifier. Otherwise, the provider may read your baby's continuing desire to suck as a hunger cue and overfeed.

Know the satiation (fullness) cues.

A pleasant ending to a feeding is just as important as a responsive beginning. Stop feeding when your baby demonstrates satiation cues. If you have four ounces of formula or breast milk in a bottle and your baby drinks three, then spits out the nipple and turns away, stop. Do not attempt to push him to eat past his satiation point. The same is true for one more bite of cereal, or chicken. If the feeding ends with discomfort and tears, your intense baby will associate the feeding experience with negative emotions. The next time you bring out the bottle, or place him in the high chair, he'll arch to get away.

If your baby has been diagnosed with gastric reflux, she may arch or cry due to pain before she is truly full. Pause, allow a short rest, a bit of gastric relief, and then offer a bit more food. If she eats, feed her. When she turns away, respect that she's finished.

Remember, your baby does not need to be coerced to eat. Your job is not to force him, but rather support him. He knows when he is full and does not want to eat anymore. Once he allows the food to dribble out of his mouth, clamps his lips shut, releases the nipple and looks around, pushes away the spoon, or throws food on the floor, listen to him. Acknowledge this by saying or signing, "All done." You may be surprised how soon he is able to "tell you" he's finished. End the feeding with smiles—not a quarrel over one more bite or ounce.

SATIATION (FULLNESS) CUES

Comfortable Satiation Cues	Pushed Beyond Satiation Cues
Food begins to dribble out of mouth	Arches as though to escape
Stops sucking	Cries and bats away bottle/spoon
Releases nipple	Wags head back and forth with lips clamped shut
Turns away	Turns red

Comfortable Satiation Cues	Pushed Beyond Satiation Cues
Pushes bottle/spoon away	Visibly upset
Tosses food off tray	
Purses lips shut but not crying	
A young baby falls asleep, content and full	

STEP 3. MAKE MEALS A TIME TO CONNECT AND CALM

In a frequently cited study, researchers from the renowned Search Institute in Minneapolis, Minnesota, identified forty positive supports that children need to succeed. They compiled their findings to create the Developmental Assets Framework. One of those positive supports or assets is shared family meals. Children who live in families who frequently eat together tend to get higher grades and are less likely to use alcohol, tobacco, and other drugs. Shared family meals reflect dependability, time spent together, and meaningful traditions. But who would think about this concept for infants?

Spirited infants need to be in the green zone of calm energy to eat well. If they are overaroused and in the tense red zone, their brain is telling their body, *You need all your energy in your muscles to fight or flee. It cannot be diverted into the digestive system now.*

Make feedings and meals intentional and calm.

For these little ones to thrive, meals must be intentional, unhurried, and comforting points of calm spaced throughout the day. A tradition of family meals as a point of peaceful connection, established during infancy, will extend into childhood and support your child as he grows and develops.

Begin by noting the hunger cues and responding. Move slowly as you pick up your baby. Talk softly. Tell her, "I see you sucking on your fist. You must be hungry, let's get you some milk." Hurriedly starting a feeding can upset slow-to-adapt babies. For example, if your baby has been sleeping, make certain she is fully awake before beginning the feeding. Pick her up. Change her diaper. Talk with her. Wait for her to indicate she's ready. If she's upset, it's easy to spiral with her. Take long full breaths—four in, four out. Listen as your baby's breathing begins to match yours. When you're both calm, begin the feeding.

Once your little one is joining you at the table you will also want to plan your transition to eating. Stop play or come inside fifteen minutes before a meal. Read a book together. Rock. Talk. Then bring your toddler to the table.

Establish a "feeding place" and feeding rules.

A consistent feeding place allows your baby to settle and focus on the feeding. Eliminate other distractions as well. (It is tempting to use feeding time to check social media sites or watch videos but doing so may mean your infant does not feed well. Even when your infant is not the one watching, the noise and light from electronics reduces her focus and attention.) Take note of lighting, noise levels, and any other sources of stimulation, including pets that may distract or disrupt the feeding process.

Once the ambience is calming, make certain everyone is comfortable. Select a chair that supports your arms, back, and bottom. Create a "throne" that feels just right. Check the position in which you are holding your baby. Is he comfortable? Is his body calm? If needed, use a light blanket to swaddle him so he can slow his body down. Or drape it over your shoulder, covering his upper body and head, to help him focus on feeding. Anything can distract this baby, even the zipper teeth on your hoodie, or sparkly earrings. The key is creating a setting that allows your baby's brain to say, *All is well. It's okay to feed.* When your baby begins to eat, use this time to mindfully focus on his essence. Breathe in his baby smell. Notice his tiny, perfect fingernails. How his lips form a near perfect rosebud. Fall in love with your baby as you nourish him.

During the second year of life, a child is also learning what the rules are. If she's allowed to take a few bites, walk around, then return to the table, she doesn't tune in to her natural hunger and satiation cues. When instead you establish the table or the feeding chair as her eating place, you are not being mean. You are helping her settle so she can eat. The key to making her comfortable there is to sit down with her. Avoid leaving her alone to eat while you get a few more things finished or plunking an iPad in front of her for entertainment. Mealtime is not just about food. Just as important is the conversation and interaction. Talk about your day. Let her try out feeding tools. Stop, engage, and connect.

. . . .

Mealtime is not just about food. Just as important is the conversation and interaction. Talk about your day. Let her try out feeding tools. Stop, engage, and connect.

. . . .

There is restorative power in a leisurely family meal. Spirited infants naturally teach us this often, sipping, pausing, then eating again. They savor each bite of food as though they were enjoying a cup of hot chocolate in a Paris café. Slow down. Enjoy this time together. Rather than focusing on how much your baby is eating, pay attention to how it feels to come together to share a meal as a family. Allow it to be that point of connection and calm.

STEP 4. FAMILIARIZE YOUR BABY WITH A BOTTLE (IF YOU WISH)

If you've chosen to breastfeed your baby, the question arises, do you introduce a bottle, and if so, when?

The decision is completely yours. There is no right or wrong answer. But if you'd like to introduce a bottle, babies who are slow to adapt and sharply aware of differences in their environment tend to be more open to learning about this new feeding tool earlier rather than later. If your baby is older than six weeks and you have not introduced a bottle, but now wish to do so, it's not too late. The secret to success is taking teeny, tiny steps, and knowing when to give it up altogether and move on to a cup, as early as four months of age.

Typically it is recommended that you wait to introduce a bottle until breastfeeding is well established. That means your baby is:

- Consistently latching well, as in getting it right almost every time.
- Effectively transferring milk and gaining weight as expected.
- Staying awake for feedings.

Usually this occurs sometime between two and six weeks of age. Once your baby is feeding well, you can introduce the bottle. The process of sucking a bottle nipple is like drinking from a straw. Sucking on a breast requires much more tongue action. They are quite different skills. Your baby needs unpressured practice and time to learn how this new equipment functions.

When teaching bottle feeding, you'll want to keep as many things the same as possible. Otherwise your baby may become overwhelmed by too many new sensations. With that in mind, think about:

- Taste—initially offer breast milk rather than formula.
- Temperature—warm the milk to match Mom's body temperature. Follow standard safe warming practices. Do not microwave, as that can result in uneven heating and hot spots that burn.
- Flow—try, to the best of your ability, to match the nipple flow with one similar to Mom's. For most breastfed babies, a slow flow is best. If you have a strong letdown and your baby is used to a fast pace of eating, try a faster nipple so she doesn't get frustrated. When your baby has been taking a bottle and then suddenly refuses it, she may be telling you it's time for a new nipple flow.

Once your baby is a pro at switching back and forth from breast to bottle nipple, you have the option of slowly introducing formula by mixing a few drops into the breast milk then gradually adding more. Teeny, tiny steps are always the best with your spirited baby.

Continue to regularly offer your baby a bottle, potentially at least once a week. Select a time of day when your baby is happy. Fussy time is not a teaching time. Note early hunger cues so the baby is calm when the feeding begins. If baby is ravenously hungry, start with breastfeeding and then switch to the bottle as your baby calms so she has the patience to explore this new apparatus.

That's what Megan did. Initially Ben sputtered and screamed when Megan offered him the bottle. Megan stopped the practice session and breastfed him. The next time she tried, she started the session breastfeeding. After a few minutes she released Ben from the nipple and offered him the bottle. His initial hunger pangs satisfied, he relaxed in her arms and took the bottle for a few moments. At the first hint of frustration she went back to the breast and let him finish the feeding. The next day she did it again, alternating bottle and breast. Soon Ben took the bottle. (The teeny, tiny steps like the ones Megan used are included in the Gentle NUDGE section later in this chapter.)

Your baby may be proficient after just a few practice sessions or require many. She'll let you know. If your baby struggles to suck in general, work with a lactation consultant or an occupational or speech therapist to strengthen those muscles.

And then again, your baby who is intense, persistent, and committed to her goals—even at three months of age—may reject a bottle completely, no matter how many practice sessions or how miniscule the steps. No worries. We are problem solvers! You can introduce a cup as early as four months. (I once fed a very hungry breastfed baby from a beer mug. I had tried and failed with a bottle and a sippy cup. Then I remembered watching her grab for her dad's beer. It worked! Fortunately, Mom returned shortly after so I didn't have to repeat it, but sometimes we have to get creative . . .)

Whether it's a bottle or cup, when you introduce it with no imminent deadline in mind, it's easier to remain calm while your baby licks, spits, and mouths to discover how it works. There's no pressure or worry. This is merely a practice session, not a feeding.

Caring for a spirited baby is demanding. While every mom is different, some breastfeeding moms have described to me a sense of relief with the knowledge that their baby would feed from a bottle or cup.

Jana explained: "Initially I didn't think I would or should give my baby a bottle. Nursing was going well. But after a few months I was feeling weary. My baby nursed to sleep. She nursed when she woke. She nursed frequently throughout the day. I was losing friends because I did not feel comfortable leaving her, nor taking her with me and nursing in public. I need to be out with people. My mental health was at stake. I couldn't do this any longer. She was four months old when we started the bottle. My father-in-law came over and practiced with her. It took a while, but gradually she became comfortable with it. Just knowing I could take a break was priceless for me."

Breastfeeding is a relationship. The well-being of both Mom and baby is critical. Not every woman is comfortable nursing in public or is successful pumping. Family leaves end and your best friend may decide that her wedding is an adult-only event. The knowledge that the baby will take a bottle or drink from a cup can bring Mom peace of mind and baby, food.

Child rearing is not a hard science. Mixed in with scientific research are opinion, cultural expectations, and individual experiences. If a rule is so rigid it leaves you crying, scrutinize it. Does it make sense for you and your baby? Let's end the shaming over how we feed our babies. Caring for a spirited baby is hard work. Allow yourself to do what you need to do to care for yourself, too. Bottles and cups are tools. You can choose to use them or not. As Sara Bennett Pearce likes to say, "There are a thousand ways to mother a child, and feeding is just one of them."

STEP 5. INTRODUCE YOUR FAMILY'S FOODS AND EATING TOOLS

Cautious by nature and wanting to get it right, first-time mom Victoria asked her pediatrician when to begin offering her daughter, Pippa, solids. "Six months," he advised, following the current recommendations of the American Academy of Pediatrics.

Evidently Pippa did not agree. At four months, while sitting on her dad's lap at the table, she began reaching for food. Following doctor's orders, Paul pushed the plate out of her reach. At five months, determined and persistent, Pippa lurched forward, mouth wide open, ready to grab food off the plate. Heeding the pediatrician's advice, Paul again pushed the plate away. Pippa erupted in howls of protest.

Victoria called her pediatrician, who once again advised waiting. But in the next few days a typically happy five-and-a-half-month-old Pippa transformed into a fussy baby. Victoria contacted me. After listening to her questions, I affirmed her for listening to her baby and explained that there were predictable signs Pippa would demonstrate when she was ready to begin solids.

In case you like checklists, here's one compiled from a variety of sources to help you decide if your baby is prepared to handle solid foods. While six months is typically the recommended age it is not a magical point. Every baby progresses at her own pace. Readiness is a matter of skill development. Your baby will demonstrate her readiness sometime around six months of age when she:

- ❑ Is able to hold up and control her head.
- ❑ Sits up comfortably.
- ❑ Begins to grasp objects.
- ❑ No longer reflexively thrusts her tongue.

❑ Mouths toys, preparing for different textures, tastes, and shapes.

❑ Grabs for your food.

❑ Lurches toward a spoon filled with food.

❑ Points at food.

❑ Expresses anger when food is removed from her reach.

All indicators were present for Pippa. Victoria offered her rice cereal, but with her sensitivity to textures and a cautious first reaction, Pippa spit it out. The next day Paul tried. Pippa spit it out again. But on the third attempt, she accepted it. Oatmeal and banana were quickly added to the options. Pippa loved it all, but especially loved the spoon, insisting that she have one of her own. Paul gave it to her. Pippa stopped fussing.

What foods to introduce varies widely by culture and present standards, which can change so frequently that "advised" foods for your firstborn may be banned by the time your third-born is ready to join you at the table. Recently research from the University of Turku found that the type of gut microbes present in two-and-a-half-month-old infants were associated with the temperament traits displayed at six months of age. It is well known that there is communication between the bacteria in the gut and the central nervous system. Perhaps one day we will be able to select specific foods to feed babies according to their gut microbes in order to influence behavior and prevent potential medical issues. Until then I defer to the latest standards and recommendations, whatever they may be when you read this. Do check the guidelines for iron-rich foods such as eggs, black beans, and lentils. Introduce them as early as deemed suitable. Low iron levels can disrupt sleep. If your family has a history of food allergies move forward selectively and cautiously; introduce one food at a time over a period of a week.

While I cannot tell you exactly when and what to serve your baby, I can share with you predictable behaviors associated with the cautious, sensitive, persistent, and irregular temperament traits of spirited babies.

Cautious first reaction

What is food? What does it feel, taste, look, and smell like? Your cautious infant is a scientist methodically answering these questions. That is why when you first offer him a new food, he may frown, scrunch it in his hand, sniff it, pound it, smear it across the tray, poke and squish it, before he ever puts it in his mouth. If the "average" child spits out a new food ten times before swallowing it, expect your spirited little one to do so twenty-five times before he takes the plunge.

When you experience that first negative reaction don't assume he detests this food and never serve it again. His first reaction is just that, a reaction. With unpressured exposure and practice, he is likely to conclude these foods are delicious. He is not a picky eater. He is a scientist conducting his research. During this exploratory process he will also be observing you. Be aware of your own expressions. Your grimace, trepidation, or delight communicates important information about this food.

Initially, your baby will be acquiring his calories from formula or breast milk. Feed him before offering a solid food. You don't want him to be starving when he is completing his "scientific analysis." This is about practice, not nutrition. Tart, sweet, sour, hot, cold, salty, or spicy—every sensation of food is new! He's got a great deal of work to do.

Your little scientist is also in a stage of cognitive development in which he is learning about two key concepts: causality and object permanence. When he looks right at you and throws the peas on the floor this is not an act of defiance, nor an indication of how he feels about peas. It's an experiment. What happens? Does the food still exist even though he can no longer see it? When you stoop to pick it up, or the dog comes running to gobble it down, he laughs in glee. Again, not because he's being contrary but because he's amazed. The peas still exist! He can make the dog come running! This is fantastic!

Be proactive. Minimize the amount of food within his reach. Serve three pieces of finger food at a time. You will know he is satiated and moving on to experimenting when he opens his mouth, grabs food off his tongue, and throws it on the floor, or the frequency of tossing morsels is greater than the rate of eating them. Say or sign to him, "All done, my little scientist. Let's find a better way to practice." Then take him out of his feeding chair and engage in a game of peekaboo, hide the toy under a blanket, or fetch with the dog to teach these very same concepts.

Begin offering a solid food or foods one meal a day. Once that is going well, add another, and then another. Just remember a serving for a child this age is a mere one tablespoon or just three bites. Again, this is an estimate. Your baby will let you know what *his* serving is! During the first year your baby triples his birth weight. If he continued this pace into the second year, he could weigh sixty pounds by twenty-four months. Prepare for your toddler's appetite to slow. This is expected.

Persistent

Spirited babies are committed to their goals. "I do it myself" is their motto. Long before their peers they will demonstrate a desire to self-feed. That may mean they are scooping food with their palm or finger feeding. If your baby wants her own spoon, give it to her. Support her efforts by serving mashed potatoes, avocado, and other foods that are easy to scoop and stick to the spoon. Do not worry that more food is on her face than in her mouth. She's engaged and exploring.

And then again there is the little neatnik, who is just as committed to having you feed her so she doesn't get messy. She will burst into tears and vigorously shake her hand in a desperate attempt to remove the applesauce clinging to her fingers. The wild antics may feel like a ploy to mess up your kitchen, but they are not. The feel of wetness or food on her skin drives her wild. Keep a damp, warm cloth handy. Ask permission before wiping by holding the cloth in front of her, and wait for her to turn to you or reach out her hand. Offer her a cloth, too, and she'll help you keep things tidy. Begin each meal by asking her if she'd like to use the spoon or pick up the morsel herself. If she demonstrates no interest, feed her. Know she's mentally rehearsing the actions and one day she'll be ready.

Sensitive

Taste, temperature, and texture matter. Sensitive babies discern the differences in brands of applesauce. The "right" temperature is critical and if the boiled carrots have touched the chicken, they are no longer edible. And don't even think about offering her the blue cup instead of her favorite red one.

Along with that sensitivity can come gagging. The coughing, sputtering, retching, and watery eyes of gagging look and sound scary, but your baby is simply pushing the food to the front of her mouth to get it into position for chewing.

Do not assume when she gags that she dislikes this food. It's more likely she is working on getting control of her tongue and the position of the food in her mouth. Help her out by placing the spoon in the front of her mouth rather than farther back. Her gag reflex is easily triggered. Observe closely as she moves the food into the proper position then swallows it.

Gagging to the point of vomiting is not typical and instead could reflect an oral motor issue. If your infant is under six months of age, she may not be ready for solid foods. Wait until she is no longer thrusting her tongue and try again. If she is older than six months, make an appointment with a speech therapist for an exam to verify that your baby's tongue and oral muscles are working properly. If your baby is of the appropriate age for solid foods but seems to be struggling, there may be a developmental or physical reason. Best to check it out.

Unlike gagging, a choking baby may be silent. Choking occurs when an object becomes stuck in your baby's throat or windpipe, making it impossible for her to breathe or make a sound. This is serious. Take immediate measures. Pluck any visible offending object out of her mouth. However, if the obstruction is not visible, do not blindly probe as you may push it farther down into the windpipe. Instead, with the heel of your hand strike firm blows between the baby's shoulder blades. Typically this will be enough to pop out the obstruction. Always remain with your baby when she is eating. Potential choking is another important reason for you to sit down and be present at the meal. It is also why I recommend you enroll in an infant first aid course.

Irregular

Irregular spirited infants are unpredictable as to when they will eat and how much food they will consume. Accept that they can eat continually one day and hardly at all the next. Yet they remain steady on their growth chart. That is the key.

While you will be following your baby's hunger cues, you can begin to gently nudge him into a rhythmic routine of family meals with cues from the environment. When spirited babies awaken on their own to the sounds of your household, they are typically calm and rested. This is a great time to offer a feeding. Regular sleep and mealtimes set the body clock and help establish your baby's circadian rhythm. If your baby is not hungry, let it go, but begin the day with this "check in and cue." Ultimately it will become a cornerstone of your daily routine.

During our interview Charrisse Jennings explained to me that at drop-off in her child-care center, babies are handed from their parent to a caregiver, who then offers the baby a feeding. There are multiple reasons for this entry ritual. First the baby shifts from the arms of one loving caregiver to another. Second, by offering a bottle the caregiver has a few moments to focus on the baby to observe how she's doing this morning. Finally, the caregiver has a sense of when the baby may be ready for her next feeding. If she eats, it will be a while. If she does not eat, the caregiver knows to stay tuned in. Hunger cues may appear shortly. While the babies are *never* pushed to eat, the reliability of this meal offering sets their clock: Soon the babies begin to fall into a rhythmic pattern of arriving, eating, playing, and then sleeping.

STEP 6. DEVELOP YOUR BABY'S INDEPENDENT FEEDING SKILLS WITH A GENTLE NUDGE

No matter what feeding skill you are working on, set your baby up for success. The ability to manage frustration is learned. Spirited infants are working on this skill but they are not there yet. Always keep in mind that the initial practice sessions are just that—practice. Follow your baby's pace. You want her to remain calm so she can easily sense when she's hungry and when she's full. You, too, benefit as her cues are now distinct, no longer perplexingly mixed up with signs of overarousal.

The Gentle NUDGE to solid foods

The Gentle NUDGE method allows you to gradually introduce your baby to the variety of food your family loves.

<u>Note where your baby is now.</u> Review the readiness checklist provided earlier in this chapter. Once you can check off all the necessary skills begin the introduction process. If your baby is not yet demonstrating those skills, no worries. Simply continue to bring him to the table when you eat, so he can observe the process.

<u>Understand your ultimate goal.</u> Hopefully a healthy relationship with food is your goal. That means there is no celebrating or pushing of food consumption. If you wouldn't want someone insisting to you, "Three more bites," or exclaiming over every swallow, "Yay, you ate it!" then don't do it to your baby. Your job is simply to select the foods, serve them, and then sit down and enjoy them with your baby. He gets to decide if he wants to eat, what to eat that's been served, and how much.

<u>Determine the teeny, tiny steps.</u> Observe your baby. What food or utensils interest her most? Obviously you won't be giving her a food that she would choke on, but if she's reaching for your bowl of oatmeal or banana she's letting you know where she'd prefer to begin. If food allergies run in your family, adjust accordingly. Here are potential teeny, tiny steps to eating solid foods.

TEENY, TINY STEPS TO EATING SOLID FOODS

Teeny step 1	Teeny step 2	Teeny step 3
Let your baby sit on your lap or near the table when you eat.	When baby meets the guidelines for readiness notice what manageable food she's reaching toward.	If baby rejects being spoon-fed place small bits of food within her reach that she can palm or pick up herself.
Teeny step 4	**Teeny step 5**	**Teeny step 6**
Expect baby to mouth and spit out food many times before ever swallowing. Initial exposure is for practice, not nutrition.	Continue to expand foods offered as baby gains competence. Allow baby to choose from the foods served.	Respect satiation cues. No cajoling or pushing to eat.

<u>Gently practice.</u> Begin offering a solid food or foods once a day. Offer your baby support and assistance. If he wants his own utensil, give it to him. Stop with the first indication of frustration. The next day, try it again. Once that meal is going well, add a second, gradually building up to six mini-meals a day.

<u>Ease back.</u> As your baby's ability to feed himself grows, gradually ease back on your support. He's likely to surprise you with how competent he is.

The Gentle NUDGE to introducing a bottle

If you would like to introduce your breastfeeding baby to a bottle, respect his pace and what he's telling you about it.

Note where your baby is now. You and your baby are becoming comfortable with breastfeeding. Once you are both proficient, begin the process of introducing a bottle.

Understand your ultimate goal. Whether for feeding when you are apart from your baby or as a backup, a bottle is one tool to help meet your baby's need for nourishment.

Determine the teeny, tiny steps.

TEENY, TINY STEPS TO INTRODUCING A BOTTLE

Teeny step 1	Teeny step 2	Teeny step 3
If possible, begin within the first six weeks, after breastfeeding is well-established.	Select a feeding place that is quiet and allows the baby to focus on the feeding.	Calm the baby before beginning. If he's starving, consider breastfeeding initially then offer the bottle of breast milk.
Teeny step 4	Teeny step 5	
Allow baby to mouth and spit out the nipple. At this point baby's simply exploring how the equipment works. Stop if baby becomes frustrated and switch to breastfeeding.	Establish a regular practice time. Perhaps every day, or at least once a week. If baby takes it, great; if not, try again the next time.	

Gently practice. Consistency and regular exposure are your friends. Set up a schedule that allows your slow-to-warm baby frequent opportunities to practice. Experiment. Does your baby seem more comfortable if you begin breastfeeding and then switch to the bottle, or does it work better for her to start with the bottle? The same is true of the feeding space and feeding position. Notice if your baby does better when you keep it the same or establish a different one for bottle feedings. Instead of offering the bottle yourself, allow another adult to try. Let your baby show you what works best for her.

Ease back. Once your baby is comfortable with a bottle, she likely will want to hold her bottle herself. You can allow her to do so, but do not prop the bottle, allow her to walk around with it, or leave her to finish it on her own. Continue to hold her and make mealtime an opportunity to focus on and bask in your love for your baby.

The Gentle NUDGE to weaning from breast or bottle

When to bring breastfeeding or bottle feeding to a close is a private decision. Many factors come into play. The American Academy of Pediatrics recommends exclusive breastfeeding for the first six months and then continued breastfeeding combined with solid foods for one to two years or *as long as mother and baby desire*. Sometimes your baby simply loses interest in either breast or bottle. Other times a breastfeeding mom is ready to transition before her baby. Return of your menstrual cycle or pregnancy may influence your decision. Your pediatrician may have recommended weaning from the bottle. Or perhaps it's apparent this beautiful relationship has run its course for you and your baby. No matter how or why you come to the weaning process, you can use the Gentle NUDGE to get there.

Note where your baby is now. If your baby is less than twelve months old and continues to take most of her nutrients from breast milk, but you have decided to or need to wean, you'll want to switch from breast milk to formula. If your little one is older than twelve months and her skills are well established with both solid foods and a cup, you may be able to wean directly from breastfeeding to family meals. However, spirited infants often need the opportunity to suck long past their peers. If you are weaning before eighteen months, weaning from breast to bottle may be necessary.

Understand your ultimate goal. Know why you are weaning. Is this a decision you are freely making, or are you feeling pressured by others? Do not allow others to push you to wean before you and your baby are ready. If you are breastfeeding and your partner is insisting on weaning, address the underlying issues. Is there a lack of intimacy? What is your baby saying about this process? Does she push away from the breast or bottle, too busy to stop for a meal? Or, would she prefer this to continue for a while? If that's the case, is there another way to address the concerns that led you here? Could you maintain her favorite times for breastfeeding but bottle feed for others, thus making it work for both of you awhile longer? The weaning process is most comfortable when you can confidently say, "I believe my baby is competent and ready to wean." *And* "I am ready to wean." When and how you come to this decision is your choice. Even if circumstances force weaning before you wish, breaking the process down into teeny, tiny steps can decrease your angst.

The following charts provide examples of the steps you might take. The first illustration delineates steps for weaning from breast to bottle. The second one demonstrates weaning from either breast or bottle to family meals.

Determine the teeny, tiny steps.

TEENY, TINY STEPS OF WEANING FROM BREAST TO BOTTLE

Teeny step 1	Teeny step 2	Teeny step 3
Begin with your baby's least favorite feeding, when she is easily distracted.	Offer a bottle instead of the breast. If baby resists or becomes upset, allow her to finish with a breastfeed. If another adult is available to give the baby the bottle, that may be ideal.	Offer the bottle again. Once baby is comfortable taking a bottle at this feeding, move on to the next least favorite feeding.

Teeny step 4	Teeny step 5	
Gradually continue to replace the breast with bottle feedings. Continue to hold baby during bottle feedings. Do not allow baby to walk around with bottle.	Continue replacing the breast with bottle feedings until weaning is complete. You can choose to maintain a favorite breastfeed longer if you and your baby wish. Continue to offer lots of cuddles and snuggles when baby seeks contact.	

Determine the teeny, tiny steps of weaning from bottle/breast to family meals.

Teeny step 1	Teeny step 2	Teeny step 3
If baby is competently taking solids and is over a year old, begin offering solid foods and then breast milk or formula.	Select the least favorite bottle/breast feeding time and offer a cuddle, meal, or cup instead.	Once baby has dropped that bottle/breastfeed, move on to the next least favorite.

Teeny step 4	Teeny step 5	
Offer baby 6 mini-meals a day spaced about 2.5 to 3 hours apart. Always include a little protein, carbohydrate, fruit/vegetable, and fat.	As baby drops bottle/breastfeedings continue to offer lots of cuddles and snuggles whenever baby seeks contact.	

Gently practice. Whenever possible allow your baby to set the pace. Give her time to adapt. If she becomes upset, slow down. Unless there is cause for an emergency weaning, move through the process slowly, gradually eliminating bottle feedings or breast-feedings. This allows you and your baby to feel relaxed and comfortable with her growing independence.

Ease back. When your baby is content and competently joining you at meals and drinking from a cup, you can feel comfortable offering cuddles instead of a breast or bottle feeding. Your baby can be trusted to eat the right amount of food for her body. She also wants to join you at family meals. Allow her to self-feed as much as she is capable of doing, but do continue to sit down with her. Family meals support your baby's growth and development. Make your mealtimes dependable, calm points of connection dispersed throughout your day.

The Gentle NUDGE allows you to break down independent feeding skills into teeny, tiny steps that lead you and your baby to success. When you suddenly experience a backslide, know something is up. Slow down. Accept where she is now, even if she's demonstrating fewer skills than yesterday. Meet her needs. Once things are back to normal, she'll rebound quickly, ready to take on the next challenge. Let feeding time with your baby be enjoyable for all. This tradition of family meals will support her growth and development throughout her life.

CHEAT SHEET FOR HAPPY AND HEALTHY FEEDING

1. *Define the responsibilities of healthy eating.* Your job is to decide how to feed your baby—breast or bottle. Your baby's job is to decide everything else—when, where, how much, and how fast.

2. *When your baby is steadily gaining weight as expected, trust his cues for hunger and fullness.* Pay attention to his signals, and trust he knows how much he needs and when.

3. *Make meals a time to connect and calm.* Stay focused. Eliminate distractions. Be mindful of the moment and allow yourself to take in the very essence of your baby.

4. *If you choose to introduce the bottle, do so sooner rather than later.* Familiarize your baby with a bottle and other feeding tools with unpressured practice and teeny, tiny steps.

5. *Use the Gentle NUDGE to practice independent feeding skills.* Gradually allow your baby to increasingly take over responsibility for feeding herself by offering finger foods and her own utensils. Respect her choices as she selects from the foods you have served.

REFLECTION QUESTIONS FOR YOUR JOURNAL

- What makes it difficult for you to trust your baby around feeding and food?

- What steps could you take to make feedings a point of calm and connection?

- What's the most important thing you wish to teach your baby about food?

Chapter 9

Enjoyable Outings

Socializing and Traveling with Less Stress and More Fun for Everyone

*"Whenever we go out, we find ourselves in this state
of hypervigilance, terrified that if she slips past the
point of tired, she will end up in an inconsolable
meltdown. When we get home it's yet another issue
trying to get her to sleep. Honestly, I just want to stay
home, lock the door, and avoid the whole thing."*
—Kevin, the father of Olivia

Bethany was eager to join her moms' group for lunch at a local restaurant. But fifteen minutes before it was time to leave, three-month-old Abe melted down. "Oh, no!" Bethany thought. She really wanted to go but it was obvious Abe was very tired. If she went, she knew the cacophony of voices and the sounds of the restaurant would keep him awake. Initially he'd enjoy it. Then, inevitably, he'd lose it, his distress spilling over well into the evening.

It was at this moment Bethany remembered a tip I'd offered in class:

Before you go out the door ask yourself if you would be willing to bet Dr. Mary $100 your baby will be "successful" on this outing.

Bethany sighed. "No way," she thought. "I wouldn't even bet a dime."

Whether it's an hour or two for errands or a get-together, a day trip, or an overnight journey, going out into the world with any infant is challenging. Add to the mix a spirited baby's slow-to-warm, intense, alert, active, and sensitive temperament and stepping out the door can be petrifying. Your brain whirls. Will there be a meltdown? Will other people stare at us, their glares telegraphing their judgment? Will we pay for this venture with disrupted sleep and fussing for the next two days? Should we forget the whole thing, or do we go and hope for the best?

Sometimes with a spirited baby the best choice is to remain at home, but it does not have to be the only solution. Socializing and outings are important for everyone's well-being. Fortunately, with forethought, preparation, and an exit plan in place, the decision to remain at home can be the exception rather than the rule. There are steps you can take to ensure things go better. Maybe not perfectly—but definitely better.

> With forethought, preparation, and an exit plan in place, the decision to remain at home can be the exception rather than the rule.

Local excursions and even long-distance trips can be sparkling successes and the beginning steps for a little person who may grow up to be an intrepid traveler, a citizen of the world, and the life of the party.

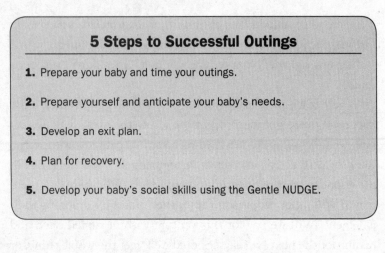

5 Steps to Successful Outings

1. Prepare your baby and time your outings.

2. Prepare yourself and anticipate your baby's needs.

3. Develop an exit plan.

4. Plan for recovery.

5. Develop your baby's social skills using the Gentle NUDGE.

STEP 1. PREPARE YOUR BABY AND TIME YOUR OUTINGS

A hungry, tired baby will have a limited capacity to cope. Set your baby up for success by intentionally protecting sleep and feedings as you make your plans. The timing of excursions can make all the difference.

Focus first on when you go.

Learn what works for your baby and routines. For example:

- Whenever possible schedule activities when your baby is rested and satiated.
- Meeting friends? Try your best to go *after* a nap and feeding and return home *before* the next one.
- Nix late-evening activities that disrupt bedtime, unless you can get a sitter.

- Going out in the afternoon? Keep morning activities low-key to conserve coping energy for when you need it.
- Catching a flight? That slightly more expensive ticket for an ideal departure time may well be worth it if it means you're not awakening your baby at 4:00 A.M. to catch it.

Courageously maintain your baby's sleep and feeding routines.

Don't stop with planning the timing of outings. While you are out, and during your travel, courageously maintain your baby's sleep and feeding routines. I say "courageously" because not everyone will support your efforts, especially when those efforts include skipping an activity to protect a nap, leaving early to avoid baby's exhaustion or overstimulation, or stepping away from an activity to provide enough calm for your baby to settle to feed or go to sleep.

Sleep and food at the right time keep your baby regulated. Unfortunately that right time is not always convenient, yet ignoring her needs can push her beyond her ability to cope. Before you step out the door, observe your baby's present state of fatigue and hunger. Consider her skill level to shut down enough to sleep or eat in the situation you'll be in. Then decide to go or to stay home.

> Before you step out the door, observe your baby's present state of fatigue and hunger.

When Bethany thought about Abe's present state of fatigue, she realized there was little to nothing she could do to help him be successful. She couldn't control the time of the moms' group. He was too alert to nap in the busy restaurant environment, even if she put him in a carrier or covered him with a light blanket. Nor was there anyone else to take him out of the restaurant if needed. The odds he'd make it through were too low, the potential costs too high, and she knew there would be additional opportunities to visit in the coming weeks.

Bethany texted her friends, explaining what was happening, sent her regrets, and stayed home. Abe napped for three hours, his longest nap ever. While Bethany did not get to see her friends, she did get three hours of peace and a happy baby the remainder of the day.

It's difficult to put your baby's needs ahead of your own and to deal with the disappointment and frustration of others when you don't show up. But sometimes the winning bet is recognizing your baby's state of arousal and protecting his sleep. When that decision is a deliberate one, it's easier to cope. You know why you are doing what you are doing. This is what your baby needs right now. It's okay. This will not be forever. It's just for now, while your baby is young and still developing self-regulation skills. Your true supporters will understand.

However, deciding to remain home today does not mean you are required to always make that choice. The next day Bethany's friend Rachel texted, "Wanna get together? You and Abe can come here. Any time works." Bethany sighed with relief. She could pick the time and it would just be the three of them, in Rachel's home. Bethany replied, "YES! :)"

. . . .

It's difficult to put your baby's needs ahead of your own. . . . This will not be forever. It's just for now, while your baby is young. . . . Deciding to remain home today does not mean you are required to always make that choice.

. . . .

After Abe's morning nap, she grabbed his wrap and headed for Rachel's home, smiling to herself as she thought, "Today I *would* be willing to bet $100 things will go well!" And they did. Rested when he arrived, Abe greeted Rachel with a grin. Later, tucked in the wrap against his mother's body, he slept forty-five minutes and remained content for the remainder of the visit. That evening he fussed for about thirty minutes, but all in all, a well-deserved win for both of them.

Unfortunately, not every friend or family member is as informed and flexible as Rachel. It's unlikely they realize how important naps and feedings are for your baby. Nor will they initially understand your baby is so alert that sleeping and eating in a stimulating environment is nearly impossible—especially when his first cousin, who is two months younger, can sleep or eat anywhere! Give them a copy of this book.

If, despite your efforts to educate them life happens and potential outings disrupt your baby's sleep and feeding times, before you automatically decide to stay home, think creatively. Are there ways to protect your baby's sleep and still go? Could you go early and leave early? Would it be possible to allow your baby to finish the nap and arrive late?

If the event is hosted by your family, could you set it up that your co-parent takes the baby home or to a quiet spot for a nap, while you continue to enjoy the event, or vice versa if it is your partner's family?

Is it possible for her to sleep if you bring along the carrier that tucks her against your body or a light blanket to drape over the two of you to block stimuli?

She hates the hoodie or blanket? Think about where you might find a quiet, dim spot to hide out to feed her.

Potential solutions may exist. Consider your options and then decide if your baby is prepared to handle this event. Your answer will change as conditions vary and your baby's skills develop.

Whether you choose to go or not go, the decision is yours. Just don't leave it to chance. Be kind to your baby. Let your baby arrive at and leave gatherings smiling rather than squalling. If others give you grief about being too protective, think about what your baby is telling you he needs. That's what matters.

. . . .

> Be kind to your baby. Let your baby arrive at and leave gatherings smiling rather than squalling. If others give you grief about being too protective, think about what your baby is telling you he needs. That's what matters.

. . . .

STEP 2. PREPARE YOURSELF AND ANTICIPATE YOUR BABY'S NEEDS

I was attempting to coordinate a walk with my friends Cassidy and Heather and their two-month-old daughter, Sage. Our text exchange read:

Cassidy: *Let's plan on 7:30 PM.*

Me: *That would be lovely.*

Me at 7:00 PM: *Weather is looking a little dicey. What do you think?*

Cassidy: *That hopefully it doesn't rain—we could try to go now—but not Sage—she's just finishing eating.*

Me: *I'm flexible—just let me know.*

Cassidy: *Okay, let's try it—we can be out the door in 5 minutes.*

Me: *Okay, I'll meet you there.*

Cassidy: *Wait. Major spit-up. Give us 10.*

Me: *No problem.*

Cassidy: *We are going to try to leave here in 5 minutes.*

Me: *Got it.*

Cassidy: *Oops—now changing diaper—need another 5.*

One of the most anxiety-provoking things about taking your baby out is that you never know exactly what's going to happen or when a meltdown will strike. This is a great time to make that switch from *what if* to *even if* that we discussed in chapter 3. When you stop worrying about *what if* and instead replace those thoughts with *even if*, you begin to empower yourself. *Even if* your worst fears become a reality, you are a problem-solving family.

You can put in place measures to keep things running smoothly and improve your odds for success. Little things, like allowing yourself extra time, being organized, and having the right supplies with you, will reduce your stress and help make outings enjoyable.

Give yourself more time and avoid rushing.

While it is impossible to foresee every surprise, it is predictable that at least one will occur just as you're attempting to get out the door. If, to arrive on time, you need to leave by 8:00 A.M., plan to depart at 7:45. Give yourself a cushion to manage those inevitable surprises. Then even if your baby spits up all over you, you won't be late. Rushing and the accompanying skyrocketing stress levels trigger your baby, but no worries for you—you've created a buffer.

Get organized.

Pack your diaper bag with the typical supplies you'll need: diapers, wipes, hand sanitizer, change of clothing, extra pacifier, duplicate lovie, sweater, snacks, formula and water, and light blanket or shawl if you use one to nurse or quiet your baby. You'll also want to include a few toys, board books, and activities to help your baby be successful. Look to your baby's temperament profile to assist you in selecting useful items to bring along.

Make it a practice to restock the bag whenever you return home and establish a spot by the door to store it. One hassle is now eliminated during those precious last minutes before departure.

Anticipate needs for activity and exploration.

Spirited little ones are active and inquisitive! You can predict they'll be on the move. Plan opportunities for activity throughout the day. Prevent the dirty looks when your baby is busy exploring by bringing along a ball. A toddler chasing a ball is delightful. People smile. No glaring judgments that this child is hyper, especially if you also point out how inquisitive and curious he is as he explores every nook and cranny. If you have a choice between meeting in a restaurant or the park for a picnic, choose the park, where your little one can freely run. Too cold or hot outside? Hit the children's museum or the play area at the mall if it's not a busy time of day.

If your baby is not yet mobile, bring a variety of toys and books you can hand to him. One at a time he'll explore each item and give you a chance to talk with friends or watch the game. You can exponentially increase the intrigue for older babies if you have a few minutes to wrap the toys. It doesn't matter that it's the truck he's seen one hundred times. This is a new and exciting presentation! The goods do not need to be elaborate. Simply harness your baby's curiosity and need to be active.

Plan protection for sensitivity levels.

Protect your baby's sensitive ears and eyes. Bring sunglasses, a hat, and even sound-blocking headphones. When flying, plan to feed your baby or allow her to suck on a pacifier during takeoff and landing. The change in air pressure can be excruciating to sensitive ears.

Manage stimulation levels when choosing timing, locations, and events.

Teach yourself to always consider the environment and stimulation levels of anticipated outings. Meeting for dinner? Can you go early before the crowds hit? Not only will it be quieter, but you'll also be served faster, increasing the odds you'll actually get to eat before a potential meltdown occurs. If there's seating available outside and the weather permits, take it. Meeting a friend for coffee? Consider a picnic at a playground with take-out cappuccinos you pick up on your way. Lower stimulation levels allow your baby to remain regulated longer.

Support your slow-to-adapt or "cautious first reaction" baby.

If you know from your baby's temperament that you have a slow-to-adapt little one, you can guess that your baby's cautious first reaction will impact your entrance into a social situation. Strategically plan your entry. Whenever possible arrive early. Give your baby time to become accustomed to the new place before the crowd arrives.

Instead of carrying your baby into a gathering in a car seat or your arms, put her in a front carrier strapped to your body. That way she can calmly observe while in a safe place. Plus, no one can grab her before she's ready. If during your drive she did not nap, which is highly likely, it also makes it easier for you to greet everyone and then move to a quiet location for her nap. You won't be "stealing" her from someone's arms to get her the rest she needs.

When she exhibits cues that she is ready to leave the carrier, the ideal situation is to find a place where you can sit on the floor with her. If she's mobile this allows her to easily move away from you, her safe haven, and return when she wishes. You can invite others to join you so she can move toward them and engage if she wishes. She'll choose to interact sooner when given a choice. Demonstrate to others how they can reach out their hands and ask your baby permission to be picked up. They'll be amazed how even a young baby will turn, look at them, or reach toward them if she wishes to make the transfer. If your baby turns away, tell the others, "She's letting us know she's not ready." Allow her to make that choice. She gets to say no. Adults can be expected to adapt to the needs of the baby. Don't ask your baby to adapt to theirs.

- -

Adults can be expected to adapt to the needs of the baby. Don't ask your baby to adapt to theirs.

- -

Plan for sleep.

If this will be an overnight journey, think about your baby's sensitivity in relation to sleeping. Look for the darkest room. The best spot may be in a portable crib tucked in a windowless walk-in closet. Depending on how far you want to take this, you can also create temporary "blackout shades." Purchase heavy paper that's used to protect wood floors during construction and a roll of electric tape (which won't lift wall paint). You can tape the paper over windows and remove it before you leave.

Bring a sheet from home so the smell is familiar. If you've been using a sound machine, bring that, too.

Is this a lot of work? Yes! But if it makes the difference between everyone being well rested versus exhausted, it's worth the effort. And no, you are not being neurotic. You are hedging your bets.

Consider your baby's internal systems.

It's not just external stimuli that can pose a problem for these sensitive babies. Intestinal upsets are also common on trips. A change in water from one location to another can result in tummy aches and loose bowels. Carry bottled water.

Rather than emptying the intestinal system, your baby's brain may instead direct the body to shut down the digestive system just in case the blood is needed in the muscles to flee. The result is constipation. This buildup of body waste can, inevitably, ooze out of the diaper, down the legs, and up the back. Pack an extra set of clothing for baby *and* for you, especially if you'll be sitting on an airplane.

If your baby is eating solids you can often prevent constipation by offering a daily small serving of bran cereal or prune puree. It will help to "keep things moving."

Help manage your baby's sensitivity to emotions.

Your baby's sensitivity to the emotions of others must be monitored as well. Like the canary in the mine, these babies sense trouble long before anyone else notices. Walk into a doctor's office, airport, a tense family situation, or any space where adults are stressed and this infant will wail.

Give yourself a heads-up by stopping as you enter a space to check if it is a red zone, yellow zone, or green zone environment. Note what is happening in your body. Are you tensing, suddenly wary as you pick up the vibe in this environment? If everyone is in the red zone, your baby will need your help to remain calm. And don't be surprised, or embarrassed, when in these edgy situations your sensitive, perceptive little person turns or bats away the person who is too loud, too invasive, too excited, or talking too much. He's doing his best to "flee" from the source of this disquiet. Do listen to him.

If you're in the doctor's office and it's the professional your baby is pushing away, ask the person to review the questions with you first, giving your baby time to adapt and calm before he's touched. Ultimately you will teach your little one to respectfully say, "No touch, please." Your baby will have a great sense of boundaries! Look for the professionals who explain to your child what will be happening and involve him in the process.

Well-thought-out, preventive measures like these drastically increase the likelihood of a fun, enjoyable outing for everyone.

STEP 3. DEVELOP AN EXIT PLAN

Just as you select the timing to begin an event, know when to bring closure. Even when the entire day has gone superbly, if your baby is screaming as you leave, that's what you will remember. Better to experience a bit of disappointment by departing early than roil with a sense of failure as you dash out the door. The key to success is tuning in to your baby's cues—sometimes hidden by his extreme perceptiveness and curiosity—and having an exit plan in place.

Max's parents, Justin and Kristi, noticed immediately how Max appeared to be watching their every move. They often noted how he seemed more perceptive and contemplative than other babies. What Max was seeing and processing became blatantly apparent a few years later.

Max was four years old the first time Justin caught him attempting to start the car. A momentary phone call temporarily caused Justin to lose sight of Max. During those few minutes, Max managed to push a chair to the hook where his mom's purse hung, dig out her car keys, drag the same chair to the laundry room, climb up on it, and unlatch the lock to the carport. Once inside the carport, he successfully opened the car door, slid into the driver's seat, and started the car. That's when a frantic Justin found him. Pleased with his accomplishments, Max greeted his dad's sudden appearance with a grin, then innocently asked, "Dad, how does the gearshift work?"

Amazing, yes, but not unusual for spirited children. Attentiveness is a sign of intelligence, and these young ones zero in on the world around them and note what is happening: how things work, the tone of voices, sights, sounds, smells, sensations, stress levels, and more. Frequently their attentiveness also attracts the notice of strangers. And if by chance you have spirited twins, multiply exponentially the level of attention and stimuli bombarding them.

Especially in social situations, colors, images, light, voices, touching, and other sensory data can flood the spirited infant's system. Initially the little charmer may seem to love all the excitement, but later, when the barrage of stimulation becomes overwhelming, he sobs as though everything hurts.

Watch for the first indication your baby is moving from the green zone of calm energy toward the red zone of meltdowns. Notice how she shifts from super-smiley to sober to frowns. Her state of well-being is waning before your eyes. Observe signals of fatigue or hunger. Be aware of how long since she's eaten or slept. If she's begun to fall into a predictable routine, set your phone to those times as an alert to monitor your baby's cues. However, do expect that your baby may need to sleep and eat more frequently than at home. She's expending a great deal of energy.

As you respond, you may realize you are facing a hurdle. Rather than feeling empathy, your first reaction to her needs may be anger or fear. Anger because you do not want to step away to let her feed or sleep, much less leave! You are having fun. (Unless, of course, you are an introvert and revel in the excuse to take a break yourself!) Or fear because your anxiety level rises just imagining the reactions of others when you tell them you are departing.

You may hope your assessment is incorrect, especially if your baby did well last time. Or, if her cue is to ramp up her energy level, laughing, grabbing toys, engaging in a flurry of activity that leads others to insist she's having a great time, you might be tempted to think, Maybe they are right. Maybe if I just ignore the cues . . . But of course, that's when your baby loses it. Now you're frustrated with her and yourself because you saw it coming but didn't want to believe it.

Just as you forgive your baby, forgive yourself. We are social beings. Spending time with others is as important to well-being as breathing. It's hard when sensitively responding to your baby puts your needs second and leaves family and friends disappointed. That's where a planned exit can make things better.

....

When your baby loses it, just as you forgive your baby, forgive yourself. We are social beings. Spending time with others is as important to well-being as breathing.

....

Often it's the surprise of your sudden disappearance or departure that upsets others. Eliminate that surprise by informing them beforehand that you will be respecting your baby's sleep and feeding times, which means you may disappear or depart. This is a fact. No need to justify it. It's not up for debate. If someone accuses you of being obsessive, rather than loving and attentive, simply shrug. Intense babies need Momma/Papa Grizzlies to protect their sleep and support their highly tuned arousal systems. The cost of disrupted sleep is too great. The recovery time too arduous and long. If someone has not lived this reality, it's difficult for them to understand. But you are fully aware that the more attuned and responsive you are, the better your baby copes.

Once others have been informed, you can simply slip away when your baby needs a feeding or a nap. No one will be madly searching for you, wondering why you've disappeared or if something is wrong. They will know what you are doing and why.

I saw this plan in action while attending a recent community event. Dad, Mom, their six-month-old, and grandparents were attending together. Dad holding the baby noted the first yawn. Without a word to anyone, he simply stepped out into the lobby. Ten minutes later he returned with a sleeping baby. No raised eyebrows or frowns occurred; the family members were obviously in accordance.

Include in your plan a quick getaway. Keep your possessions gathered together. When it's time to leave, load the car, return for the baby, and say a simple good-bye. A friendly wave to the group suffices. You want to be out the door before your baby loses it. There's not a lot of extra time. Later, if you wish, you can call or text individuals.

If you'll be heading home for bedtime, change your baby into pajamas before you exit and plan to depart earlier than the typical sleep time. Then when you arrive home, your baby will already be prepared for bed and you'll have additional time for the essential wind-down. The shift from socializing to sleep is a big leap. If you don't plan for that wind-down time, your baby will remain so wound up that, like a missile, he'll shoot right past his typical window for sleep. Then it may be an hour or two before he finally crashes. Now overtired and dysregulated he will likely wake frequently throughout the night. Adjust your timing and expectations accordingly.

After you have made it out the door, take a deep breath. Recenter yourself. You did it! Maybe you even got out without a single tear. But if you have a toddler, despite your preparations she may be loudly protesting your decision. That's to be expected. She has no other way to say, "Hey, I was having fun! I do not agree with this decision!" Empathize. Let her know you understand it's difficult to leave, but as her parent, you are doing what she needs.

STEP 4. PLAN FOR RECOVERY

Let's face it. Going out with a spirited baby requires both physical and mental energy. It is not just your baby who may be worn out afterward but you, too. As Becky told me, "I need a vacation from my vacation!"

Plan downtime. Temporary regressions in nighttime sleep and naps are predictable after excursions. Avoid scheduling an 8:00 A.M. meeting the first day back from vacation, or one family gathering weekend immediately after another. Even better, when your vacation period is seven days long, arrive home on day six, to give yourself a chance to recenter, catch up, and prepare for the week ahead.

Be certain to record in your journal what went well. After the successes are noted, reflect on what did not go so well. Hindsight is golden.

No matter how organized you are, every outing or trip is not going to be perfect. Life is messy. There will still be moments when everything falls apart. If that occurs, remember your baby is not intentionally embarrassing you. He simply got pushed beyond his ability to cope. Be cognizant of what plans require tweaking to make things run smoother next time. Then call a friend, take a nap, or hand over your baby to your partner. You deserve a break!

Trust that one day as you reflect upon how things went, you'll realize your little one made it through the morning at the zoo *and* lunch!

STEP 5. DEVELOP YOUR BABY'S SOCIAL SKILLS USING THE GENTLE NUDGE

The skills to cope in social situations are the same skills your baby uses at home. The difference is that social situations tend to be more demanding and higher in stimulation. The self-regulation "muscles" to navigate them must be stronger. Even if your baby is napping in a crib at home, it may be several months later before she can do so at Grandma's house. The same is true for feedings. Older siblings running around the room at home may not be an impediment to a good feeding but make those individuals strangers or unfamiliar cousins, add in a new "room," and she just can't get the brakes to hold. Gradual, supported practice with you results in the formation of new pathways within the brain that strengthen her skills and enhance her ability to manage these situations. Use the Gentle NUDGE to get her there.

The Gentle NUDGE to accomplish a successful errand

<u>Note where your baby is now.</u> A trip to the grocery store on a busy Saturday morning sends your baby over the edge. She starts to scream before you have ten items in the cart. Recognize the level of stimulation is too high.

<u>Understand your ultimate goal.</u> Life is easier when you can run an errand with your baby in tow. Your goal may be to make errands with him a pleasant and enjoyable event for both of you.

Determine the teeny, tiny steps. If your baby is falling apart in the store on busy Saturday mornings, try Monday. She fell apart after ten minutes? Plan to go for five. Find the sweet spot where your baby is successful. Gradually, move forward from there.

TEENY, TINY STEPS TO ACCOMPLISH A SUCCESSFUL ERRAND

Teeny step 1	Teeny step 2	Teeny step 3
Select a low-stimulation time, when your baby is rested and fed, and you are in the green zone of calm energy. Perhaps 8:00 on Sunday morning.	Plan to pick up no more than 3 to 5 items. Leave while your baby is still content, even if you only have one item in the cart.	Next week, go again.

Teeny step 4	Teeny step 5	
Once your baby makes it through selecting 5 items, increase to 8 or 10. Again, leave the store while baby is still content.	Sunday at 8:00 has been going well. Shift to a slightly later, busier, but not overwhelming time—after your baby's had a nap and feeding. Make sure you are in the green zone, too.	

Gently practice. Your spirited baby may never cope well with a wild Saturday morning crowd at the grocery, and since being spirited has a genetic element to it, you may be just fine with that.

But rather than avoiding the store completely, simply select a quieter day and time to practice. Keep the sessions short and successful. Gradually lengthen sessions, still protecting nap and feeding times. Slowly increase the stimulation level.

Ease back. Over time your baby's self-regulation skills will strengthen to the point that she can move through the store successfully, but do recognize when enough is enough. Leave when you see the first indication that she's struggling to remain calm. There are also certain stores where the lighting, music, chaos of items, and crowding are so overwhelming that even an adult finds them excruciating. These stores are best avoided, no matter the day or time.

The Gentle NUDGE to a successful car ride

While driving, you may have become accustomed to the fumes of diesel engines, horns honking, sirens blaring, sunlight streaking through the windshield, and the *whoosh* of five lanes of traffic flying by. Your brain has sorted it all and for the most part determined that all is fine. But for your spirited baby it's all new and quite astonishing. Add to this challenge being locked in a five-point harness facing backward and it can be easier to understand why your baby is screaming.

Note where your baby is now. Is your baby comfortable in her car seat? If not you'll need to start here, making the adjustments necessary for her comfort. Can she make it down the driveway and around the block, or does she lose it the minute you shift into drive? Is she content on side streets but freaks out on the freeway? Identify at what point during a car ride your baby begins to struggle to regulate. Then back up one step.

Understand your ultimate goal. It is dangerous to drive with a baby screaming in the back seat. You want your baby comfortable and content while in the car.

Determine the teeny, tiny steps. Whether it is your baby's sensitivity being triggered or her need to move that is activating her arousal system, determine the teeny, tiny steps necessary to help her be successful.

TEENY, TINY STEPS TO A SUCCESSFUL CAR RIDE

Teeny step 1	Teeny step 2	Teeny step 3
Place your baby in the car seat. Adjust straps and lock buckles. Check the support the seat provides your baby's body, especially neck and head. Make certain he's comfortable.	Once your baby is comfortable in the car seat, turn off the radio or video, drive around the block. Is he calm?	If he didn't make it around the block without fussing, try a different time of day. Is he comfortable when it's dark, but not midday when the sunlight pierces his eyes?
Teeny step 4	Teeny step 5	
Add a sunshade if needed. Try again. Success? Turn on the radio. No success? Try again.	Gradually lengthen your drive but avoid exceeding more than an hour before taking your baby out for a stretch.	

Gently practice. By slowly adding in new elements, and progressively increasing the length of the ride, you can identify what is difficult for your baby to manage. Is she content when there is no sound other than the road? Is music playing acceptable, but not the news? Does she manage the ride better when the light is less intense? Support her, work with her, make changes accordingly.

Ease back. Repeated practice will gradually strengthen your baby's coping skills. If at four months the radio triggers her, don't assume you will never be able to play music in the car. Try again when she's six months and her skills a little stronger. See how she does. If at six months the radio continues to add too much stimulation, wait until she's ten months, but do try again.

The Gentle NUDGE to a successful trip in a different time zone

If you live in New York and your baby typically awakens at 6:00 A.M., when you travel to Los Angeles to visit family, your baby's body clock will continue to tell him to wake at six. The trouble is in Los Angeles it will be 3:00 A.M. While electronic clocks switch quickly and automatically, our body clock does not. When your journey will shift you into a different time zone, use the Gentle NUDGE to successfully transition.

Note where your baby is now. Check time zones. Know what zone you live in and the zone of the area you are going to. Do the math. How many hours' difference is it?

Understand your ultimate goal. Determine your goal by answering two key questions: Will you be traveling west and gaining time, or traveling east and losing time? How long will you be in the new time zone? Your answers will influence your goal. If you will be in the new zone for only a couple days, and the difference in time is a mere hour, it may be simpler to maintain your baby's routine on *your* time zone. In New York she wakes at 6:00 A.M.; in Chicago that's 5:00 A.M. Early, but livable, especially for just a day or two.

But if you will be traveling for a week or more, and/or the time difference is two hours or greater, your best bet may be to maintain your baby's routine sequence but shift to the new time zone.

Determine the teeny, tiny steps. To avoid a cold turkey approach, you will need to begin the teeny, tiny steps a week or two before you leave home. Shift in fifteen-minute increments.

TEENY, TINY STEPS TO A SUCCESSFUL TRIP IN A DIFFERENT TIME ZONE

Teeny step 1	Teeny step 2	Teeny step 3
Begin a week or two before departing to shift your baby's wake time and bedtime closer to your destination's time zone. Move in 15-minute increments.	If you'll be flying, decide if it would be easier for your baby to arrive at nighttime and shortly thereafter go to sleep, or to arrive during daylight.	If it's daytime when you arrive, walk outside. Delay bedtime as long as your baby can handle it to move closer to the new zone's bedtime. If it's nighttime when you arrive, dim lights, wind down, try to sleep.

Teeny step 4	Teeny step 5	Teeny step 6
Minimize plans for the first day or two after arrival. A change in time zone makes it harder to fall asleep and stay asleep.	Maintain your baby's nap and bedtime schedule in your destination's time zone.	Reverse the process going home. Expect that it can take weeks to shift a mere hour or two. Plan recovery time accordingly.

<u>Gently practice.</u> If you are traveling west, shift bedtime fifteen minutes later. Once your baby is falling asleep at that time, move bedtime another fifteen minutes later.

If you are traveling east, wake your baby fifteen minutes earlier than normal and put him to bed fifteen minutes earlier. Once that is working, shift another fifteen minutes earlier.

Even if you don't get all the way to the time zone of your destination, you'll be closer than if you had done nothing.

It is typically more challenging to adjust to traveling east, which requires an earlier sleep time, than west, which delays sleep time. No matter which direction you are going, though, once you arrive, plan to start each morning outside for exposure to morning light. This will help to reset your body clocks.

<u>Ease back.</u> Upon returning home expect that it can take one to three weeks for your baby to return to his home schedule. Once again, getting outside for exposure to morning light will help to ease the transition. Watch cues. Adjust sleep times as needed, gently nudging your baby back into your time zone.

The Gentle NUDGE allows you to gradually help your baby strengthen self-regulation skills. The stronger your baby's self-regulation skills become, the easier it is for your baby to maintain and implement the skills he demonstrates at home under more challenging conditions. The key is teeny, tiny nudges, not shoves. It can be a slow process, but when you allow your baby to set the pace, his confidence grows along with his competence. Once comfortable these alert, energetic, persistent, passionate individuals roar out into the world. Which is why I receive photos from parents of their now young-adult spirited children riding camels in the desert, climbing in the Himalayas, and winning the improv competition. Hold that vision. This little one who now fusses and vomits in new situations may one day be inviting you to accompany her on a hike along the coast of Italy. Life with spirit is rich. It just takes patience and practice to get there.

The stronger your baby's self-regulation skills become, the easier it is for your baby to maintain and implement the skills he demonstrates at home under more challenging conditions.

CHEAT SHEET FOR SUCCESSFUL OUTINGS

1. *Always begin with you and your baby's readiness for success.* Whenever possible, before you go, ask yourself, "Would I be willing to bet Dr. Mary $100 my baby will be successful on this outing?" Don't leave the decision to chance.

2. *Prepare your baby for success.* Fiercely protect sleep and feedings as you make your plans. A hungry, tired baby will have a limited capacity to cope. The timing of events matters.

3. *Prepare yourself.* Allow extra time to get out the door. Always have your bag packed with supplies and activities. Be mindful of potential pitfalls like stimulation and tension levels. Plan your entry to allow time for your baby to acclimate.

4. *Plot your exit.* Stay tuned in to your baby's cues. At the first indication of dysregulation, be prepared to step away for a break, or leave. Inform others beforehand that you'll be honoring your baby's sleep and feeding needs. Stay organized for a quick getaway.

5. *Plan recovery time.* Going out with a spirited baby requires both mental and physical energy. Allow yourself time to recenter and recharge. Maintain a journal with successes and tips for next time.

6. *Use the Gentle NUDGE to strengthen skills.* High-stimulation environments require stronger "self-regulation muscles." Break this challenge down into teeny, tiny steps.

REFLECTION QUESTIONS FOR YOUR JOURNAL

- What is my biggest fear when going out with my baby?
- What is the number one cue I need to look for—and respect—when I'm out with my baby?
- What is the most successful outing I've had recently? What works best for us?
- What new social skills did my baby demonstrate today?

Chapter 10

Moving Forward with Confidence

Living, Loving, and Thriving with Spirit

*"You promised me she would grow up to be
an awesome person, and she has."*
—Lydia, mother of two

My husband and I traveled into the Bridger Mountains of Montana on a recent day trip. The road, rutted and slick with mud, narrowed as we climbed. A cliff tumbled off precipitously on our left. This was not what we had expected when we planned our small adventure but now there was no turning back.

Dropping into four-wheel drive, we crawled forward toward the promised trailhead and accompanying parking lot. A marker said 2.5 miles to our destination—how bad could it be? Plenty, it turned out. With a mile left to go, the ruts were so deep they grazed the undercarriage of our truck, roughly rocking it. I braced myself and breathed deeply. The road shrunk further. What had we gotten ourselves into? Finally, the trailhead appeared and with it the most glorious panorama of snowcapped mountains and golden aspen leaves shimmering in the sun. Magnificent, marvelous, magical, the view alone was worth the knocks, worry, and endurance it had required to get there. I grinned, pumped my fist in the air, and shouted, "Yes!" Yes to tenacity. Yes to my friend June, who had told me it would be worth it. Yes to the privilege of being here. And yes to the possibilities of the hike yet to come.

This journey, I realized when I got home, was a bit like life with a spirited baby. Tumultuous, tingling, and at moments terrifying. Your baby, who is fierce yet fragile, may have hurled you to emotional peaks and valleys you have never experienced before. Elation, despair, exhaustion, joy, wonder, frustration—you are learning to meet them all head-on. You realize you are forever changed. Tougher, more resilient than you ever imagined you could be, and at the same time possessing within you a level of vulnerability that leaves you shaken. Finding your way is a daily challenge. But on this journey, you are learning about yourself, your baby, your relationship with your partner, and the importance of asking for help.

Throughout this book I've been honest with you. I won't stop now. The hike yet to come with your little one will still be strewn with boulders to be clamored over and steep grades to climb. But my hope, as you finish reading this book, is that your backpack is filled with the tools and nourishment you need. By your side are friends and helpers, some who have walked this path before you. You are not alone. You are one of many.

Guided by your newfound understanding of temperament, you will find yourself thinking differently about everyday life. "Why me?" will be replaced (on most days) with a sense that this baby is extraordinary rather than a burden. True, he is still a handful and you are tired and working harder than any parent whose baby is not spirited, but there is joy in the realization that this extra effort is worth it. Your baby is normal but your baby is also different—more intense, alert, sensitive, and energetic. These traits are wired into her very essence. They cannot be denied. They influence every interaction, experience, and sensation of the day and must always be taken into consideration.

But you are learning you can trust what your baby is telling you. Her piercing screams reflect the intensity of her emotions, not a desire to make you look bad. You know that responding is not spoiling. Responding calms your baby and changes the wiring of her brain so one day she can settle on her own. Indeed, one day she does. You find yourself chuckling, remembering the muddle of movements and cries that confounded you. Now they are like cue cards in large print signaling: I'M TIRED. I'M HUNGRY.

When your baby heads to the door after thirty minutes at the community play group, you no longer attempt to convince him to stay. It's obvious he's telling you in the only way he can right now, *It's time to go.* You depart with no one in tears and give yourself a mental high five: *Yes, we are figuring this out!*

You also have a new awareness of the richness of the world around you. Every sight, sound, smell, and nuance has meaning. Each transition, no matter how small, has significance. Before, you may have been oblivious to the brightness of the light or the tension in the room. No longer is that the case. You've learned the hard way you can't ignore how each detail impacts the level of your baby's arousal system. Your consciousness is keener and your life is more focused in the moment because of it.

Daily routines become your assistants as they support you in bringing more predictability to your baby's feeding and sleeping patterns. You reap the rewards with your baby's longer stretches of sleep. Again, not perfect, but better.

I hope you are also becoming kinder to yourself, mindful of your own arousal system and how your baby synchronizes to it. Rather than trying to ignore or power through your rising stress level, my wish is that you are beginning to monitor it, giving it a name, and taking steps to bring yourself and your baby back into the green zone of calm energy. I want that harsh voice in your head that berates you for taking a break or reaching for a helping hand to become quieter—not silent but allowed less time. Even if you haven't yet done it, I encourage you to at least consider scheduling small hiatuses in your day to meet your own basic needs, especially those quiet moments in the morning before others rise.

Despite all your effort and hard work, not every day will be perfect. Just as there are blizzards and tornadoes, some days everything blows up. Seek shelter in the arms of your support team. If you are married, your marriage has been affected by this experience. Know, however, that rather than pulling you apart, the challenges of parenting a spirited baby can bring you together at a new and higher level. Never have you needed one another so much. If you are struggling, schedule an appointment with a marriage counselor or someone you trust who can help you get back on track.

As you move forward, the good days that were once few and far between have now stretched to being *most* days, and your appreciation of your baby's abilities has grown. I now have a request of you: When you see other spirited babies in your community, reach out to their parents. Share with them your knowledge, joy in your baby's spirit, empathy, and encouragement for the hard days, and most important, your confidence and hope. Have at hand your own tales of "spirit" to share. Be ready like the dad laughing in delight as he told me the tale of his eighteen-month-old who used a broomstick to unlatch the back door so he could wander next door for cookies and like the mom who proudly described how her ten-year-old can take apart anything and put it back together again. This is not bragging. This is creating a vision of possibilities. An image to grab on to for those days when the thirteen-month-old is, once again, despite childproofing, opening and shutting the dishwasher for the hundredth time to figure out how it works.

Raising your spirited baby is a roller-coaster ride. Up and down, exciting, exhausting, demanding, and delightful. Every day has its moments, its wins and losses. Ashlie described it well: "At the end of the really tough days I can talk myself off the ledge by asking myself, 'Did I find something to love about my baby today? Did I do my best today?' Then I was a great mom today."

While this book draws to a close, our journey continues. I won't leave you alone. Keep this book close at hand, a gift of reassurance, knowledge, and sense of community. Let it be a reminder that you are one of many. Join your fellow parents in the Raising Your Spirited Child support group at https://www.facebook.com /groups/2348651727/.

There you will find additional support and help—and moments of delight and humor. When you are ready, or your baby "graduates" from infant to child, grab a copy of *Raising Your Spirited Child*. Together we'll move forward, excited to discover even more about this amazing little person who has come to live with you.

Index

About the Author

MARY SHEEDY KURCINKA, Ed.D., is a renowned parent educator, lecturer, and founder of ParentChildHelp, providing training and consultations for families and professionals in North America and around the world. She is the originator of the "spirited child" concept, and her bestselling books *Raising Your Spirited Child; Raising Your Spirited Child Workbook; Kids, Parents, and Power Struggles;* and *Sleepless in America* have been translated into more than twenty languages. Her work brings a practical whole-family, research-based approach to creating healthy and thriving families.